PENGUIN

KE.
NEKRA
THE TROJA

Jean-Paul Sartre – possibly one of the best-known and most discussed modern French writers and thinkers – was born in Paris in 1905. He was educated in Paris and later taught in schools at Le Havre and Laon. In 1934 he spent a year in the French Institute in Berlin where he became acquainted with modern German philosophy. He then taught at the Lycée Condorcet in Paris. He played an active role in the Resistance during the war, and afterwards left the teaching profession. After 1946 he spent his time writing, and editing the magazine *Les Temps modernes*.

Sartre was a Marxist and the founder of French existentialism. His philosophical works such as *L'Être et le néant* (1943) have had a profound effect on modern thought. His plays include *Huis clos* (1944); *Altona* (1960), *Men Without Shadows* (1946) and *The Flies* (1942; three plays published in one volume by Penguins in 1962); and *The Respectable Prostitute* (1946) and *Lucifer and the Lord* (1951; both published in Penguin Plays). His novels include *La Nausée* (1938; published in Penguin as *Nausea*), and the trilogy, *Les Chemins de la liberté* of which *The Age of Reason* (1945), *The Reprieve* (1947), and *Iron in the Soul* (1949) are also published in Penguins. Sartre's other works include *Words*, reminiscences of his childhood (1964; published in Penguins), *Baudelaire* (1964), *Saint Genet, Actor and Martyr* (1964), and *Situations*, a volume of essays (1965). His *Literary and Philosophical Essays* were published in 1968.

Jean-Paul Sartre died in 1980.

Jean - Paul Sartre

THREE PLAYS

KEAN
Translated by Kitty Black

NEKRASSOV
Translated by Sylvia and George Leeson

THE TROJAN WOMEN
English version by Ronald Duncan

PENGUIN BOOKS
in association with Hamish Hamilton

Penguin Books Ltd, Harmondsworth, Middlesex, England
Penguin Books, 625 Madison Avenue, New York, New York 10022, U.S.A.
Penguin Books Australia Ltd, Ringwood, Victoria, Australia
Penguin Books Canada Ltd, 2801 John Street, Markham, Ontario, Canada L3R 1B4
Penguin Books (N.Z.) Ltd, 182–190 Wairau Road, Auckland 10, New Zealand

—

Kean first published by Éditions Gallimard 1954
First published in Great Britain by Hamish Hamilton 1954
Translation © Kitty Black, 1954

Nekrassov first published by Éditions Gallimard 1956
First published in Great Britain by Hamish Hamilton 1956
Translation © Sylvia and George Lesson, 1956

Les Troyennes first published by Éditions Gallimard 1965
The Trojan Women first published in Great Britain
by Hamish Hamilton 1967
Translation © Ronald Duncan, 1967

First published in one volume by Penguin Books 1969
Reprinted 1982

—

Set, printed and bound in Great Britain by
Cox & Wyman Ltd, Reading
Set in Monotype Bembo

CONTENTS

*Application for performing rights
should be addressed to Eric Glass Ltd
28 Berkeley Square, London W1*

KEAN
OR
DISORDER AND GENIUS

Based on the play by Alexandre Dumas

Translated by Kitty Black

CHARACTERS

KEAN
THE PRINCE OF WALES
COUNT DE KOEFELD
SOLOMON
PETER POTT, *landlord of the Black Horse*
LORD NEVILLE
A CONSTABLE
DARIUS, *a hairdresser*
STAGE MANAGER *at Drury Lane Theatre*

ANNA DANBY
ELENA, COUNTESS DE KOEFELD
AMY, COUNTESS OF GOSVILLE
GIDSA, *Elena's maid*

Major-domo, Footmen, Acrobats, Stage-hands,
Theatre Attendants, Firemen, etc.

ACT ONE

Scene: *The hall of the Danish Embassy in London.*

>   [*When the curtain rises, the orchestra is playing a waltz.* FOUR FOOT-
>   MEN *enter down the grand staircase, carrying candelabra, and line up,
>   centre. The* MAJOR-DOMO *enters, speaking to the orchestra, off.*]

MAJOR-DOMO: Thank you, gentlemen. Your brilliance and tempo
are sure to please His Excellency. Be ready to open the ball as soon
as His Royal Highness arrives. [*He crosses to the* FOOTMEN, *inspecting
each one in turn.*]

[*To the first.*] Serve tea and punch in the boudoir.

[*To the second.*] Set up the card tables in the conservatory – two of
Whist and three of Boston.

[*To the remaining two.*] Announce the guests. To your places!

>   [*The* FOOTMEN *turn back to the stairs and exit.* GIDSA *enters from
>   Elena's room.*]

GIDSA: Mr Matheson! Her Excellency. [*She draws aside a curtain.*
ELENA *appears.*]

ELENA: Oh – Matheson – I hope you remembered the cigars.

MAJOR-DOMO: Yes, indeed, your ladyship. Nothing is lacking to
make this the ball of the year.

ELENA: Very good. I shall expect you to be within call the whole
evening.

>   [*The* MAJOR-DOMO *bows and turns to go. The* FOUR FOOTMEN
>   *enter and take up their places on each side of the stairs.*]

IST FOOTMAN: The Countess of Gosville!

ELENA [*aside*]: Good heavens! Already! [*She quickly takes up a graceful
position on the sofa. The* MAID *hastens to arrange her train,* ELENA
dismisses her with a gesture. The MAID *exits discreetly.*]

>   [AMY *enters with a great rustle of skirts. A moment later, obeying a
>   wave of the hand from* ELENA, *the* FOOTMEN *withdraw.*]

ELENA: Amy, my dear, how kind of you to come so early; I have a
thousand things to say to you.

AMY: My dear, I wanted to have you to myself for a moment. It's impossible – we can no longer see our friends, we only meet them at parties. Those races at Newmarket – naturally, one had to be seen there . . .

ELENA: I thought you had a horror of racing . . .

AMY: So I have. It's absurd to drive dozens of miles behind one's own horses merely to watch other people's gallop. Horses gallop – what is surprising in that? It's natural. And most of the men one knows can do nothing but ride. Put a dozen men on the backs of as many horses, set the whole lot to whooping and shouting, naturally, one or other will arrive at the finishing post before all the others. Still, one has one's obligations. You have them too, Elena, but I find you observing them less and less . . .

ELENA: I'm not English, my dear, and I have no . . .

AMY: You may not be English, but your husband is an Ambassador. How are we to remember we are no longer at war with Denmark if we never see the Danish Ambassador's wife at our receptions? I have had to endure four dinners, two balls and three visits to the Opera this week alone. I tell you, Elena, I am not made of iron, and when I see my friends fail in their duties, I find my own courage ebbing.

ELENA: I was at Drury Lane last night.

AMY: Drury Lane – at least that is better than nothing. But the play is not fatiguing. You can relax, close your eyes, even go to sleep, in the privacy of your box. While you were enjoying a rest, I was dancing with the old Duke of Leinster. You know how lame he is, and when I reached home, I found I was limping myself. What was the play?

ELENA: Hamlet.

AMY: Again! The trouble with old authors is they never give us anything new.

ELENA: Their plays are renewed each time they are created by a new actor.

AMY: So they say. But when one has seen Othello stifling Desdemona twenty times with a pillow, they may change their Othello, or their leading lady, it is still the same pillow. The first time I saw Hamlet, when he cried 'A rat, a rat!' I was so frightened, I screamed and jumped on my chair. Now the surprise has worn off, and whether Hamlet is Kemble or Young, I know quite well the rat is Polonius!

ELENA: Last night you would have been frightened.

AMY: Enough to scream?

ELENA: And jump on your chair.

AMY: Then your Hamlet must have been Kean.

ELENA: It was Kean.

AMY: Why do you find him so wonderful?

ELENA: I don't know. I . . . I felt I was seeing Hamlet himself.

AMY: What a play! A man who need only draw his sword to kill off his uncle, and takes five acts to make up his mind! Your Hamlet is a bore, my dear. Why go to the theatre to spend three hours with people one would refuse to receive in one's own home? Go to the theatre to see Hamlet! Now if you told me you went to see Kean . . .

ELENA: Kean? Is there such a man as Kean? The creature I saw last night was the Prince of Denmark in person . . .

AMY: Yes – as he was Romeo the night before, and the Thane of Glamis the night before that. How agreeable for his mistress – if he has one. Tonight she can sleep with the Prince of Denmark, and tomorrow in the arms of the Moor of Venice. The most fickle would find satisfaction. Elena – you won't be angry with me?

ELENA: Never with you. What is the matter?

AMY: Oh, the maddest story. I only tell you to make you laugh.

ELENA: Then I promise not to disappoint you.

AMY: No one can hear us?

ELENA: You're frightening me, my dear.

AMY: Do you know what they're saying?

ELENA: Who are they?

AMY: Everyone.

ELENA: I can guess. They say a husband is unfaithful to his wife, or a wife is unfaithful to her husband. Isn't that it?

AMY: Not altogether.

ELENA: And of whom are they saying this 'not altogether'?

AMY [*taking her hands*]: Elena, my dearest Elena ... [*Pause.*] Of you.

ELENA: Of me?

AMY: They say you have fallen in love with Shakespeare.

ELENA: If it were true, the English should be proud.

AMY: You may be sure of that.

ELENA: If Shakespeare is their god, why shouldn't he be mine?

AMY: But you see, they wonder if it is for the sake of the god that you visit the temple.

ELENA: What else?

AMY: For the priest.

ELENA: Young?

AMY: Pooh!

ELENA: Macready?

AMY: My dear!

ELENA: Kemble?

AMY: Ha! Ha! [*A very slight pause.*] Kean.

ELENA: A madcap story, as you said. Where do these rumours come from?

AMY: Who knows? Such stories fall from the sky.

ELENA. From the sky straight into the ears of our best friends. [*She touches Amy's ear.*] So? I am in love with him?

AMY: Passionately.

ELENA: What would I do for him?

AMY: Everything.

ELENA: Flattering. I have Italian blood and I neither love nor hate by half measures. What else do they say?

AMY: Everyone is sorry for you.

ELENA: A pity. I should prefer to be condemned.

AMY: To think of such a thing. In love with Kean!

ELENA: Not so fast, my dear, I have admitted nothing. Why should I not be in love with Kean?

AMY: The man's an actor.

ELENA: No doubt. And why not?

AMY: Those creatures are not received in our world ...

ELENA: And therefore should not be admitted to our beds. Amy, I met Edmund Kean in the company of the Prince of Wales.

AMY: A prince may be permitted his caprices. . . . Seriously, Elena, as a man he is utterly detestable.

ELENA: Indeed?

AMY: Good heavens – only you could be unaware of his reputation. Do you know he has had a thousand mistresses?

ELENA: A thousand?

AMY: A thousand.

ELENA: Neither one more nor less?

AMY: Exactly a thousand. He says that after the next he will be the equal of Don Juan.

ELENA: So according to your rumours I shall be the thousand and first . . .

AMY: Yes – unless before then . . .

ELENA: I see. Poor man . . .

AMY: Oh, he has been famous for ten years. A thousand in that time . . .

ELENA: If it is true, where is the crime? The women were willing, I suppose? Your Mr Kean knows how to manage his life, that is all.

AMY: My Mr Kean? I implore you, this is no joking matter. He is a lost soul, a monster of pride, driving himself mad because of his low birth, scattering his money in an endeavour to compete with the prodigalities of the Prince of Wales. He is crippled with debts – he should have been in prison months ago were it not for the kindness of certain great ladies . . . a parvenu whose vulgar habits proclaim his lack of breeding . . .

ELENA: Kean, vulgar?

AMY: Every night he leaves his kingly robes in the theatre and frequents the lowest taverns dressed as a common sailor.

ELENA: Is that true?

AMY: Entirely true.

ELENA: Ah, my dear, I can see you're right – he is utterly detestable.

AMY: You see!

ELENA: A vile man!

AMY: Now you have learnt reason!

ELENA: With revolting habits.

AMY: Alas!

ELENA: And it is this man you have decided to give me as a lover? How you protect my reputation!

AMY: Elena, I have never believed it!

ELENA: Of course not, my dearest. Believe me, I never believed that you could believe it. [*Pause.*] I do exactly the same for you. Wherever I go, I defend your reputation.

AMY: My reputation? Good heavens, against whom?

ELENA: Against vile slanders. The little stories that fall from the skies. How is Lord Delmours?

AMY: Lord Delmours. . . . But . . . how should I know? I . . . I hardly know him.

ELENA: I always ask everyone how he is these days. He is so charming, don't you think? I like him so much – so young, so handsome, so fragile one fears he may break at a touch. Every virtue, in fact, except one. He is not very discreet.

AMY: Not discreet?

ELENA: No, not altogether. But who can believe what he says? Everyone knows he is a fool and a coxcomb. You were saying?

AMY: I? Nothing at all.

ELENA: Then I have said nothing, either. [*They laugh.*] How time flies when one is saying nothing.

AMY: How times flies when one has said nothing. [*She picks up a fan.*] What a beautiful fan!

ELENA: It was a present.

AMY: From whom?

ELENA: A Don Juan who has loved a thousand women, a prodigal, crippled with debts . . .

AMY: From . . .

ELENA: No, my friend; from the Prince of Wales.

AMY: Indeed!

ELENA: Will rumour now credit me with a tenderness for the Prince?

AMY: It credits him with a tenderness for you. But are we not to see His Excellency your husband?

ELENA: Your desires are his orders; here he comes.

[*The* COUNT *enters.*]

COUNT: Tomorrow I bow to the crowned heads of Europe; tonight I only acknowledge one queen. [*He kisses* AMY's *hand.*]

AMY. How provoking that one can never believe you.

COUNT: And why not?

AMY: I know you diplomats too well – when you say yes, you mean no.

COUNT: Then I shall say your dress has been cobbled together, and you have been made to look a perfect fright. [*He laughs.*]

AMY: How am I to know you don't mean what you say?

COUNT [*startled*]: But, dear lady . . .

AMY: If I were as hideous as a scarecrow you would take advantage of my lack of confidence in diplomats and tell me the truth to make me believe you were lying. That is diplomacy of the second degree.

ELENA: Yes, but supposing I were jealous and he wished to pay you compliments without arousing my suspicions? He could play on the different degrees of our belief. By telling you he thinks you ugly, he would make you believe he lied, while making me believe he was speaking the truth. That is diplomacy of the third degree.

AMY: Then this is the fourth; supposing he believes you fickle, and wishes to make you jealous. He will say I am ugly to make you think he wants to make you believe he does not like me. As for the fifth . . .

COUNT: Ladies, ladies, for pity's sake! I swear to you diplomacy was never so complex; if it needed so much reflection, we should have to appoint women as ambassadors.

AMY: Well, count, what do you say? Am I fair, or ugly?

COUNT: Madame, I no longer know what to say . . .

AMY: You have chosen the better part. I will believe in your silence.

ELENA: Are we not to see Lord Gosville?

AMY: I fear me not. He is helping Lord Neville ruin himself.

ELENA: I thought him ruined already?

AMY: This time it is tragic, my dear. He is getting married.

ELENA: Married?

AMY: A fortune – an heiress – a disaster.

ELENA: Surely the disaster has a name?

AMY: If you like. But it is a name without meaning – and utterly unmemorable. Annie . . . Anna . . .

COUNT: Danby.

ELENA: Danby? It has a meaning – at least for me. But what?

COUNT: Anna Danby, my dear, is the child who has the box at Drury Lane opposite ours.

ELENA: And never takes her eyes off Kean? She is delightful.

AMY: Indeed?

ELENA: I mean, she is quite pretty. My one complaint is her lack of manners; she never misses a single performance, and indeed it was her – persistence, which made me remark her.

COUNT: Be sure she has noticed you too, my dear.

ELENA: Why should she notice me? Do I lean over the edge of my box? Do I applaud till I split both my gloves?

AMY: Perhaps she likes Shakespeare?

COUNT [with a glance at ELENA]: Obviously!

ELENA: Shakespeare! Imagine! I hope for her sake that marriage will calm her down.

AMY [aside]: This gallant seducer begins to intrigue me. [To the COUNT] Your Excellency, may I be so bold as to ask for a seat in your box the next time he plays?

COUNT: What? You too wish to see him?

AMY: Yes, and at close quarters. From your stage box one must be able to see his every expression.

COUNT: With pleasure: but tonight you will be able to see him still closer.

AMY: Tonight?

COUNT: He is coming to the ball and will sup with us later.

ELENA: Did you invite him? Without asking me?

COUNT: Invite? Invite? Does one invite these people? Let us say I engaged a buffoon. He will give us Falstaff with the dessert.

ELENA: Without asking me!

COUNT: Elena, I must do my best for the royal prince who con-
descends to find him amusing. Ladies, ladies, I was keeping this
for His Royal Highness, and you have surprised my secret. Now
can you say I am a diplomat?

[*The* MAJOR-DOMO *enters with a letter.*]

Excuse me. [*He reads.*] A strange era when an actor refuses the
invitation of an ambassador!

ELENA: From Kean?

COUNT: Yes.

ELENA: He declines?

COUNT: Yes. I can hardly believe my eyes.

ELENA: I hope your invitation was polite?

COUNT: Judge by the reply. [*He reads aloud*] 'Your Excellency, I am
deeply distressed. The rare honour you were gracious enough to
do me was addressed, I have no doubt, to the actor. Although you
had the delicacy not to put it into words, I am sure you would have
been disappointed had I not played for your guests after supper, and
I would have been delighted to give my best endeavours for your
entertainment. Unfortunately, I know of no way of inviting the
actor without the man, and the man is otherwise engaged at an
appointment he cannot cancel. I beg you to be kind enough to
accept my most sincere regrets, and to lay my respectful homage
at the feet of the Countess your wife.'

AMY: Insolence!

COUNT [*annoyed*]: Of course not.

AMY: No?

COUNT: No. If it had been insolence, I would have had to be
angry, and my dignity as Ambassador forbids me to lose my
temper.

[ELENA *sinks into a chair, almost fainting.*]

Elena, what is the matter?

[*The* MAJOR-DOMO *announces.*]

MAJOR-DOMO: His Royal Highness the Prince of Wales.

[The FOUR FOOTMEN *take their places on the stairs. The* PRINCE *enters, laughing.*]

PRINCE: Ha! Ha!

COUNT [*amused at seeing the* PRINCE *laugh*]: He! He!

PRINCE [*his laughter growing*]: Ha! Ha! Ha!

COUNT: He! He! He!

ELENA: Your Royal Highness is very gay.

PRINCE [*kissing her hand*]: You must forgive me, ladies, but the most extraordinary story is going round London.

ELENA: We will only forgive you, sir, if you tell us what it is.

PRINCE: Tell you! I would tell the reeds of the Thames if I had no other audience.

ELENA: I warn you I shall not believe a word.

AMY: I implore your Royal Highness – we can repeat it without believing it.

PRINCE: Lord Neville . . . [*He begins to laugh*] Ha! Ha!

COUNT [*laughing*]: He! He!

       [*Everyone laughs.*]

AMY: Have pity on us, sir . . .

PRINCE [*through his laughter, painfully*]: Left flat.

COUNT: Flat? But I thought . . .

PRINCE: That he was getting married? So did he, I suppose. The proof is that he bought a new wardrobe, refurnished his house, refilled his stables and equipped himself with a host of new creditors. Then tonight, when he went to claim his bride . . . [*He laughs again.*] Gone!

COUNT: Gone?

AMY: Gone?

PRINCE: Flown! The door wide and the cage bare! [*He laughs.*]

ELENA: Poor child! Were they marrying her against her will?

       [*The* PRINCE *is still laughing.*]

   Sir, how can you laugh! Supposing some harm has befallen her!

PRINCE: Where's the harm in running away with the man you love?

ELENA: The man you love?

AMY: Then they know the name of her abductor?

PRINCE: Know it? It's the best-known name in London!

AMY: Tell us – tell us! I cannot endure the suspense!

COUNT: Ladies, don't press His Royal Highness – you may be embarrassing him.

PRINCE: I? No, no, dear friend, I never interfere with the middle classes. Ladies, the hero of the adventure is the man who wears his crown while I still wait for mine – long live the King!

ELENA: Tell us who it is!

PRINCE: Don Juan! Romeo! The Richelieu of three kingdoms! Edmund Kean.

ELENA: Kean!

PRINCE: At this very moment, madam, he is with her on the road to Dover.

ELENA: It's . . . it's impossible.

AMY: But why, Elena? You were saying yourself that the child never takes her eyes off him . . .

COUNT: So this is the reason he declined my invitation.

PRINCE: Your invitation? To come here?

COUNT: I invited him, hoping to give you pleasure, sir.

PRINCE: It may be as well that he refused; otherwise you might have been taken for his accomplice and we'd have had a war between Denmark and England. . . . Ladies, we must celebrate this happening which has restored peace to our firesides. It is a victory for public morality, and I swear that half London will be illuminated tonight.

AMY: Was he so irresistible?

PRINCE: Ah! Ah!

AMY: They say that certain great ladies have been complacent enough to raise him up to their level.

PRINCE: Madam, they have been kinder still, for they have descended to his.

ELENA [violently, in spite of herself]: Your Royal Highness, I cannot allow . .

COUNT: Elena . . .

ELENA: Forgive me, sir, and be good enough to think of me as a country girl. After all, I have only spent one season in London and our Danish husbands are barbaric enough to respect their wives. Be sure that by next autumn my foolish scruples will have drifted with the leaves; I shall laugh at my sex with the best of your wits, and I shall slander my best friends to cause you amusement.

PRINCE: Madam, it is I who should ask forgiveness, and give you my thanks.

ELENA: Thanks?

PRINCE: I know your smiles and your graces, but I thank you for giving me occasion to admire your anger. Your husband is fortunate – I hope you find many occasions to scold him.

COUNT: Yes, indeed – very many.

PRINCE: As for our great ladies, I have no desire to speak ill of them; I merely pity them. It isn't their fault if our court grows effeminate. If they lose their hearts to Kean, they are chasing a shadow.

ELENA: A shadow? Is Kean then not a man?

PRINCE: Indeed no, madam. He is an actor.

ELENA: And what is an actor?

PRINCE: A mirage.

ELENA: And our princes? Are they also mirages?

PRINCE: That is something you can only verify by touching them.

[*The* MAJOR-DOMO *and the* FOUR FOOTMEN *enter.*]

MAJOR-DOMO: Mr Edmund Kean.

ELENA: Kean!

COUNT: Kean!

PRINCE: Kean? This is growing complicated. [*He rubs his hands.*] I adore complications.

COUNT: Let him come in.

[KEAN *enters.*]

KEAN: Ladies. . . . Your Excellency . . . [*Seeing the* PRINCE.] Your Royal Highness.

[*No one moves.*]

I ask you to forgive my erratic behaviour. I did think I should be unable to accept your gracious invitation, but an unexpected

happening altered my plans and forced me to come here and ask
for your help.

COUNT: We were no longer expecting you, sir.

KEAN: Alas, your Excellency, I was sure of that myself. For one
moment you honoured me by desiring my presence, and I, to my
shame, was unable to take advantage of your kindness. Believe that
I regret most sincerely having to appear when no one wishes to
see me.

   [*Pause. No one replies.*]

I find myself in a false position, but after all, false positions are a part
of my profession – I live through them every night. The man I meet
is the one who wishes me a thousand miles away – the woman to
whom I declare my passion grasps the knife with which she intends
to kill me. You have no idea of the situations our authors imagine;
sometimes I declare my passion to my brother, not knowing he is
my rival, and he hears me in silence, as you are doing now. Another
time, the woman I love believes me false, and I must prove my
innocence before her very husband. Yesterday, the King of
Denmark – your country, Excellency – decreed my banishment
and death. I escaped his vengeance, though it was this same king
who had killed my father. It seems I am unfortunate in my relations
with Denmark. Today I have mortally offended the Danish
ambassador – but I shall survive your scorn, Excellency, and do
you know why? I have become impregnable. We actors, when we
have to demonstrate scorn must make it perceptible to a thousand
eyes. It must flame and blaze, it must dazzle the spectator. Falstaff
endures the scorn of the King without the flicker of an eyelid. That
is why, Excellency, I can survive your reprobation without sinking
into the earth; your disdain is terrible, of course, but it has the
drawback of being real. Sometimes I wonder if real emotions are
not merely false emotions badly acted. Come, Excellency, and you
too, sir, will you trust me? In a moment we shall be laughing at
this together. Our playwrights plunge me into a false situation
every night – but every night they extricate me. I shall know how
to get us out of this one as easily as all the others.

COUNT: I can see only one way of doing that, sir – your immediate departure. The rumours attendant on your name, which His Royal Highness has related to us, must certainly make you feel . . .

KEAN: That my presence here is unwelcome? Excellency, I am deeply aware of my indiscretion – nevertheless, it was those rumours that brought me here.

AMY: Are they false, sir?

KEAN: No, madam, they are true; Miss Anna Danby came to my house this evening.

ELENA: Well, sir, and what is it to do with us? Do you expect my husband to condone your love affairs?

KEAN: Madam, everything is true, except one point; the lady left again without seeing me.

PRINCE: Yet I was told . . .

KEAN: That she had stayed? Ah, sir, the spy who saw her come in did not have the patience to see her go out. [*With vehemence.*] The result of his fine work is that her reputation is compromised.

PRINCE: What vehemence! I thought you were not always so prompt in defending a woman's honour!

KEAN: Sir, I enact – consequently I have to experience – every feeling. Every morning I put on the one that matches my coat. Today I decided on a generous mood. [*To the* COUNT] Excellency, my one hope is in you.

COUNT: In me? What the devil do you expect? If you are innocent, you need only deny the story.

KEAN: Deny the story? Ah, Excellency, you are unaware of what people think of me? [*He turns to* ELENA.] If I were to say to you, madam, quite simply, 'The story is false, I do not know Miss Danby, and I could never love her', would you believe me?

ELENA: Without further proof?

KEAN: Without further proof than my word of honour.

AMY: Elena, you wouldn't believe him!

ELENA: No, I should not believe you.

KEAN: You see, Excellency, Madam de Koefeld herself cannot discern the honour of the man behind the habiliments of the actor. Kean's honour – that makes you laugh. But you, your Excellency, you who have a natural right to command respect, if you were to say.... No, to silence gossiping tongues requires more than respect, it demands veneration. Madam, all London venerates you. Would you condescend to utter this denial yourself?

ELENA: Mr Kean, I cannot deny the story unless I believe you sincere.

KEAN [*holding out a letter*]: Deign to glance at this letter. You can declare to the whole world that Miss Danby's honour is without stain.

COUNT: Read it yourself, sir, we will hear you.

KEAN: Pardon me, Excellency, we must allow each of us to keep his station; honour to men of the world, intelligence and talent to actors, delicacy of feeling to the ladies. A secret on which the happiness, the future and perhaps the very life of a woman depend can only be revealed to another woman. Read, madam, I implore you.

PRINCE: Does my rank give me the right to enjoy this confidence?

KEAN: Sir – before a secret all men are equal.

PRINCE [*drawing* KEAN *aside*]: Kean, what game are you playing?

KEAN: What game? Sir, what else do you expect of a player? I am playing a part, that is all. [*To* ELENA] Madam, I urge you to hear my prayer.

COUNT [*growing impatient, tapping his foot, loudly*]: I cannot decide . . .

AMY [*taking his arm*]: Come, Count, you are a diplomat: as soon as your wife knows, you will be able to guess at this secret.

PRINCE [*taking his other arm*]: And when you have guessed it, you will be able to tell us.

ELENA [KEAN *draws her aside*]: This letter alone will justify you?

KEAN: Read!

ELENA [*reading*]: 'Sir, I came to see you and found you away from home. I have not the honour of your acquaintance, but when you learn that my whole life depends on the advice you alone can give me, I am sure you will not refuse to see me tomorrow. Anna Danby.' Thank you, Mr Kean, thank you a thousand times. But what reply have you given?

KEAN [*in a low voice*]: Turn the page, madam.

ELENA [*reading in a low voice*]: 'I did not know how to see you, Elena, I dared not write to you; an opportunity has arisen and I have seized it. The rare moments you steal from those who surround you are so brief and tormenting they are marked in my life only by their remembrance . . .' [*She stops.*]

KEAN: I beg you to read to the end, madam.

ELENA [*reading*]: 'I have often wondered how a woman of your world, who loved me truly, could grant me one hour without compromising herself. . . . If this woman loved me enough to accord me this hour, in exchange for which I should give my life, she would come to Drury Lane, stop her carriage and enter the theatre as if to purchase a ticket. The man she would find there is devoted to me, and I would instruct him to open the secret door to my dressing-room if a woman veiled and dressed in black might perhaps condescend to visit me tomorrow night . . .' Here is your letter, sir.

  She kisses the letter lightly and holds it out to him, but gazing at him passionately, slips it into her dress before he can take it.]

KEAN [*bowing*]: A thousand thanks, madam – your Excellency – my lady. . . . Your Royal Highness . . .

  [*He makes as if to go, but remains a little apart.*]

AMY [*close to* ELENA]: Well, Elena?

PRINCE: Well, madam?

COUNT: Well, my dear?

ELENA: Mr Kean has been wrongfully accused of abducting Miss Anna Danby.

  [KEAN *bows.*]

PRINCE [*taking* AMY's *arm and going upstairs*]: Ah, Mr Kean, you have been acting a charade – but I swear on my honour I shall have the last word.

  [ELENA *turns and smiles at* KEAN *as she passes him with the* COUNT.]

KEAN [*in a murmur*]: Thank you, madam.

  [*A* FOOTMAN *blows out the candles on one side, throwing* KEAN *into shadow.* ANOTHER *extinguishes the candles on the other side, putting the forestage into darkness. In the shadows,* KEAN *watches the countess disappear, then in the light coming from the ballroom, we see the silhouettes of the two couples beginning to waltz.* KEAN *blows a kiss in the direction of his beloved while the music swells and the curtain falls.*]

CURTAIN

ACT TWO

Scene: KEAN's *dressing-room.* KEAN *and his factotum,* SOLOMON.

SOLOMON: Guv'nor!

KEAN: Eh?

SOLOMON: Can I have a word with you?

KEAN: Later, later. What time is it?

SOLOMON: Six o'clock.

KEAN: She will not come.

SOLOMON: Of course she will!

KEAN: You'll see – you'll see.

SOLOMON: Then she will be the first, sir.

KEAN: I wasn't in love with any of the others. There's no one in the world more punctual than a woman one does not love. . . . The door opens easily, I hope?

SOLOMON: I oiled it myself this morning.

KEAN: Supposing she had been and tried to open it, and couldn't get in?

SOLOMON: Impossible.

[*He goes to the secret door, opens it. It squeaks badly. He closes it again.*]

A child could open it with one finger.

KEAN: Very well. There's nothing to do but wait. I hate waiting.

[*A street musician is playing outside and the noise gets on* KEAN's *nerves. He picks up a purse.*]

Throw the fellow this and tell him to leave me in peace.

[SOLOMON *pulls a few coins from the purse, throws half to the musician and puts the rest back in the purse which he lays on the table.*]

KEAN: What are you doing?

SOLOMON: Dividing the spoils; half for you, and half for him.

KEAN: What's the matter with you? I detest half measures.

SOLOMON: Then you should have kept the lot.

KEAN: *You* trying to stop my charitable impulses?

SOLOMON: Yes, when you perform them with other people's money.

KEAN: Those miserable guineas . . .

SOLOMON: Those guineas, we earned them last month, but for nearly three years we've been spending them with all the others we will earn for the next six years to come.

KEAN: You mean the money belongs to my creditors?

SOLOMON: Alas!

KEAN: All the more reason to give it away. I'm saving their souls. [*He moves to throw the purse from the window.* SOLOMON *stands in his way.*]

SOLOMON: Over my dead body. [*Clutching the purse*] Guv'nor, it's all we've got left.

KEAN: All?

SOLOMON: All the ready, that is.

KEAN: So we're broke to the wide?

SOLOMON: Cleaned out – plucked like a chicken.

KEAN: Well, I'll be able to pull in my belt. It's all good for the figure, Solomon.

SOLOMON: Not so good when you have to go round mother-naked.

KEAN [*severely*]: Solomon!

SOLOMON: I must make you see sense, Guv'nor.

KEAN: Why should I trouble myself about money? What good does it do?

SOLOMON: It pays for what you buy.

KEAN: Why do I need it when I buy everything without paying?

SOLOMON: Why do you need it? You'll know in a moment even if you won't listen to me.

KEAN: I always listen to you, Solomon.

SOLOMON: In the end.

KEAN: But not today.

SOLOMON: I might have known. Tomorrow?

KEAN: Yes, tomorrow.

SOLOMON: We'll never get a better chance! You can't keep still – you're yawning your head off – you're bored and restless.

KEAN: I'm expecting a woman, simpleton . . .

SOLOMON: That's what I said.

KEAN [*continuing*]: And I'm bored because love is a boring experience.

SOLOMON: Let me give you a statement of your financial position, and I promise you won't find it boring – the time will slip by like a dream.

KEAN: And if I want to be bored, eh?

SOLOMON: What for?

KEAN: For the love of love. Seriously, when do you expect me to meditate on the charms of my beloved?

SOLOMON: Heavens! When she arrives.

KEAN: When she arrives, I shan't have a moment to see her; I shall be very much too busy watching her. Come now, let me rest. [*He stretches on the divan and closes his eyes.*] Elena!

SOLOMON [*approaching on tiptoe and shouting in his ear*]: The game's up!

KEAN [*startled*]: Eh?

SOLOMON: You're bankrupt.

KEAN: You shouldn't have told me. How do you expect me to make love to her now? [*Pause.*] Bankrupt. Charming! It's been going on for thirty-five years – d'you think I don't know? Twenty times I've thought of hanging myself; a hundred times I thought I should die of starvation. When I was a child . . .

SOLOMON [*protesting*]: Oh, no, no, no! Everything, but not your childhood. I haven't deserved it.

KEAN: Not my childhood? What's wrong with my childhood?

SOLOMON: I respect it, I pity it, but I know your childhood off by heart. We'll never get anywhere if you insist on telling me the story every time I want to discuss money matters. We're not talking about the child now, but the man. The child lived in poverty and thought of nothing but how to grow rich. The man has lived in luxury for ten years . . . and we've got to find a way of keeping him in it. Guv'nor, you've got to listen to me.

KEAN [*indignant*]: Luxury? What on earth are you talking about?

SOLOMON: All this ... your house, your carriage, your six servants ...

KEAN: But that isn't my concern, idiot! The house is crumbling under a mortgage, the bill for the carriage has been outstanding for years; the servants are owed three months' wages. This divan belongs to poor Gregory McPherson, dealer in antiques. This dressing-gown ... You want to see the likeness between the man and the child; the child owned nothing but the holes in his Harlequin jacket and the man owns nothing but his debts, which are the holes in his budget. If all my creditors took it into their heads to take back their wares, I should find myself in Piccadilly, feeling a dozen years younger.

SOLOMON: To listen to you, anyone would think you desired it.

KEAN. I want to be free. They are keeping my place for me – old Bob and his troupe of acrobats. I should put on my mask, pick up my bat, and get into my Harlequin jacket.

SOLOMON: When?

KEAN: Whenever I wish. I have nothing, nothing keeps me here. Everything is provisional – I live from day to day in a fabulous imposture. Not a farthing, nothing in my hands, nothing in my pockets, but I need only snap my fingers to summon spirits of the air who bring me Orient pearls, jewels and bouquets of rare flowers.

[*He snaps his fingers. There is a knock at the door.*]

Who is it?

SOLOMON [*who has gone to open*]: Flowers.

KEAN: Well? What d'you say? Am I a magician or an illusionist? Put them down – they are for her. [*Pause.*] You're looking very sour.

SOLOMON: They must cost a guinea apiece.

KEAN: What?

SOLOMON: Those flowers.

KEAN: Where do you see flowers?

SOLOMON: There.

KEAN: Nothing but illusion. Have I paid for them?

SOLOMON: Certainly not.

KEAN: Then who is the legitimate owner?

SOLOMON: The florist of Soho Square.

KEAN: Is he a prodigal? A ninny? A fool?

SOLOMON: He is the meanest of skinflints, who gives nothing for nothing.

KEAN: You see: having given nothing, I have received nothing: therefore, they are still in his shop and you are the victim of an optical illusion. Shadows of roses, all hail! Enter into fantasy. I prefer to rule over mirages, and I love you all the more because you do not exist in truth. See how they open, how they unfold themselves: if I had bought them, I should already be tired of them: but I still desire them because they will fade without ever belonging to me. Play, Solomon.

SOLOMON [*startled*]: Eh?

KEAN: Play the game.

SOLOMON: What game?

KEAN: Everything that doesn't belong to you. The wind of the skies, the wives of other men, these flowers. [*He throws him a rose.*] Enjoy but never possess.

SOLOMON: To enjoy without possession is to lay up debts for the future.

KEAN: Very well, let us have debts. Look, am I not adored if my admirers send me such flowers? As long as you don't pay your debts, they are gages of love, proofs of human generosity. Ah, the good florist – the noble heart – it is too much – very much too much – he is spoiling me – I shall have to scold him! And be sure he prays God every day to send me long life. Solomon, do you love me?

SOLOMON: You know I do!

KEAN: Then you must love those who love me. Instead of reproaching me for my debts, help me to multiply them.

SOLOMON: Impossible.

KEAN: What? What is impossible?

SOLOMON: The multiplication of your debts.

KEAN: Why?

SOLOMON: Credit exhausted.

KEAN: Exhausted? But even yesterday . . .

SOLOMON: That was yesterday.

KEAN: Can the hearts of men change in a night?

SOLOMON: The hearts of men, no: but we're speaking of creditors. They have passed round the word. No more dealings except for ready money.

KEAN: And this is the moment you choose to tell me?

SOLOMON: For an hour I've been trying to get in a word.

KEAN: Let them all go to the devil! Moneylenders at least will never lack.

SOLOMON: A word concerning you has been sent round all London.

KEAN: What word?

SOLOMON: 'Not a penny to the actor Kean.'

KEAN: But what do they all want?

SOLOMON: To be paid.

KEAN: The sharks! [*He strides up and down.*] Will they allow me to continue my work? Do these people imagine I can rehearse *Richard III* in a hovel? Assassinate the greatest actor of the age and see how tedious your evenings become. [*To* SOLOMON] What do you think you are doing? I'm being strangled, stabbed to the heart, and you stand there yawning your head off! Run! Find us some money!

SOLOMON: Where?

KEAN: That's your affair. My business is to spend it and yours is to find it. [*Abruptly*] Just a moment . . . Come here! What has been happening? What is all this about? If they have stopped my credit, it must be because they don't trust me any more. And if they have lost faith, it must mean I have lost my reputation. . . . Go to the manager at once and ask to see the house returns . . .

SOLOMON: What do you care about the receipts? The money doesn't belong to you.

T – T.P. – B

KEAN: I want to know if business has gone down. . . . Because if it has, Solomon, then it means I have gone down as well.

SOLOMON: Yesterday, we turned away six hundred people.

KEAN: And the day before?

SOLOMON: Seven hundred and fifty.

KEAN: You see! You see! Why this discrepancy?

SOLOMON: Because of the difference of opinion between our Government and the Kingdom of Holland.

KEAN: To the devil with politics! Politics fill prisons and empty theatres. Solomon, you swear the people love me still?

SOLOMON: Passionately.

KEAN: Listen to me, my brother, my friend – you who teach me my parts and hold the book every evening, tell me frankly, am I slipping? Don't be afraid to hurt me; I want to leave the stage before I cover myself with disgrace.

SOLOMON: You never acted better in your life.

KEAN: Never better. But have I been as good?

SOLOMON: Well . . .

KEAN: I understand. [*He walks about in a frenzy.*] I am not slipping, but I am not rising either. That means I am lost; in the theatre as in love, there is only one law; improve, or slip back. But good heavens, what do they expect of me? That I should surpass myself? How? Our authors are all dwarfs. If you want a Super-Kean you must give me a Super-Shakespeare. Solomon, I am Aladdin, my lamp is my genius. If one day it were to go out . . .

SOLOMON: It will never go out; that lamp will shine till the day of your death.

KEAN: It . . . touch wood, fool! Touch wood! [*He grasps the arm of a chair in a changed voice.*] Well, what must we do?

SOLOMON: Firstly; economize.

KEAN: On that point, I am adamant. Never. Go on to the next.

SOLOMON: It would be so easy!

KEAN: How the devil do you expect me to economize?

SOLOMON: You care so little for company: do not give these supper parties.

KEAN: I have given none for a very long time.

SOLOMON: You are giving one tonight. The dresser told me.

KEAN: Tonight? It isn't a party. I'm going to Peter Pott, to the Black Horse – the haunt of cut-throats, down by the river.

SOLOMON: What for?

KEAN: A christening party.

SOLOMON: How many guests?

KEAN: How should I know? Two or three dozen.

SOLOMON: Not counting the thieves and murderers you will collect on your way.

KEAN: Solomon, what do you want? To stop me treating my friends?

SOLOMON: Those footpads were never your friends.

KEAN: Not footpads, you fool! Acrobats! Old Bob and his company. To me, they are sacred. I touched the depths of poverty with them, I begged, I danced at street corners, they taught me everything. Do you expect me to forget them? All my childhood, Solomon. Do you insist I renounce my childhood . . .

SOLOMON: For the love of heaven, leave your childhood in peace.

KEAN: Good. I will never mention it, if you won't mention my debts. Come with me, Solomon, you are warmly invited. Old Bob has just had his twelfth, and I am the godfather. Why don't you come!

SOLOMON [mournfully]: It will only mean one more mouth to feed.

KEAN: Peter Pott still gives us credit. Come along, Solomon, why don't you laugh? Why do you always look so sour? Why won't you smile? What else is there to tell? Holding something back? Another question of money, eh?

SOLOMON: The . . .

KEAN: I won't hear a word – I won't hear a word! You are going to spoil my good humour! Solomon, she is a countess, I shall need all my patience. [Pause.] Very well. Tell me; what is the matter?

SOLOMON: It's the jeweller. You gave him your note for £400. For the necklace you gave Miss Fanny Hearst.

KEAN: How can you speak of it! . . . They are things one does without thinking.

SOLOMON: Yes, but you haven't honoured your signature.

KEAN: My signature? When and what did I sign?

SOLOMON: Your note of hand, six months ago.

KEAN: Since then I have played Hamlet, Romeo, Macbeth, Lear, and you say I haven't honoured him.

SOLOMON: I mean you haven't paid him.

KEAN: Are you mad? You choose the moment I love Elena to make me pay for a necklace I gave Fanny? It would be the worst of betrayals.

SOLOMON: But the jeweller lives on such betrayals . . .

KEAN: What has he done?

SOLOMON: Your lawyers told me he has asked for a warrant for your arrest.

KEAN: My arrest! He'll never obtain it.

SOLOMON: They say they are quite sure it will be granted.

KEAN: And if they obtain it?

SOLOMON: You will be arrested, certainly – and imprisoned, most probably.

KEAN: We'll see if the people of London will leave me to be imprisoned. Kean, in prison? All the theatres of the world will close in sign of mourning. [*Changing his tone, sadly*] So it has come! You have spoilt it at last!

SOLOMON: What?

KEAN: My good mood. I know I am ruined – lost – cleaned out – broke to the wide. Only I have the good manners not to talk about it.

SOLOMON: I thought . . .

KEAN: What now?

SOLOMON: That you might . . . ask the Prince of Wales.

KEAN: Good heavens! His debts are three times greater than mine.

SOLOMON: He might be able to intercede with the King.

KEAN: We'll see. Now I won't hear another word!

SOLOMON: A very little money . . .

KEAN [*violently*]: From today, I forbid you to pronounce that obscene

word in my presence. What am I to say to Elena? How shall I
open my arms to her? You have besmirched me.

SOLOMON [*sticking to his idea*]: If the King would pay half your
debts – only half, with the money you earn . . .

KEAN: I, earning money! I'd rather die!

SOLOMON: All the same, you . . .

KEAN: What are you talking about? Do you believe I am paid to
act? I am a priest; every evening I celebrate mass, and every
week I receive the offerings of my public, that is all. Money
stinks, Solomon. You may steal it; at most, receive it as an
inheritance. But the money you earn, there is only one way to
use it. [*He has crossed to the window. The musician has started to play
again.*] Throw it out of the window. [*He throws his purse to the
musician.*]

SOLOMON [*with a great cry*]: Oh, my God!

KEAN [*a little disconcerted by his own gesture, shrugs his shoulders*]: Oh
well, can't be helped. [*Charmingly*] You'll lend me a guinea tonight,
for my cigars.

SOLOMON: Yes, Guv'nor.

   [*There is a knock at the door.*]

KEAN: Again? Is this a public house? I can see no one.

   [SOLOMON *has opened the door.*]

SOLOMON: It's . . .

KEAN [*impatiently*]: Well? Who?

SOLOMON: The Prince of Wales.

KEAN: Tell his Royal Highness that I cannot see him.

PRINCE [*entering*]: Why cannot you see me, Mr Kean?

KEAN [*continuing, as* SOLOMON *goes out*]: That I cannot see him
without the greatest pleasure.

PRINCE: Naturally. But you find this visit inconvenient and you
would like to see me in Hades.

KEAN: Your Royal Highness can never inconvenience me.

PRINCE: You flatter from force of habit, but your teeth are so tightly
clenched the words can scarcely get past your lips.

KEAN: Imperfect diction? That is serious. [*He repeats – articulating as if at an elocution lesson*] Your Royal Highness is never inconvenient.

PRINCE: Never?

KEAN [*smiling*]: Never.

[*The* PRINCE *picks up a cigar.*]

Please . . .

PRINCE: Thank you. But if you expected a woman? Kean, you must tell me at once, and I will retire.

KEAN: Sir, I am expecting nobody.

PRINCE: Liar! And these flowers?

KEAN: Bouquets sent by admirers.

PRINCE: And this elegant dressing-gown?

KEAN: Every night I have to dress to please my audience. May I not dress in private to please myself?

PRINCE: Who made it for you?

KEAN: Perkins.

PRINCE: I shall order one like it tomorrow morning.

KEAN: Again?

PRINCE: What do you mean?

KEAN: This is the sixth time your Royal Highness has been pleased to copy my taste . . .

PRINCE: What harm is there in that?

KEAN: In a week's time, all Europe will be wearing this identical garment.

PRINCE: In your place I should be very proud.

KEAN: Sir, for a long time my voice and features have belonged to the world, and the actors of the United Kingdom have copied my style of acting. At least in the old days I had a few rags I could call my own – behind locked doors, this mirror could reflect the image of the true Kean that I alone could be said to know. When I survey myself today, I see only a fashion plate. Thanks to the condescension of your Royal Highness, I have become a spectacle down to the last detail of my private life.

PRINCE: And you complain? It is the price you pay for my friendship. [*Pause.*] What do you play tonight?

KEAN: Romeo.

PRINCE: Romeo? At your age? My poor Kean – he was eighteen when he died, was he not?

KEAN: More or less.

PRINCE: So you have survived him by twenty years?

KEAN: For twenty years I have kept him from dying.

PRINCE: And your Juliet – who is she?

KEAN: Miss MacLeish.

PRINCE: Good heavens! She was my father's first mistress. Between you, you must be a hundred years old. The stage will bend beneath the weight of your combined years. I cannot imagine how the public can endure the sight of an old couple enacting middle-aged amours.

KEAN: Where is my talent if I cannot persuade them I am eighteen?

PRINCE: Oh you – you can always manage. But what about Mac-Leish?

KEAN: Where is my genius if I cannot convince them she is a child?

PRINCE: How will you do that?

KEAN: By insuring they see no one but me – that they see her only through my eyes.

PRINCE: And when she speaks?

KEAN: What do you expect them to hear? They will wait until I answer her. Besides, Juliet's part isn't a good one. It has long tedious speeches. I have had the whole play cut and considerably lightened.

PRINCE: All the same, she must speak if we are to notice her existence.

KEAN: I shall observe the audience. If they watch her too closely, I will cut in on her lines.

PRINCE: I see. Why do you look at your watch?

KEAN: To see if it is time to take my goat's milk. I drink it to clear my voice.

PRINCE: Indeed? An hour and a half before the performance? And for your nerves?

KEAN: I beg your pardon?

PRINCE: What do you take for your nerves? You seem very agitated this evening.

KEAN: It is the unexpected pleasure of your visit.

PRINCE: Come now, Kean, we all know the cause of your impatience
– everyone knows your secret.

KEAN: I have never had a secret from your Royal Highness.

PRINCE: That was true – until yesterday.

KEAN: Yesterday?

PRINCE: The letter you showed Madam de Koefeld.

KEAN: Ah, sir, that contained Miss Danby's secret.

PRINCE: I thought I recognized your handwriting. And I wondered
if the secret you were confiding to the lady were not your incor-
rigible heart. [*He repeats*] 'I have often wondered how a woman
who loved me truly . . .'

KEAN: Sir!

PRINCE [*continuing*]: . . . 'could grant me the favour of an hour
without compromising herself . . .'

KEAN: Sir, sir – who told you?

PRINCE: Ah, indeed? Who could possibly know? . . . [*Pause.*] What is
the matter, Mr Kean?

KEAN [*white with passion*]: Merely a touch of fury, sir.
[*He sits down.*]

PRINCE: Mr Kean! Did I ask you to sit down?

KEAN [*laughing, with an effort*]: I, sitting down? Before your Royal
Highness – never. I have merely sunk into a chair.

PRINCE: You stammer – you can hardly speak!

KEAN [*bitterly*]: Yes, indeed. Can you imagine that on a stage? I am
Othello – I learn that Desdemona is false, and I sink into a chair.
I can hear the hisses from here. The public expects us to give more
nobility and amplitude to the expression of our feelings. Sir – I
have all the gifts; the trouble is they are imaginary. Let a sham
prince steal my sham mistress, you would see if I knew how to
lament. But when a real Prince tells me to my face: 'You trusted a
woman and last night she and I made a fool of you,' anger turns
my limbs to water, and I am incapable of speech. I have always said
that Nature was a very inferior copy of Art. [*He has recovered.*]
So, Sir, Madam de Koefeld told you everything?

PRINCE: You confess? You confess you asked her to meet you

tonight at the theatre, and you are waiting for her now? Very well, I shall be generous – since I have your confession, I will put an end to your torment. She told me nothing. [KEAN *is silent.*] Nothing – not a word. I was joking. [*Pause.*] Come, Kean, must I give you my word?

KEAN: I believe in your Royal Highness' word as I believe in Holy Writ – except when it is a question of a woman. Sir, we have lied together to too many husbands.

PRINCE: Husbands, yes. But not to you, my friend!

KEAN: To me? Oh, sir! What about Jenny? And May? And Laura? [*Another pause.*] Someone must have read you that letter, otherwise how would you have known?

PRINCE: How? But my poor fool, you yourself have read it to me a thousand times! Firstly, three years ago – before you sent it to Lady Blyton; secondly, last year, before you slipped it into Countess Potocha's hand. . . . Thirdly. . . . No, the third time I took the liberty of learning it by heart, and sent it on my own account to Lady Portarlington.

KEAN [*laughing*]: So that's the way of it.

PRINCE [*laughing*]: Yes, indeed! Nothing else.

KEAN [*laughing*]: I read it to you myself! And you knew nothing at all?

PRINCE: Nothing! I took a chance. [*Reproachfully*] Oh, Kean! The selfsame letter! Have you no shame?

KEAN [*raising his head – ironically*]: Am I not the selfsame man? Besides, this time everything is changed.

PRINCE: How changed? You wrote the same letter?

KEAN: I wrote it, yes. But I didn't show it to you.

PRINCE: Then you really love her?

KEAN: She is my life!

PRINCE [*laughing*]: Romeo!

KEAN: No, no, I am no Romeo. Romeo loved to the death. I tell you I love her with my life. In an hour, I shall make my entrance and enact an imaginary love story; but what I feel now is real. It cannot be acted, nor sung, nor spoken. It makes me stammer – it bewilders me.

PRINCE: Very well – cure yourself.

KEAN: If I could!

PRINCE: And you cannot?

KEAN: Sir, this time, I am not in love for my pleasure.

PRINCE: Kean, if I asked you to give up this woman?

KEAN [*strongly*]: So that was why you came tonight?
     [*He rises.*]

PRINCE [*coldly*]: That was why . . .

KEAN: Then you, too . . .

PRINCE: Am in the same case? [*Laughing*] God, no. I have already
enshrined three women in my heart – what should I do with a
fourth? What I have to say is for your own sake. You are cutting
a very poor figure in all this. Last night you behaved like a lunatic.
These mad passions are not fitted to your years, Kean – they
deprive you of reason, you have said it yourself, and England
cannot afford to lose her finest actor.

KEAN: If England wishes to keep me, she must leave me my private
affairs. I have to experience them all to act them better. Until now,
I have only known the joys of love – at present I am enduring the
horrors, and you shall see the profit I have drawn if you come
tomorrow night to see me play Othello.

PRINCE [*without moving, firmly*]: Kean, give up this woman.

KEAN: I beg your Royal Highness to pardon me.

PRINCE: If not from good sense, then at least from obedience.

KEAN: Oh, forgive me, sir. I believed I was addressing the gay gallant
I have often followed in his nocturnal adventures – and more than
once brought home on my shoulders. But I realize my fault; I am
speaking to the Prince of Wales. Obey? It is the first of my duties.
But if your Royal Highness insists that I submit to his commands,
then at least he must excuse me from sharing his pleasures. It makes
it difficult for me to – respect him.

PRINCE [*sharply*]: Kean! [*Pause.*] Let us say I am speaking in the name
of the king.

KEAN: Of the king? Does His Majesty concern himself with my love
affairs?

PRINCE [*sharply and very quickly*]: His Majesty desires you not to meddle with his ambassadors. Count de Koefeld is an important diplomat who serves the interests of his country while at the same time helping ours. Supposing it were discovered. . . . Come, Kean, you know that he would be recalled immediately. And who would they send in his place? Do you know we have important commercial treaties with Denmark?

KEAN: Cheese.

PRINCE: I beg your pardon?

KEAN: I say that these important treaties are reduced to the purchase of cheese in Copenhagen. What a strange bargain. Sir! In one scale you place a cheese, and in the other you weigh my heart.

PRINCE: If I were to add gold?

KEAN: On the side of my heart?

PRINCE: No – on the side of the cheese. You have debts . . .

KEAN: Who should know better than you, sir. We incurred them together.

PRINCE: If you agree, the king will see them paid. Come, Kean, I know your heart, and you cannot make me believe it is worth more than six thousand pounds. There! [*He holds out a paper.*]

KEAN [*approaching*]: What is it?

PRINCE: A written renunciation.

KEAN [*reading*]: 'In consideration of the sum of six thousand pounds, I agree to renounce the pursuit of . . .' Pooh! Six thousand pounds! Sir, I have no doubt you are valuing my love at its correct level, but I should have believed you attached more value to my word! It is not enough for you that I sell my soul to the devil – you want me to sign a contract as well.

PRINCE [*laughing – still seated, he folds the paper and holds it in his hand*]: Kean – on any other occasion, your word would have been enough. But would you expect me to trust it when it is a question of a woman? How many times have we lied to their husbands? How many times have you betrayed me with my own mistresses? With this letter in my possession, I can be at peace. If you tried to see Elena, I should have it sent to her immediately. Come, sign, and the money will be brought to you this evening. [*Pause.*] Well?

KEAN: If His Majesty is concerned with the money-lenders of his kingdom, he should begin by settling your own debts. Your creditors have been waiting longer than mine, sir.

PRINCE [*calm, but furious*]: Mr Kean, is this a way to address me?

KEAN: Sir, is this a way to treat me?

PRINCE: There, there – I own I was wrong. But I am not used to seeing you take your love affairs seriously. Lady Blyton herself – I believe you would have preferred six thousand pounds. And Lady Montague . . .

KEAN: Lady Blyton, sir, wished to feel Othello's hand laid on her fair shoulders, and Romeo's mouth pressed to her fair lips. I sometimes wonder if she had ever heard the name of Kean. As for Lady Montague, I never meant anything to her. At the beginning of our affair, I would not have left her for six thousand pounds, but that was because she had offered me seven thousand to stay.

PRINCE: Kean! Cynicism does not become you.

KEAN: What's this, sir? You have the bad grace to reproach me for selling myself at the very moment you endeavour to buy me? What am I, if not the man you have made of me?

PRINCE: I?

KEAN: You, and all the others. We believe that men need illusion – that one can live and die for something other than cheese. What have you done? You took a child, and you turned him into an actor – an illusion, a fantasy – that is what you have made of Kean. He is sham prince, sham minister, sham general, sham king. Apart from that, nothing. Oh, yes, a national glory. But on condition that he makes no attempt to live a real life. In an hour from now, I shall take an old whore in my arms, and all London will cry, 'Vivat!' But if I kiss the hands of the woman I love, I shall find myself torn in pieces. Do you understand that I want to weigh with my real weight in the world? That I have had enough of being a shadow in a magic lantern? For twenty years I have been acting a part to amuse you all. Can't you understand that I want to live my own life?

PRINCE: Who can prevent you?

KEAN: What rights have I left? We players have been declared outside the law. Can I be a member of Parliament? Buy a commis-
sion? Fight a duel? Act as witness in a court of law? More than that
– I cannot even get a licence to sell cheese. You have debarred me
from every profession – except the practice of love. I can only be a
man in your wives' beds – it is only there that I can become your
equal. Very well – but let no one disturb me there!

PRINCE: Listen to me, you lunatic. We are not thinking of you,
but of her reputation. Your encounters are the talk of London.
Did you see how Lady Gosville's eyes sparkled last night? That
serpent guessed your game, and Lord knows how many times she
has repeated the story this morning.

KEAN: Every ambassador's wife has a lover and no one complains!

PRINCE: Lovers, yes. But . . .

KEAN: But not Kean! As long as their lovers have titles, even if they
are dishonoured, or fortunes, even if they are Shylocks, everyone
bows before them. But if one of them glances at an actor – even
the greatest in the land – let her look to herself! She would be
more easily pardoned if she had slept with a stable boy! [Pause.] I
don't give a damn for the scandal.

PRINCE: Are you mad? She would be . . .

KEAN: Repudiated? Driven from court? Pointed at by the mob?
All the better, she would have no one in the world but me. Do you
think I cannot replace the world?

PRINCE: You want her happiness, and yet you are ready to harm her?

KEAN: Who said I wanted her happiness?

PRINCE: You love her!

KEAN: I love her and I want to destroy her. That is how we actors
behave. Do you not think I have dreamed of heaping honours on
the woman I love? But since that is denied me, I accept the risk of
dishonour for her. If I must destroy myself and her with me, I
accept; at least, I shall have marked her for life.

PRINCE: Kean, you hate her!

KEAN: I? I would give everything . . .

PRINCE: To destroy her reputation? What good does it do you? To cure your sick pride, a woman would have to renounce her pride of her own free will; to save you, she would have to desire her own shame; you will never feel you are a man like us until she has preferred the dishonour you bring her to the honours we could give her: you will never be revenged on the world until the woman who loves you destroys the nobility in herself to follow you. In pursuing Elena, it is we, the real men, you are attacking. [*He laughs.*] It is we you would like to overcome.

KEAN: And supposing it has happened?

PRINCE: But Kean, she would have to love you!

KEAN: Well?

PRINCE: Poor Kean! [*Pause.*] Do you believe that?

KEAN: I believe it so firmly, sir [*glancing at his watch*], that I must implore your Royal Highness . . .

PRINCE: To leave you? [*He laughs.*] I will lay you a wager she never comes.

KEAN: I say she will. She has already started . . .

PRINCE: Do you accept the bet?

KEAN: I accept.

PRINCE: What stakes?

KEAN: If she does come, you will satisfy my creditors.

PRINCE: Agreed. And if she does not come . . .

KEAN: I sign your paper.

PRINCE: I see – in either case I pay your debts. [*Pause.*] She will not come: there is a ball tonight at Marlborough House and I sent her an invitation myself this morning. She is dressing this very moment . . .

KEAN: Can you believe she would prefer a ball . . .

PRINCE: To your dressing-room? Yes, I do believe it. Kean, do you think *our* wives would prefer *you* for ever?

KEAN: To convince you, your Royal Highness need only remain with me until you hear a knock at this door.

PRINCE: I will stay with you till you are called down for your first scene.

[*Knock.* KEAN *turns to the secret door.*]

Ah, no, Master Kean. It was that door. [*He points to the other door.*]

KEAN: Come in!

SOLOMON: A note, sir.

KEAN [*taking the note and reading*]: Very well, sir, you have won your
bet. The salon of Lady Marlborough has more attraction for the
Danish ambassador's wife than the dressing-room of a humble
actor. Laugh if you will! No, there is no need. I know I am nothing
beside her husband – although he is almost senile. But why can I
be nothing? I must be a fool, for I cannot understand why all
England places me at once so high and so low. [*Crying out*] You
are tearing me apart! Between your admiration and your scorn,
you are destroying me. Am I king or buffoon? Tell me! . . . Ah,
I must be mad with pride – it is impossible for me not to believe
I am a king. . . . Come, Sir, you need not be afraid. It is only
Kean the actor, acting the part of Kean the man. I am the man who
makes himself disappear, night after night. And you, who are you?
You are playing the part of the Prince of Wales? Very well, we
shall see which of us wins the greater applause. And the countess?
I would say, of we three, she is by far the best actress. [*He laughs.*]
What shall we call the play? 'As You Like It', no doubt. Or 'Much
Ado about Nothing'? Wait, we must make sure of a happy ending.
The prince and the countess must have plenty of children, and the
old count must receive a great many decorations. As for the buf-
foon – ah well, his debts will be paid. Give me your paper, sir!

PRINCE [*gently*]: No.

KEAN: No? But surely you want me to sign.

[*There is a knock at the door.* KEAN *opens, but there is no one there,
then he begins to laugh.*]

What . . . again?

[*Confronted with emptiness he stands for a moment, then closes the
door.*]

This seems to be a night of deceptions.

[*Another knock.* KEAN *smiles, a hand on his heart.*]

I fear our conversation has lost its purpose.

[*The secret door opens slowly.*]

PRINCE: I fear it too.

[*A veiled woman appears.*]

KEAN [*rushing forward*]: Elena!

PRINCE [*bowing*]: Goodnight, Mr Kean. Good evening, madam. [*He goes.*]

KEAN *pulls the beard of one of the masks hanging on the wall, and the door closes.*

KEAN: I knew you would come; your letter convinced only reason; my heart refused to believe your words. I had despaired of seeing you, but I still hoped. Thank you, Elena, thank you for justifying my faith. [*He drops on one knee and kisses her hands.*]

ANNA [*pulling away her hand*]: How beautiful! But alas, I ... I am not Elena.

KEAN [*abruptly*]: Then who are you who dared ... ? [*He draws back her veil.*] You are Miss Danby.

ANNA [*sadly*]: Yes, but for your sake I wish I were Elena.

KEAN: Who allowed you to use this door?

ANNA: I should never ... I see you are displeased. [*Quickly*] It wasn't entirely my fault; I was told at your house that you had gone to the theatre, so I came here, and found all the doors closed except one by the main entrance. I pretended I wanted to buy a ticket, and asked the man if I could see you.

KEAN: You were veiled?

ANNA: I have to be. My guardian and Lord Neville are looking for me.

KEAN: Then it was a misunderstanding, that's all. [*He laughs.*] And my lady is dressing to go to her ball. She will find it hard to convince the Prince of her innocence. Today is indeed a day of deceptions.

ANNA: Then you are not angry with me?

KEAN: On the contrary. You have won my bet and saved me a humiliation.

ANNA: I?

KEAN: Yes. Are your surprised?

ANNA: No. I bring luck to my friends – you will notice it more when we know each other better. So I can stay . . .

[*She sits down, very much at ease, smoothing her dress.*]

KEAN: You . . . er . . . . Yes, indeed, why not stay? I like company. What do you want of me?

ANNA [*as if reciting*]: Sir, a moment ago . . . I no longer knew if I could ask your help, or if I should have to go for refuge to the convent in Mayfair.

KEAN: To a nunnery, go! And quickly too . . . [*He laughs.*] Are you a Catholic?

ANNA: Yes.

KEAN: Irish, perhaps?

ANNA: Yes.

KEAN: I like the Irish: they never drown their whisky. Would you like a drink?

ANNA: No thank you.

KEAN: In that case, allow me to drink alone. [*He drinks.*] To the Emerald Isle! [*He drinks.*] To the state of Denmark! You see, I am making free with you. Have you heard I am a great drunkard?

ANNA: I have been told so.

KEAN [*refilling his glass*]: It wasn't true these last few weeks. But I feel I am about to return to my wicked habits. You will have the honour of seeing the great Kean in a state of stupefaction.

ANNA: Mr Kean! You . . . you should not drink at all this evening . . .

KEAN: Because you are in my room? You come in by mistake, and on top of that, you expect me to change my habits. You will lose nothing: wine makes me more gallant. [*He advaces on her, glass in hand.*]

ANNA: I wasn't thinking of myself, but . . . you have to appear tonight.

KEAN: If I am not mistaken, madam, you came here to ask my advice – not burden me with a lecture. [*He drinks.*] Besides, don't be afraid. There is no better actor than a drunkard. The public is so stupid they see nothing but the general effect. You yourself, I have seen you cheering me a hundred times. How your eyes sparkled!

ANNA: Did you really notice me?

KEAN: Yes, and you made me laugh, because I was drunk – my little Irish nun – drunk as an Irish lord. [*He laughs and goes to the table, laying down his glass. Then he goes behind the screen where he changes his clothes for his Romeo costume.*]

ANNA: I know.

KEAN [*behind the screen*]: Pooh!

ANNA [*bringing a diary from her reticule and consulting the pages*]: You were drunk on December 15th. You staggered when you bowed to the queen, and you called her Polonius. [*Turning the pages*] You were drunk again on December 18th, and you spoke the Fortinbras soliloquy so beautifully you had the whole house in tears.

KEAN: You see!

ANNA: Yes. Only that night, the play was *Lear*.

KEAN: What did the audience do?

ANNA: Well, King Lear is supposed to be mad, so it wasn't surprising he should take himself for Hamlet. December 22nd . . .

KEAN [*furiously*]: Enough, enough! So you knew I was drunk, and you applauded all the same?

ANNA: I wanted to encourage you.

KEAN: Encourage me? Me!

ANNA [*concealing her laughter, teasing him*]: Each word cost you such an effort, and besides, you looked so frail. I was afraid all the time you would forget your part, and stand there lost in the middle of a sentence with all those people watching you. Ah, it was then I appreciated your technique. On a night like that, I am cold with fear. Fortunately, you have an excellent prompter.

KEAN: In other words, you applauded the prompter?

ANNA: And you too. There is nothing so moving as a man fighting his tongue. Besides, I knew you must be unhappy.

KEAN [*annoyed*]: Unhappy! [*He appears wearing his Romeo wig.*] I, Kean, unhappy! It is the first time that has ever been said to me. Normally, I am envied far more than I am pitied. That man who left just now, he envies my success, my talents, even the women who love me. Do you know who it was? The Prince of Wales.

ANNA: Then Romeo isn't unhappy?

KEAN: 'Are you unhappy? Are you in love?' Every woman asks the same questions. To be or not to be. I am nothing, my child. I play at being what I am. From time to time, Kean himself plays a scene for Kean. Why should I not have my private audience too? [*He drinks.*] You are lucky tonight! You are going to see a private performance. You will see the whole gamut, from the sublime to the obscene. [*He laughs. Then, changing his tone.*] I am suffering the tortures of the damned!

ANNA: Kean!

KEAN [*experimenting with three different intonations*]: The tortures of the damned! The tortures of the damned! The tortures of the damned! Which intonation do you prefer? Dear Miss Danby, I torture myself in my spare time in order to experience everything. [*He drinks.*] Leave me alone . . .

ANNA [*rising. Slowly, afraid*]: Why?

KEAN [*glass in hand*]: I feel I am going to make you hate me.

ANNA: You will find that very hard to do. [*She smiles.*] I shall stay.

KEAN: You have been warned! You won't be startled if Romeo changes into Falstaff. I think you would have done better to go to your nunnery in the first place. [*Pause.*] Do I frighten you?

ANNA: No.

KEAN: No? You are right. Kean is a pistol charged with blanks. He makes a noise, but he doesn't do any harm. He can be mocked and insulted – insulted, do you hear? – and what happens? Nothing at all. He sinks into a chair and stammers! [*He laughs.*] Words, words, words! Remember! [*He drinks.*] You may be making a great mistake, my little nun. You are making the acquaintance of the actor Kean at a very bad moment. Tonight the great Kean loves very few of the genus woman, and if one should come into his clutches . . . Beauty . . . nobility . . . they are out of my reach. [*He goes to her.*] Do you know my secret ambition? To have a beautiful woman between these four walls and humiliate her. [*Sharply, as she makes no move*] Fly from me! Why don't you fly from me?

ANNA [*sitting down again and spreading her skirts*]: Because I feel perfectly safe.

KEAN [*on his knees beside her*]: Will you sleep in my bed?

ANNA [*calmly*]: No.

KEAN: I should treat you like a sister. [*Quoting*] 'Lady, shall I lie in your lap?'

ANNA: 'No, my lord.' That's Ophelia's line. I know the whole part by heart.

KEAN: Indeed. [*He rises and looks at her carefully.*] What do you want?

ANNA [*rising*]: To be an actress.

KEAN [*bursts out laughing*]: Forgive me – it's ridiculous: the cheese-monger's daughter wants to be an actress! Your father would turn in his grave, Miss Danby! You an actress! But it's the lowest profession of all! What a strange idea! Who put it into your head?

ANNA: You.

KEAN: I?

ANNA: Your example proved that it can be glorious and honourable.

KEAN [*During the following scene he finishes getting into his Romeo costume.*] Honourable! [*He drinks and rises, swaying a little.*] Do I look honourable? My poor child, you were born honourable; it is the privilege of purveyors of cheese. Famous, yes, I am famous. And then? If the gossips of your village stain your good name, that is dishonour: but if all England knows you are a whore, that is fame. If I had time, I should offer you my arm, and we should take a walk through the streets of London. You would hear the murmurs as we pass: 'Is that really Kean? I thought him much better-looking. How much stouter he's grown! And doesn't he think a lot of himself! How old he looks! Have you seen his hair? He must be wearing a wig. I should like to try if it's real!' In the old days, when a man had committed some terrible crime, every loyal citizen had the right to shoot him at sight, like a mad dog. That is fame. Go home, Miss Danby, there is no place for you here.

ANNA [*smiling*]: Mr Kean, I ran away from home last night; that is quite enough to ruin a woman's reputation.

KEAN: Wasn't it enough?

ANNA: Since I have begun, I might as well go on to the end.

KEAN: You asked my advice, and I gave it you.

ANNA: That was not what I asked you. I wanted to know if you thought I could become an actress.

KEAN: I should have to hear you first.

ANNA: I know every woman's part in the whole of Shakespeare.

KEAN: Indeed. [*Pause.*] Who taught you?

ANNA: You.

KEAN: I again? [*He begins to put on his make-up.*]

ANNA: I played the parts with you. I have heard you so often, and then I imagined the criticism you would give me.

KEAN: Let us see the results. What will you try?

ANNA: Desdemona, Juliet, Ophelia – whatever you please.

KEAN: Ophelia will do.

[*As she recites, he drinks.*]

ANNA: 'There's rosemary, that's for remembrance: pray you, love, remember: there's pansies, that's for thoughts. ... There's fennel for you, and columbines: there's rue for you: and here's some for me: we may call it herb of grace o' Sundays: O, you must wear your rue with a difference.'

KEAN: You want the truth.

ANNA: Yes.

KEAN: The whole truth.

ANNA: Yes. [*Frightened by his tone.*] Very nearly the whole truth.

KEAN: Get thee to a nunnery!

ANNA [*gazing at him*]: Is there – no hope?

KEAN: Not the slightest.

ANNA: Was I ... very bad?

KEAN [*scornfully*]: Worse than bad. Very good.

ANNA [*her eyes still on him*]: Then ... then ... if I work hard ... I know how to work, you know – and I'm very strong-minded. I always get what I want.

KEAN: You have to be strong-minded to grow rich among cheese: and the daughters of cheesemongers inherit their strength of will from their fathers. You will try and acquire your talent in driblets, as your father amassed his pennies. How hard you're going to work! It makes me tired merely to think of how hard you're going to work. And you will make progress – you will make such progress. You will never stop making progress. It will begin by being bad, then not too bad, then really not bad, then good, very good, better still, perfect, better than perfect. And then? [*Imitating her*] 'I always get what I want.' [*In his own voice.*] With determination, my child, you can even get the moon which, after all, is only made of green cheese. But you cannot *become* an actress. Do you think you have to act *well*? Do I act well? Do I look as though I could work hard? You are born an actor as you are born a prince. And determination and hard work have nothing to do with that fact.

ANNA: Mr Kean, I *have* to become an actress.

KEAN: What for?

ANNA: To earn my living.

KEAN: Have you no money?

ANNA: I left everything when I ran away.

KEAN [*bursting out laughing*]: Left everything! So you've come to the gutter to make an honest living! We'll save our pennies like papa! Hard work and economy: what an edifying picture! Shakespeare, Marlowe, Ben Jonson, d'you hear? You cannot act to earn your living. You act to lie, to deceive, to deceive yourself; to be what you cannot be, and because you have had enough of being what you are. You act because you want to forget yourself. You act the hero because you are a coward at heart, and you play the saint because you are a devil by nature. You act a murderer because you long to poison your best friend. You act because you are a born liar and totally unable to speak the truth. You act because you would go mad if you didn't act. Act! Do I know myself when I am acting? Is there ever a moment when I cease to act? Look at me; do I hate all women, or am I acting at hating them? Am I acting to make you afraid, or do I very truly desire to make you pay me for your whole sex? Get thee to a nunnery, and give your virtues to God. Go home to your golden guineas, and leave us in peace with our cardboard coins!

ANNA [*gently*]: Mr Kean, could you try to act at being kind?

KEAN [*startled*]: Kind? After all, why not? It isn't a part in my repertoire, but I don't mind improvising . . . [*Pause.*] If I were kind . . . if I were kind . . . [*Acting*] You have seen the gilded surface of our life, and it has dazzled you; now I must show you the reverse of this brilliant medal – it has two crowns; one of flowers and one of thorns.

ANNA [*laughing*]: You are funny when you are kind.

KEAN [*imperturbably*]: There are many things difficult for a man of my years to say, difficult for a child of your age to understand.

ANNA [*acting*]: Edmund Kean would never utter a word that was unfit to be heard by Anna Danby.

KEAN [*in a changed voice*]: Are you prepared to sell yourself?

ANNA [*as herself*]: Is it absolutely necessary?

KEAN: Indispensable. You must go to bed with . . . Let me see . . . [*He counts on his fingers.*] The director, the leading actor, the author . . . not counting the understudies . . .

ANNA: To start with the author – that's easy, Shakespeare is dead. As for the director, he does as the leading actor tells him.

KEAN: Now for the leading actor. Supposing you come to see our national hero, the great Kean. . . . Let us play the scene. We shall see if you can improvise. I am Kean, you are yourself. You have just arrived. Go out. Pretend to go out.

[*She runs to the door and turns to face him.*]

Now come in.

[*She comes forward.*]

Don't we knock?

ANNA: Oh, forgive me. [*She goes back to the door and knocks.*]

KEAN: Come in. [*She comes forward.*] Shut the door.

[*For a moment she is at a loss, then makes as if shutting a door.*]

CALL BOY [*off*]: Five minutes, please.

KEAN: Good. Now come in. No, no, don't raise your veil. There, that's perfect. [*He acts.*] What do you want, my child?

ANNA [*sincerely, but very much the ingénue*]: Mr Kean, I want to act.

KEAN: No, no, no. Not like that. You are throwing away your

chances. This is a vain creature. You must flatter him. Begin again. Invent – create.

ANNA: I don't know how.

KEAN: Speak as you feel.

ANNA [*improvising*]: Here I am in his very room. . . . Should I have the courage to tell him what has brought me here? . . . Ah, dear God – give me strength, for I feel my courage failing.

KEAN [*acting*]: What do you want of me?

ANNA [*in ecstasy*]: Ah, it is his voice! [*To* KEAN] Forgive me, sir, however modest you may be, you must understand that your reputation – your talent – your genius . . .

KEAN: Very good – very good indeed . . .

ANNA: . . . disturb me far more than your kind reception reassures me. Yet they say you are as good as you are great.

KEAN: I am not good.

[*He walks up to her, looking her up and down, touching her chin, her arms.*]

Not bad – not bad at all.

ANNA: Are you really saying that, or is it in your part?

KEAN [*vicious*]: I don't know. What does that prove? That you could drive a man to distraction? How am I to know that you can make an audience happy? Show me your legs.

ANNA [*acting*]: Oh, sir!

KEAN: What? Does that embarrass you?

ANNA [*spoken*]: I? Not in the least! [*She lifts her skirts.*]

KEAN: Are you mad? You should have refused! [*He beats her dress down.*]

ANNA: Why? I want to be an actress.

KEAN: It's out of character. Say: Horror!

ANNA: Horror! [*She giggles.*]

KEAN: Better than that.

ANNA [*trying to get it right*]: Horror! Horror . . . horror!

KEAN: Good. Now walk. Better than that. Like a queen. Not bad for a cheesemonger's daughter. Now be ashamed.

ANNA: Why?

KEAN: Because I have humiliated you. Good God, I told you! I detest all women. I touch your shoulder . . .

ANNA: Ah! . . .

KEAN: I bend over you . . . I shall break your pride. Perhaps take revenge on you for a woman I hate. Are you a virgin?

ANNA [*after a pause*]: No.

KEAN: Of course you're a virgin. Say, yes.

ANNA: Yes.

KEAN: Better than that.

ANNA: Yes.

KEAN [*annoyed*]: Make up your mind – are you or aren't you?

ANNA: Whatever you like.

KEAN: You are a virgin and you're afraid of me.

ANNA: Oh, no, Mr Kean.

KEAN [*pushing her into a chair and leaning over her*]: Little fool, you wanted to cheat me, eh? You planned your comedy well; the brutal fiancé, the midnight flight, the secret stair, the fortunate coincidences. You wanted to have your game without paying. To earn the right to make a fool of me, you have to be at least a countess. You will pay your shot. You are proud, aren't you? Stubborn and proud. You are all proud, you devilish regiment of women. Well, you shall never set foot on a stage unless you do all I ask. Choose.

ANNA [*rising*]: I have made my choice; I will do anything you ask.

KEAN: Incapable of improvising.

ANNA: I speak how I feel. I will do anything you ask . . .

KEAN [*quickly*]: You can work with me, and if you have the smallest talent, I will engage you in my company. Don't be afraid; unconditionally.

ANNA: Without asking – anything?

KEAN: No, no, of course not! I was only acting.

ANNA [*disappointed*]: I see.

KEAN: I told you!

ANNA: One never knows with you.

KEAN: Nor with you either, little nuisance! Run along. You've won.

ANNA [*amazed*]: Are you acting at being kind?

KEAN: I don't know. I'm drunk – that's all I know. Take advantage of it.

ANNA: I will. [*She kisses* KEAN *on both cheeks and runs away lightly.*] I'll be here in the morning! [*She has gone.*]

KEAN [*left alone, continues to dress, singing to himself. Suddenly he realizes he is singing, stops himself with a scandalized* 'Oh!' *Then*]: Elena . . . Elena . . . [*annoyed*] No! [*more sombrely*] Ah, Elena, you hurt me very much tonight . . .

CALL BOY: Beginners, please.

KEAN [*with a sidelong glance in the mirror*]: Elena, you hurt me very much . . . [*articulating*] Hurt me ve-ry much . . . Ele-na, you hurt me ve-ry much. [*He puts on his stage shoes, takes his hat and cape.*] Elena . . . [*He looks at himself in the mirror.*] Juliet . . . Juliet . . . [*He recites.*] 'It was the lark, the herald of the morn, No nightingale.'
    [SOLOMON *enters.*]

SOLOMON: Your call, sir.

KEAN [*a glance in the mirror*]: Solomon, how old am I?

SOLOMON [*promptly*]: Eighteen, sir.

KEAN [*reciting*]:
  'Night's candles are burnt out, and jocund day
    Stands tiptoe on the misty mountain tops:
    I must be gone and live, or stay and die.'
    Stay and die! Ridiculous! Anyone in front, tonight?

SOLOMON: House full boards out.

KEAN: Idiots! They have come to see a Romeo of forty-five whose Juliet has furnished him with a pair of horns! [*He laughs.*] I'll give them Romeo. I'll give them Romeo. [*Before he goes, he turns to the audience and cries.*] The public are all fools!

    [SOLOMON *throws open the door.* KEAN *disappears towards the stage (off). We hear the National Anthem in the distance, the rustle of the audience, then silence as the people rise. We see the theatre in reverse, with the lighted stage, and the actors preparing to begin the play.*]

                          CURTAIN

ACT THREE

Scene: At the Black Horse.

   [*The members of old Bob's troupe of acrobats, among them* FANNY,
   DAISY, KITTY *and* PIP *are practising a number.* PETER POTT *the
   landlord is watching them. There are various customers in the background.*

      KEAN *enters, dressed as a sailor. He settles at a table, and calls
   loudly*]

KEAN: Wine!

PETER POTT [*who is watching the dance*]: All in good time, sir!

KEAN [*furious*]: What's this? Bring me a drink, you villain, or I'll
   burn the place down over your ears.

PETER POTT [*joyfully*]: Oh, it's you, sir!

KEAN: No.

PETER POTT: What?

KEAN: No, it isn't I!

PETER POTT: Mr Kean!

KEAN: Gone away till the end of the month.

PETER POTT: But I know you!

KEAN: Have you ever seen me like this? [*He does look very depressed,
   almost mad.*]

PETER POTT: Oh no, fortunately!

KEAN: Then you can swear this isn't I. Go and fetch me a bottle, and
   bring me a harlot to share it.

PETER POTT: Well, sir . . .

KEAN: What is it?

PETER POTT: These people are waiting for you – you told them to
   meet you here.

KEAN [*looking at them dully, without recognizing them*]: The devil!
   Get me a drink.

   [PETER POTT *goes, nodding to one of the girls to go to* KEAN.]

THE GIRL: Here I am!

KEAN: What's your name?

FANNY: Fanny.

KEAN: Fanny – foolish Fanny. Do you make love on credit?

[PETER POTT *has returned with champagne. He signs to the girl to say yes.*]

FANNY: Yes, sir.

KEAN: Call me Romeo. [*He pours out the wine. The acrobats have crowded round him and stare at him in silence.*] Who are you? What do you want?

[*Disappointed, the acrobats murmur among themselves.*]

Why, it's you! [*He rises and goes to them.*] My poor friends – my brothers – forgive me – I am drunk. There's a child to be christened?

[*One of the acrobats –* PIP *– replies, still very depressed.*]

PIP: A christening party – yes. You invited us, then you forgot us . . .

KEAN: I? Forget my companions in misfortune? Kiss me – all of you. I love you from the bottom of my heart. [*To* PETER POTT] Have you a meal for us?

PETER POTT: Of course!

KEAN: Then lead us to it! [*To the acrobats*] Where is the lucky father?

PIP: Oh, sir – poor old Bob – he's had an accident . . .

KEAN: You don't mean . . .

PIP: No – but he has broken his leg and the doctor says he must stay in bed for six weeks.

KEAN: Well, that'll be six weeks of rest. God, I envy him.

PIP: Still, during that time . . .

KEAN: Well?

PIP: The whole company could die of hunger!

KEAN: Can't you do the act without him?

PIP: You know we can't.

KEAN: You'd starve while you had the chance of a good meal, and you'd have gone away with your empty bellies because you thought I didn't recognize you. Ah, I know the pride of you tumblers – my own pride of the old days. Wait . . . [*He fumbles for his purse, then remembers it has gone. Furiously*] The devil! ... I have no money ... [*He picks up a jug of water and holds it out to* FANNY.] Juliet, pour that over my head. [*She hesitates.*] Pour, I tell you – I must clear my brain. [*She pours the water over him – he shakes his head.*] Now – get back to your paying customers. [*He looks at her more closely.*] No, you're as thin as a rail, you'd better dine with us too.... A week without food ... that happened to me, you know, sixteen years ago. It seems like three weeks.... Peter – Peter Pott! Pen, ink and paper ...

   [PETER *goes out, and comes back immediately with paper and writing materials.*]

KITTY: What is he doing? [*They all huddle in a corner.*]
KEAN [*writing*]: Carry this to the director of Drury Lane. Tell him tomorrow I will play the last act of *Othello* for the benefit of one of my friends who has had an accident.
PIP: Ah, what a true friend.
KITTY: In good times as well as bad.
PETER [*calling*]: Tom! [*A sailor comes forward.* KEAN *gives him the letter.*]
KEAN: Take this – wait for a reply. Now – are you all ready? I want my dinner!
ALL: Ready!
KEAN: Then let's go!
DAISY: We mustn't keep the Vicar waiting.
KEAN: The Vicar is patient ... but a good supper should never be kept waiting. [*To* PIP] We'll give your little brother a splendid christening.
PIP: It's a sister!
KEAN: Never mind! We'll take good care of her all the same.
PETER: I'll see if the spit is turning.
KEAN [*on his way to the dining-room*]: Wine! Wine!
JOE [*appearing*]: Here, sir.
PETER: Not a drop of water in the wine you give Mr Kean!
JOE [*who wears an apron*]: And the others?
PETER: Use your own discretion.

JOE: I understand.

[*They have all gone into the other room where the music now begins.* ANNA *appears.*]

PETER [*seeing her, comes forward respectfully, wiping his hands*]: Miss?

ANNA: Can you give me a room?

PETER [*mysteriously*]: It's quite ready.

ANNA [*surprised*]: Indeed?

PETER: I was told to prepare my best room for a lady who would be coming tonight. I presume it is you?

ANNA [*aside, smiling*]: He thinks of everything. [*Aloud*] Take me to my room, please. I am so afraid someone may see me.

[PETER *shows her towards the stairs.*]

PETER [*calling*]: Dolly: show the lady up to Number One.

DOLLY [*appears, very dignified, and precedes* ANNA *up the stairs*]: Can I send you up anything, Miss?

ANNA: No, thank you, nothing. [*She disappears.*]

[SOLOMON *appears.*]

PETER: Good evening, Mr Solomon.

SOLOMON: Has Mr Kean gone?

PETER: Not yet. He's having supper with the acrobats.

SOLOMON: Tell him I am waiting and must speak to him at once.

PETER [*to* JOE]: Joe, d'you hear? Fetch Mr Kean.

[JOE *goes out to the other room. The music swells as he opens the door.*] [*To* SOLOMON] You're too late for supper and too early for breakfast – what can I give you?

SOLOMON [*bad-temperedly*]: Nothing. I couldn't swallow a drop.

[KEAN *enters with his napkin round his neck, glass in hand.*]

KEAN: Well? What's the matter?

SOLOMON: Oh, sir, a disaster.

KEAN: Oh, is that all? What else did you expect?

SOLOMON: It's the jeweller – that devilish jeweller. He has taken out a warrant for your arrest, and the sheriff and bailiffs have gone to your house.

KEAN: What the devil do I care since I'm not there myself?

SOLOMON: They say they'll wait till you come back.

KEAN: Splendid! In that case, I won't go home.

SOLOMON: Sir!

KEAN: Come along, Solomon, join us at supper.

SOLOMON: I'm not hungry!

[ANNA *runs gaily down the stairs.*]

ANNA: Here I am!

KEAN: Eh?

ANNA: I said: here I am! [*The music stops.*]

KEAN: By the lord, so I see. What the devil are you doing here?

ANNA: I was in my room and I heard your voice.

KEAN: In *your* room? D'you have a room in this brothel?

ANNA [*amused*]: Is it a brothel?

KEAN: Er . . . very nearly.

ANNA: The room you took for me is very clean.

KEAN: I? Take a room for you? [*To* SOLOMON] Go in to supper. I'll follow. [SOLOMON *goes.*] What's all this about? Why do I find you wherever I go?

ANNA [*showing him a letter*]: If you didn't want to see me, why did you send me a letter?

KEAN [*exasperated*]: Ah – ah! I never wrote you a letter.

ANNA [*reading*]: 'You have been followed: your retreat is discovered. Meet me tonight at the docks. Ask for the Black Horse. Someone will meet you to bring you to me. Fear nothing and trust me. I respect you as much as I love you. Kean.'

KEAN [*repeating the last words*]: As much as I love you. [*He shrugs.*]

ANNA [*obstinately*]: As much as I love you. Your very words.

KEAN: If I had wanted to see you, I would never have taken these precautions.

ANNA: You added a postscript: 'I have been followed. That is why I cannot come myself, and why the man who will fetch you will probably be masked.'

KEAN: Masked. [*He begins to laugh.*] It seems I am out of luck. I leave the theatre to plunge headlong into melodrama. I've had enough of the theatre, of swords and mysteries and masked conspirators. Do you know why I'm here? To eat and drink! That is life! I have the right to live, haven't I? [*Furiously*] I respect you as much as I love you! A masked man! [*Harshly*] Look at me. You wrote that letter yourself!

ANNA: No!

KEAN: Bah! You're quite capable of it!

ANNA: I am quite capable of it, but I didn't write that letter.

KEAN: Show me. [*He looks at the letter.*] It's a man's hand. You've fallen straight into their laps.

ANNA: I?

KEAN: It's obviously a trick of your guardian, or your betrothed.

ANNA: Not my guardian – he's no imagination.

KEAN: Lord Neville has enough for two. It's quite clear: they've made you come here, and they'll pluck you like a flower.

ANNA: No.

KEAN: Why not?

ANNA: Because you will save me.

KEAN: Obviously. But will you please tell me why I can't take two steps without running into you? Why all London last night whispered that I had eloped with you? Why this evening you come to my room through my secret door, and why now I find you in this thieves' den, where apparently I am going to have to grapple with a gang of masked men?

ANNA: They may not be masked.

KEAN: Why do you have to bring tragedy – and when I say tragedy, I mean tragical-comical, into the crossroads of my life? Is there so much of the romantic in this head? [*He taps her forehead.*]

ANNA: Romantic? Kean, you're wrong! I'm not romantic at all.

KEAN: No?

ANNA: I'm not romantic, but I've been horribly bored. [*Sweetly*] And this evening I'm not bored at all. [*At ease*] Won't you sit down? Can I have some champagne?

KEAN [*sitting down unwillingly*]: My guests are waiting.

ANNA: I know. [*Pause.*] I was so bored with my guardian that I actually fell ill.

KEAN: You aren't going to tell me the story of your life?

ANNA: Would you rather tell me the story of yours?

KEAN: No.

ANNA: I haven't a glass . . .

KEAN: Then you don't have to drink.

[ANNA *takes the bottle and wipes the top with her muff.*]

ANNA: Let me explain. I was bored and I pined away. I fell into a decline. Do you know what that means?

KEAN: Yes. You needed a husband.

ANNA: I needed amusement. That's what the doctors said. They said: she will die. She needs balls, parties, theatres. . . . Balls! . . . Do you like balls?

KEAN: I never dance.

ANNA: Neither do I. So, I . . . slipped. Oh, merely from boredom. So, after that, I was only allowed the theatre because they could keep an eye on me there.

KEAN [*furiously*]: You were a fool.

ANNA: Why?

KEAN: A fool to . . . to slip. It . . . it doesn't suit you in the least. Who with?

ANNA: Bah! it was so long ago . . . besides, it was so boring I became a virgin again immediately afterwards. So, I went to the theatre. To Drury Lane. The first evening, it was Romeo! The evening went by in a dream. I never spoke, I never breathed, I never even applauded at the end of the play.

KEAN: A pity; actors need encouragement. Who played Romeo?

ANNA: Next evening, I was taken to the Moor of Venice. Ah, what a magnificent creature! And how delightfully jealous! I should adore to be stifled with a pillow: I think that shows great delicacy of feeling. To die among feathers – how agreeable. I liked him better than Romeo because I have always preferred older men.

KEAN: H'm! And who played Othello?

ANNA: Next time, it was Hamlet. A poor young man who soliloquized too much. But so prettily. How unfortunate that he was in love with that goose. I should have answered him: 'I like men who have plenty to say for themselves.' Anyway, she died. Good

T – T.P. – C

riddance. But the poor boy died too. And so stupidly. That evening
I cried: oh, how I cried. But don't be afraid. I applauded too.

KEAN: And who was Hamlet?

ANNA: Kemble!

KEAN [*startled*]: What?

ANNA [*laughing*]: No, no, Kean, no. It was you, of course. And Romeo
was you. Othello was you. Hamlet was still you. But admit
Kemble isn't bad?

KEAN: Don't be foolish. Kemble plays Hamlet like a carpet-seller.

ANNA: Yet the critics have given him great praise.

KEAN: Critics don't hurt us with their bad notices. They destroy us
with the good notices they give other people.

ANNA: So I made inquiries, and I found you were a drunkard, a
libertine, crippled with debts, melancholy and mad by turns, and
I said to myself: 'That man needs a wife.'

KEAN: Indeed!

ANNA: A wife. A cheesemonger's daughter, wilful and stubborn, to
bring a little order into his ways.

KEAN: Order! I see! And genius? What happens to that while my
life is being ordered?

ANNA: You don't understand. I shall supply the order, and you will
supply the genius. Oh, Kean, everything will be tidy. Every night
from nine to midnight you will rage through your parts, and then
you will come home and find peace, luxury ... [*Lowering her
lashes*] ... and love ...

KEAN: Come here, little sister. Do you know what I think? You are
even madder and more romantic than I. [*He kisses her on the forehead.*]

ANNA: Don't you want me?

KEAN: No, of course not. With your method and my madness, the
house would blow up at the end of the first week.

ANNA: You will accept in the end – I'm sure of that. You are a very
weak character, and everything I want ...

KEAN: ... you get. I know.

　　[*The* SAILOR *runs in.*]

What is it?

SAILOR: A letter from the theatre, Mr Kean. The answer to your note.

KEAN: Let me see. [*He glances at the letter.*] Very good. [*To the* SAILOR] Go back to the theatre. Tell them to put the posters out tomorrow morning. I will find someone else to play myself. [*The* SAILOR *goes.*] You who always get what you want – do you *want* to play Desdemona?

ANNA: Desdemona?

KEAN: Tomorrow night I am giving a benefit for one of my friends: I only decided this evening, and now they tell me there is no time to get Miss MacLeish who has gone to the country until Friday. Do you want to take her place?

ANNA: But I have never . . .

KEAN: Come to the theatre at noon tomorrow, and I'll work with you until the performance.

ANNA: You mean . . . I should play . . . with you?

KEAN: Naturally. Who else?

ANNA: You see – you see! It's proof positive I'm going to marry you.

KEAN: Yes, yes, of course. In the meantime I'll have to get you out of this hornets' nest.

ANNA: What hornets' nest? Oh, I had forgotten. How amusing it all is! What are you going to do?

KEAN [*calling*]: Peter! Fetch the constable.

[*A* CONSTABLE *enters.*]

KEAN: Ah, here he is. Constable, this is Miss Danby, one of the richest heiresses in London. Her guardian is trying to force her into a marriage against her will. I put her into your care . . .

CONSTABLE: And who are you, sir, to give me orders with such authority?

KEAN: What matter *who* demands the law's protection, since in the eyes of the law all men are equal? If you wish to know, I am the actor . . . [*He rises to his full height.*] Kean!

CONSTABLE: Oh, sir! Why didn't I recognize you? I've seen you play a hundred times, sir – I'm one of your greatest admirers . . .

This lady requires protection? Naturally, sir, naturally – everything to serve your interests. May I know how . . .

KEAN: Anna, take this officer upstairs, and tell him the story. I must stay here – I am expecting a guest.

ANNA: I do hope you knock him down.

KEAN: Why not? Particularly if he is the one I hope he is.

ANNA: Then I want to stay here – to see.

KEAN: Will you kindly go up to your room?

ANNA [*with a cry*]: Ah!

KEAN: What's the matter?

ANNA: You said that exactly as if I were your wife.

[*She runs upstairs, followed by the* CONSTABLE. *It is very dark. We see* LORD NEVILLE *enter masked – he speaks in a low voice to two masked men, disguised in long capes. All three of them hide.* KEAN *has not seen them.*]

KEAN: Masked? Why should he be masked? A man who makes a bet has no need to mask himself . . . Good heavens! But it must be the bridegroom in person – Lord Neville himself. Caught red-handed in the act of rape and forgery. But . . . but . . . I have the right to strike him! I can beat him as much as I like! Prince – to take revenge on your noblemen, Kean has no need to strike through a woman. Since I cannot touch the shoulders of that lady, I can lay a noble lord on his back in the dust. A lord in the dust – I am a new man. I can beat a lord like a dog, with the law on my side. Oh, God, hear me – make him come – make him come! Here he is . . .

[LORD NEVILLE *appears alone.*]

NEVILLE: Stand aside, friend – I wish to pass.

KEAN: Stand back, friend – you cannot pass here.

NEVILLE: What does this mean?

KEAN: That I dislike masks.

NEVILLE: Indeed?

KEAN: Indeed. Masks went out of fashion with Queen Anne.

NEVILLE: A man may have good reason for hiding his face.

KEAN: Is yours so ugly? Disfigured perhaps by the smallpox? Covered

with pimples? Strawberry marks over your cheeks? Someone has
cut off your nose and ears? I'd regret that – nothing for me to do.

NEVILLE: Will you stand aside?

KEAN: No, my fine sir.

NEVILLE: What do you want? Money?

KEAN: I want to see the cut of your jib. And if you won't take off
your mask, I shall have to do it for you.

NEVILLE: Insolence!

KEAN: Well? Which is it to be? You have a free hand – use it.
For if I have to raise mine, you may hear it sing about your
ears. You won't? Very good! Come in all of you and bring some
light. I've caught a fly-by-night and I want to take a good
look.

NEVILLE: Kean!

KEAN: Why, it's my lord Neville! What a surprise – I make my
excuses. I took you for a sneak-thief, and I was about to chastise
you. I have mistaken Polonius for a rat so many times, it has
become a kind of occupational disease.

NEVILLE: This is a trap!

KEAN: Be assured, sir, it is one you cannot get out of.

NEVILLE: What do you want?

KEAN: You insulted me by using my name as a cloak for your
infamies, you must answer to me for that, here and now.

NEVILLE: There is only one inconvenience, sir. A peer of England
cannot fight an actor.

KEAN [dropping the stool he has raised]: But of course, what was I
thinking of? You're a lord and I'm an actor. How can we cross
swords? You are descended from the Plantagenets, in line direct –
I might even say you slid down. I am descended from no one – I am
the rising star. You inherited an immense fortune, which you
squandered in ten years; I have earned as much money as you have
spent, and if I choose, I can rival the luxury of the Prince of Wales.
You would not deign to appear on a stage, even before an audience
of kings, but you stoop to playing the cut-throat in the lowest
tavern in town. With me, there's this difference – from eight to

midnight I play anything I choose, even the traitor Iago, but if after midnight I had to play the part of Lord Neville, I should hold myself dishonoured. You sit in the House of Lords, you make and unmake laws; the doors of the king's palace open at the very sound of your name. But when you wish to play tricks, you borrow mine. Not for all the gold in the world would I borrow yours; my name belongs to me – it was not given me, my lord, it's my own creation.

[*He points to himself, then to* LORD NEVILLE, *and shakes his finger, meaning that they will not fight.*]

You're right. We cannot cross swords. You have fallen too low, mine would pierce the air above your head – I have mounted too high – yours would hardly touch the heel of my boot. [*Pause.*] My lord, in all this, you have only forgotten two things: that I might denounce your attempt to the police, and put you into their hands: secondly, that you are in my power. We will not fight: agreed. But what would you say if I were to knock you down? Eh? Do you know that actors have strong hands? I could crush you as I crush this glass . . . [*He laughs.*] . . . if I did not prefer to use it to propose a toast. Wine, Peter. [PETER *fills his glass.*] To the health of Miss Anna Danby, to her free choice of a husband . . . and may that husband bring her all the happiness she deserves. My lord, you are free to go.

NEVILLE: Mountebank!

ALL: Long live Kean!

[LORD NEVILLE *turns on his heel and goes, followed by the jeers of the acrobats who having seen him go, crowd back to the supper room.* KEAN *glances up towards* ANNA'S *room. His eye falls on one of her gloves, which he picks up. As he does so, one of the assassins, holding a blackjack, prepares to strike* KEAN, *who has thrown the glove aside. At this moment,* KEAN *bends to pick it up, the blackjack strikes the table. One of the drinkers, who has been asleep at the table, wakes up at the sound.* KEAN *has risen, and kicks the cut-throat in the stomach. The man falls, his arms spread wide. During this, the other cut-throat brings out a dagger and prepares to strike* KEAN. *The drinker* (JOHN) *springs at him, sends a blow crashing into his face, and sends him reeling to the foot of the stairs.* KEAN *falls back.*]

KEAN: Well done, lad. What a magnificent ending to the act!

CURTAIN

ACT FOUR

SCENE ONE

Scene: KEAN's *dressing-room.*
  [ANNA *and* SOLOMON *are rehearsing* Othello.]

SOLOMON: 'No; heaven forfend! I would not kill thy soul.'

ANNA: 'Talk you of killing?'

SOLOMON: 'Ay, I do.'

ANNA: 'Then heaven have mercy on me!' What's the time?

SOLOMON: What – again?

ANNA: Again?

SOLOMON: You asked me the time, and I said 'again'! That's the seventh time. It's half past six.

ANNA [*crying*]: Solomon, he won't come!

SOLOMON [*hiding his anxiety*]: He will. He has to play tonight.

ANNA: And if he has decided not to?

SOLOMON: Oh, that! Of course he has decided not to.

ANNA: You see!

SOLOMON [*fetching the Othello breastplate*]: Every time he gets really drunk, he swears he will never set foot on a stage again; that he will go back to being a tumbler. It always happens!

ANNA: This time he may really mean it.

SOLOMON [*putting the breastplate behind the screen*]: How could he? He has promised this benefit to his old friends; he always keeps his word to them.

ANNA: Supposing there has been an accident?

SOLOMON: An accident – to him? He is luck personified. His only misfortunes are his successes in love.

ANNA: You say that to reassure me – I can see you are as anxious as I am.

SOLOMON: Not at all. Start again. 'I would not kill thy soul.'

ANNA: What can he be doing?

SOLOMON: What do you expect? He's sleeping off his wine.

ANNA: But where? He didn't go home last night.

SOLOMON: How should I know? Once we found him in a ditch on the road to Cambridge, ten miles away. No one ever knew how he got there. He was sleeping like a child: when we woke him up, he demanded his tea.

ANNA: What are you doing?

SOLOMON [*nervous*]: Just looking at the time.

ANNA: You see – you are worried.

SOLOMON: I told you to go over your part.

ANNA: You love him, don't you?

SOLOMON: Who?

ANNA: Him.

SOLOMON: Far more than any of his women.

ANNA: Then I promise you nothing will be changed. You can live with us.

SOLOMON: With you? When?

ANNA: When we are married. 'That death's unnatural that kills for loving.'

SOLOMON [*criticizing*]: Not like that. You're putting too much fire into it.

ANNA: It's what I've got.

SOLOMON: It's not right for Desdemona. She was only a breath – a whisper.

ANNA: A breath? How could she be? She had to have courage to make her general marry her.

SOLOMON: She was an innocent victim – a martyr.

ANNA: Have you ever seen a beautiful woman being a martyr? Martyrdom is for the plain – we must allow them some compensation.

SOLOMON: That's ridiculous.

ANNA: How do you know? What do you know about women?

SOLOMON: Considering the numbers that have passed through this room, it would be very surprising if I didn't understand them.

ANNA: And Shakespeare – do you understand him too?

SOLOMON: I have held the book for more than forty years.

ANNA: That's a fine reason!

SOLOMON: And Mistress MacLeish – doesn't she understand? She always plays Desdemona with great gentleness. As soon as the curtain rises, you can see she is already dead.

ANNA: She has to play it that way because she's afraid of collapsing altogether. I am young – I have blood in my veins. I shall play it as I please.

> 'Alas, why gnaw you so your nether lip?
> Some bloody passion shakes your very frame!'

There, now you've put me off. Why isn't he here? He's the only one who knows. He said: 'Come to my room at twelve o'clock. Be on time.'

SOLOMON: He was drunk.

ANNA: Of course he was drunk. But he said it again when he was sober.

SOLOMON: He never drew a sober breath all night.

ANNA: At six o'clock this morning he was sober. You didn't see him. It was in his carriage – he was taking me home to my aunt. The sun was shining, it was a lovely day – he took my hands and called me his heart's darling.

SOLOMON: If all the women he has called his heart's darling were entitled to a pension, the Treasury would go bankrupt.

ANNA: Mr Solomon, you are a fool. And 'little sister'? Are there many he has called 'little sister'?

SOLOMON: Ah, that, no. Sisters aren't exactly in his line.

ANNA [proudly]: He called me little sister.

SOLOMON: It's nothing to be proud of.

ANNA: Solomon – I told him I had – slipped. Was I right?

SOLOMON: And naturally you have never – er – slipped?

ANNA: Of course not.

SOLOMON: People can tell, you know!

ANNA [discontented]: Oh?

SOLOMON: Yes. But it isn't important. He isn't concerned with that with you.

[KEAN's *voice is heard off – shouting:* 'Do you call that a wig! Miss Cook – my shirt cuffs are torn again.']

SOLOMON: Here he is.

ANNA: At last!

KEAN [*off*]: What's that? My fault? I make too many gestures? I shall insist on Venetian lace – this stuff isn't good enough for the Moor ... No ... I don't need anyone to help me dress ...

SOLOMON: Take my advice – slip out by the secret door.

[*He pulls aside the curtain of costumes which conceals the door.*]

ANNA: Why?

SOLOMON: You heard him. He's in a black temper.

ANNA: But he needs me: I'm going to play tonight.

SOLOMON: Needs you! He's very far from thinking of you. He'll burst in here, calling for a carpet ...

ANNA: A carpet? ...

[KEAN *erupts into the room. He is still dressed as a sailor, and is somewhat unsteady on his feet. He opens both doors wide, a cape thrown over one shoulder.* ANNA *remains seated, very calm, arranging the folds of her dress.*]

KEAN: Solomon! A carpet!

SOLOMON: What!

KEAN: A carpet – a lion skin – anything ... [*He sees* ANNA.] It's you again!

ANNA: You told me ...

KEAN: What? What did I tell you?

ANNA: That I should play Desdemona.

KEAN: Did I indeed? I must have been infernally drunk! Well then, madam, you will not play Desdemona, that's all.

ANNA [*disappointed*]: Oh! Why not?

KEAN: Because there will be no performance tonight. You hear, Solomon; I will never act again!

SOLOMON: Very good, Guv'nor.

KEAN: Not tonight, or ever again!

SOLOMON [*with a wink at* ANNA]: Yes, Guv'nor.

KEAN: You don't seem very upset?

SOLOMON: I'm heart-broken.

KEAN: Where's my carpet?

ANNA: What in the world do you want with a carpet?

KEAN: To practise my handsprings. That's the way I started and that's the way I shall end. Proclaim from the housetops that Kean, the acrobat, will do his tricks in Regent Street and St James's – on condition that he is paid eight guineas per window. I shall make a fortune within a week; while here, in this accursed theatre, I have to slave for years to earn enough to retire, with a slice of salt beef and a pot of ale to sustain my old age. Fame! Genius! Art! This time, Solomon, I have made up my mind. Do you know what I am? The victim of Shakespeare! I work my guts out for that grinning vampire!

ANNA: Give up your art! How could you!

KEAN: My art! Ha! Ha! It's easy to see you are accustomed to sell cheese. Cheesemongering is a peaceful profession – gentle and nourishing. But art is a cannibal; can't you see it is devouring me alive? I tell you, I have behaved like a fool – pulling chestnuts out of the fire for Shakespeare. To the devil with Shakespeare: he wrote the plays, why doesn't he act them!

ANNA [*gently*]: Kean! What's the matter?

KEAN: The matter is that my house is surrounded and my very bedroom crawling with bailiffs. I had to spend the night in a tavern and the whole day in a carriage. My spine is bent in two, and my skull split open by hammer blows! The matter is that I am going to be clapped in prison – and all for a miserable four hundred pounds!

ANNA: I told you! If you would only put a little order into your life, my love.

KEAN: Order! [*He laughs.*] This is the moment to discuss order! I want to create disorder! To whip a great lady and betray her to a royal prince. And if that isn't enough, I shall set fire to the theatre. Order in a desert, that's what I want. Set fire to the theatre and

Kean will perish in the flames. What an exit! God in heaven – what a head. [*Sharply*] Since when have I become your love?

ANNA: Since yesterday.

KEAN: Yesterday? [*Worried*] What happened yesterday?

ANNA: A great many things.

KEAN [*more and more worried*]: Oh?

ANNA: You took my hands . . .

KEAN: Your hands? And . . .?

ANNA: That's all.

KEAN: Your hands! You see, Solomon, I am growing old. It's time for me to retire.

SOLOMON: And you called her little sister.

ANNA: Yes.

KEAN: Did I? I see . . . So I took your hands and asked you to play Desdemona?

ANNA: Yes.

KEAN: Very well. You shall.

ANNA: I thought you were never going to act again?

KEAN [*grumbling*]: Oh, well – I shall have to go on . . . because of poor Bob! But this is the last time!

SOLOMON: Yes, sir.

KEAN: The very last time, d'you hear?

SOLOMON: Yes, sir. [*Pause.*] Guv'nor, if you are appearing tonight, couldn't you . . . out of the takings . . .

KEAN: Eh?

SOLOMON: Keep back four hundred pounds?

KEAN: But the takings don't belong to me! Do you expect me to be paid for giving my services?

SOLOMON: You can pay it back . . . in a week . . . give me time to look round.

KEAN: What's this you say? That Kean should borrow money from a mountebank. Think of some other way.

SOLOMON [*sulking*]: Oh – if you won't help.

KEAN: Come here, you, and begin. What are we playing?

ANNA: The last scene of *Othello*.

KEAN: Charming! To have to roar with this head! Lie down and
let me stifle you.

ANNA: Send Solomon away first!

KEAN: You don't want to die in front of him, eh? Solomon, behold
her womanly modesty. It's true, there's nothing more naked than
a corpse. [*To* SOLOMON] Get out!

SOLOMON [*going*]: I wouldn't mind . . .

   [ANNA *crosses slowly to the divan, but* KEAN *catches her by the arm.*]

KEAN [*at the table*]: Look at me. You would make a very lovely
corpse. Aie!

ANNA: What is it?

KEAN: My head – my head.

   [ANNA *takes a cloth from the basin where it is lying ready and
   wrings it out.*]

I wish it were false, like Richard's hump. I could take it off.

ANNA: Does it ache very much?

KEAN: I'm paying for last night. You see what a fool I am. If I had
made love to you, instead of getting drunk, I should be as proud as
a peacock now, without an ache in my bones.

ANNA: Let me do this. [*She ties the napkin round his head, like a night-
cap.*] That should be better.

KEAN: It's cool and refreshing. I must look a sight?

ANNA: You look splendid. Just like a pirate.

KEAN [*pleasantly surprised*]: A pirate? Why not? That's what I should
have been!

ANNA: I could have gone to sea with you.

KEAN: Dressed as a boy. You would have been Kean's favourite
cabin-boy – Kean, the king of the Tortoiseshell Islands.

ANNA [*tenderly*]: And we could have been hanged together . . .

KEAN: What a beautiful end: between heaven and earth – face to
face, sticking our tongues out at each other. It's symbolic of all
love stories. [*Pause.*] Good. Well – lie down and let me explain
how you die. Give me the pillow.

   [*She lies down on the divan. He takes the pillow.*]

'She wakes.'

ANNA: 'Who's there? Othello?'

KEAN: 'Ay, Desdemona.'

ANNA: 'Will you come to bed, my lord?'

> [*The secret door opens suddenly.* ELENA *appears, and bursts out laughing.*]

ELENA: Kean in a nightcap with a pillow in his arms! Am I disturbing you?

> [KEAN *snatches the napkin off in a rage.*]

I came to congratulate you. This morning, all London believes you married to this lady. But it appears the ceremony took place a long time ago: a real Darby and Joan already.

KEAN [*with dignity*]: Elena, I am rehearsing the last scene of Othello.

ELENA: Ah? And Mrs Kean plays Desdemona? It's delightful – a real household of talent. Aren't you afraid of making your debut on top of an orgy, madam? Not too fatigued, I hope. If I can believe all I hear, last night, you were . . .

ANNA [*nods*]: In a very low haunt, yes, indeed.

ELENA: Kean, your wife is delightful, but her wit smacks of her father's shop. I have no taste for disputes, and I will withdraw, happy to have been witness of your felicity.

KEAN: Madam, stay – and you, child, go to your room.

ANNA: I have no room.

KEAN: Solomon will find you one. Solomon! [SOLOMON *enters.*] Find a room for the child.

ANNA [*rising*]: I don't want to leave you alone with her!

KEAN: If you don't go immediately, you will certainly not appear tonight.

ANNA [*very dignified, crosses past them and goes out. Then she puts her head round the door and adds*]: If you want her to play instead of me, you'd better change the scene to *The Taming of the Shrew*. [*She goes.*]

KEAN: She has gone!

ELENA: So I see. Thank you, Kean; I was almost prepared to commit the greatest folly of my life, and you have prevented me . . .

KEAN [*in agitation – on his knees beside her*]: If you had come last night, if only you had come . . .

ELENA: Ah, scold me! I betray my husband's trust – I cast aside morality and modesty – I come to you at the risk of a thousand dangers, and I find your dressing-room transformed into a boudoir – a woman lying on your divan and you, Kean, wearing a night-cap! But I am the accused – I am the one who has to defend herself.

KEAN: Elena, there is nothing between Miss Danby and myself. [*She does not reply.*] I swear it. [*She is silent.*] Elena, do you believe me?

ELENA: Alas, I am fool enough to believe you. [*She smiles. Pause.*] But if you appear with her tonight, I will never see you again.

KEAN [*rising*]: It's too late to find someone else.

ELENA: I see. She is allowed to insult me, and in a few moments, I shall see her in your arms. How could I endure it?

KEAN [*imploringly*]: Elena, we are playing *Othello*. The final scene. I have to kill her. Kill her – d'you hear? With a pillow! I don't even have to touch her. If . . . that young lady has been unfortunate enough to displease you, surely you should be glad to see her stifled. Ah – none of this would have happened if you had only come to me last night!

ELENA [*rising*]: Why must you always come back to that! Do you know what you deserve? That I should not say a word! That I should not even answer your unjust reproaches. But I am not like you; your anxiety affects me, and I want you to be calm. Kean, I didn't come last night, because I was prevented.

KEAN [*harshly*]: Indeed! Is it a duty to attend a ball?

ELENA: For an ambassador's wife, yes, it is an official duty. Kean, I went to the ball because my husband ordered me to attend. There. . .

KEAN [*turning to look at her*]: Ordered you?

ELENA: Yes, ordered me. He had been instructed to pay his respects to the Prince of Wales.

KEAN: That's true – I had forgotten the Prince of Wales. So – the Count couldn't go to the ball alone? Couldn't you find an excuse?

ELENA: A headache? The vapours? Those are actors' tricks. You don't know my husband – he can be terrible.

KEAN: Indeed! I would never have thought it.

ELENA: What good would it be to be a diplomat, if one didn't know how to hide one's feelings? You force me to confess what I intended to hide. My husband is suspicious.

KEAN: Suspicious? Of us?

ELENA: Yes – of us. I was right not to want to tell you: you are upset. Do you see now why I couldn't disobey him? If I had refused to go to the ball, he would have pretended to go without me, and then come back later, hoping to surprise us. Ah – good heavens – supposing he hadn't found me at home! Kean, is this the way you love me: do you want him to hurl me into the gutter? To kill me?

KEAN [*desolate*]: Madam . . .

ELENA: He would do it . . .

KEAN [*kissing her hand*]: Elena, forgive me.

ELENA: That is how you all are, you men – unjust, cruel and ungenerous. It isn't enough to entrust you with our honour – we must still risk losing it for love of you. Very well, Kean – go on to the very end – set the limit on your unkindness – to your cruelty – to the pain you are causing me. Say it – say it – that I must be dishonoured before you can love me.

KEAN: Elena! [*He falls on his knees.*] If you knew how I have suffered!

ELENA: Yet they say you spent the night laughing and singing!

KEAN: Laughing? Elena, I was drunker than I have ever been in the worst moments of my life. I was involved in a street fight – I insulted a lord . . . I would have killed him if it would have helped me escape from these terrible sufferings . . .

ELENA: Madman! For a mere mishap . . .

KEAN: You call that a mishap?

ELENA: What else?

KEAN: I am jealous, Elena. I have vitriol in my veins.

ELENA: Jealous? You?

KEAN [*seizing her in his arms*]: Jealous – tortured – obsessed – humiliated – degraded.

ELENA: Jealous – good heavens, of whom?

KEAN: You know very well.

ELENA: No, indeed, I swear it.

KEAN: Swear nothing – I don't believe your vows. Women have an instinct that tells them we love them – long before we tell them ourselves.

ELENA: But so many young men pay their court to me.

KEAN: I'm not talking of them. Elena, was the Prince of Wales at the ball?

ELENA: Yes, naturally.

KEAN: Did he speak to you?

ELENA: Yes, for some time.

KEAN: What about?

ELENA: What do you think? Nothing.

KEAN: Ah – that's as I feared!

ELENA: Very well – everything, if you prefer it.

KEAN: Nothing – everything – it's all the same. While lips speak and say nothing, eyes can make themselves understood without words.

ELENA: He always looks at me.

KEAN: And . . . how did he behave?

ELENA: What a question! As always; he was ironic, amusing, charming.

KEAN: Charming!

ELENA: Isn't he always charming?

KEAN: Alas!

ELENA: You are intolerable! Did I come here to discuss the Prince of Wales?

KEAN: Madam, he is in love with you!

ELENA [*genuinely surprised*]: He? But, Kean, you are confusing me. The Prince of Wales! He doesn't even notice me.

KEAN [*reproachfully*]: Elena!

ELENA: Well . . . if I must tell you . . . I did think . . . once . . . when he gave me this fan. . . . And then, I never considered it again . . . I never thought of anyone but you!

KEAN [*taking the fan*]: The Prince of Wales came to this room yesterday and asked me to give you up. [*He tosses the fan on to his dressing-table.*]

ELENA [*joyfully*]: The Prince of Wales? Is it possible? What did he say? Quickly, quickly – tell me everything.

KEAN: Alas, madam – you see!

ELENA: What do I see?

KEAN: Your voice – your manner – everything shows that this news delights you.

ELENA: Kean, have you gone mad? How could the Prince of Wales know that I . . . that I wish you well? Oh, Kean – was it you who told him?

KEAN: He guessed I loved you.

ELENA: Ah well – poor prince – supposing he does love me; of course, I am only supposing it to please you. What do you expect me to do?

KEAN [*very close to her*]: I couldn't see him at your side without going mad.

ELENA: My Othello! But what can we do? It is too late to cancel our plans . . .

KEAN: Cancel what plans?

ELENA: He did us the honour of asking for a seat in our box.

KEAN: Tonight?

ELENA: Yes.

KEAN: You mean he will be in your box while I play tonight?

ELENA: Yes – while you hold that . . . creature in your arms.

KEAN: Ah, madam, for me it is only a sham, like everything else in my life. Merely another piece of acting.

ELENA: You mean that I . . .

KEAN: I am going to make you a request, which I implore you not to refuse: all the time I am on stage, do not speak to him, do not smile at him, do not listen to him. Madam, never take your eyes off me. If I surprise a trace of understanding between you, I should no longer be master of myself.

ELENA: And what would happen?

KEAN: I don't know. Listen, supposing I lost my memory, that I stood glued to the middle of the stage, unable to speak? Supposing I were to break down and weep? [*She laughs.*] Don't laugh! I should be ruined!

ELENA: Do you realize you are asking me to insult the king's brother? Kean, if he is offended it is Denmark that will suffer.

KEAN [*rising, furiously*]: Denmark! Denmark! Always Denmark and its milch cows! Madam! it is I who have been offended! Yes, I. Last night I was told that you didn't love me. That for you I was only a caprice, that you had glanced at an actor for lack of employment. For you, I was only a game, or at most a distraction.

ELENA: Madman!

KEAN: My love demands that you prove your own.

ELENA [*furious*]: Your love? No, your pride. You don't want me to prove it to you – you want me to prove it to the Prince. He humiliated you yesterday, by pretending that I didn't love you, and now you expect me to undeceive him. My love? Ah, you care little for me at this moment: what counts, in your eyes, is the opinion of the Prince.

KEAN: Elena – that proof will be understood by me alone – it will be valued by me alone. You are a great lady, and I am only an actor, but I honour you, madam, when I count on you alone to prove to the actor that he can be loved like a prince.

ELENA: Very well. But service for service.

KEAN: Ask me anything!

ELENA: Send the little Danby home, and play the scene with Miss MacLeish.

KEAN [*in despair*]: Elena! Miss MacLeish is in the country – there is no time to fetch her.

ELENA: What do I care? It's up to you. Play the part with the prompter.

KEAN: The prompter! How on earth am I to do that?

ELENA: If you really have genius, you ought to make the audience believe him the most beautiful of Desdemonas.

KEAN [*groaning*]: I'm not a magician – I'm an actor.

ELENA: Very well, Mr Kean. Your demands increase from day to day, and when, in return, one dares ask for the simplest and most legitimate favour, you refuse point blank. Very well, I tell you plainly. If that girl appears on the stage at your side, I will turn to

the Prince and smile at him till the end of the act. I will make you
pay for this. I . . .

[*There is a knock at the door.*]

[*Frightened*] Heavens!

KEAN: The door is locked. [*Calling*] Who is it?

PRINCE [*off*]: It is I.

ELENA [*in a low voice*]: The Prince of Wales!

[*During the following scene, she endeavours to open the secret door.*]

KEAN [*aloud*]: Who?

PRINCE (*off*): The Prince of Wales, of course.

COUNT [*off*]: And the Count de Koefeld.

ELENA [*low*]: My husband! I am lost! How can I open this door?

KEAN [*low*]: Pull the beard!

ELENA: Which beard?

KEAN [*pointing to a bearded mask on the side of the wardrobe*]: That one,
and go, quickly . . .

[ELENA *pulls the beard, and the door opens, squeaking.* KEAN *coughs,
to cover the sound, imitating the squeaks.*]

KEAN [*aloud*]: Forgive me, sir . . . But for the moment I have the
misfortune . . . [*in a low voice, to* ELENA] Hurry, hurry! [*aloud*] To
have at my heels certain gentlemen who pursue me for a matter of
£400 . . .

PRINCE: I understand!

[ELENA *is entangled in the costumes – the door has stuck – she beats
on it, but cannot get through.*]

KEAN [*aloud*]: And they would not hesitate to make use of your
Royal Highness' name . . .

[*He leans against the door to prevent anyone from opening.*]

PRINCE: And so?

COUNT: And so?

ELENA [*clasping her hands*]: Oh! . . . Santa Maria! . . .

KEAN [*aloud*]: Be good enough to send me a note signed by your
own hand, sir.

[ELENA *pulls the beard on the mask so hard that it comes off, but the
door opens with a great clatter.*]

PRINCE: What on earth are you doing?

KEAN [aloud]: I am fetching the key. [Low to ELENA as she goes] Farewell, Elena – I adore you – will you grant my prayer?

ELENA [low]: Will you grant me mine?

KEAN [low]: I . . .

ELENA: Service for service. I shall not go back on my word.

> [She disappears, the door closes abruptly. KEAN puts the costumes back in place. Through the keyhole of the other door comes a little roll of paper.]

KEAN [taking the note]: A note of hand for £400 . . . a truly royal card. Come in, sir, it must indeed be you.

> [He opens the door. The PRINCE and the COUNT enter. SOLOMON enters behind them and disappears behind the screen.]

PRINCE: A debt of honour I owed you.

KEAN: Owed me?

PRINCE: Since yesterday.

KEAN: Ah, sir – the stakes were very much higher than that.

PRINCE: I know, Kean. This is only a beginning. [To the COUNT] We are talking of a wager we made, and I do not yet know if I have won or lost.

COUNT: In that case, sir, why do you pay?

PRINCE: Because the result makes no difference. Win or lose, Mr Kean has arranged for me to pay.

KEAN: Then I accept. Solomon, you know what to do with this money.

SOLOMON: Yes, indeed . . . [He goes.]

> [KEAN goes behind the screen and begins to change.]

COUNT [low to the PRINCE]: Are you sure he was with a woman?

PRINCE: Certain.

COUNT: Miss Danby, perhaps?

PRINCE: It's hard to tell . . .

> [The COUNT sees the forgotten fan on the table and picks it up, slipping it into his pocket, without the PRINCE having seen.]

COUNT: I shall find out – I promise you.

PRINCE: How?

COUNT: That is a diplomatic secret.

KEAN [*dressing behind the screen, an arm or a leg protruding from time to time*]: Well, sir? What's the news?

PRINCE: Nothing of great importance – I hear an insolent fellow insulted and threatened Neville last night.

COUNT [*shocked*]: Insulted Lord Neville? . . . Why?

KEAN: A lord can never be insulted – even with words.

COUNT [*to the* PRINCE]: I am not familiar with your English habits, sir, but when we Danes believe ourselves insulted, we fight the whole world.

KEAN: Long live Copenhagen! One day I shall go there to get myself killed.

COUNT [*sharply*]: You would be welcome. Until then, I thank you for allowing me to penetrate the Holy of Holies . . . and I bow before you – the High Priest. [*He goes to the door.*]

KEAN [*aside to the* PRINCE]: Your Royal Highness – I must speak to you . . .

PRINCE [*to the* COUNT]: I will rejoin you, Count.

COUNT: Your Highness will come to our box?

PRINCE [*aside to the* COUNT]: You will tell me everything?

COUNT [*aside to the* PRINCE]: I give you my word. [*He goes.*]

PRINCE [*watching* KEAN *making up as Othello*]: Now – you scoundrel – have I won or lost? Answer me!

KEAN: Sir, you know the result as well as I do. You saw Madam de Koefeld at the ball?

PRINCE: She did appear, certainly. But very late. That veiled lady . . .

KEAN: That veiled lady . . . was a cousin of mine.

PRINCE: Then I have won? [KEAN *does not answer.*] You will not say? Did I lose?

KEAN: In either case, sir, I beg your permission to keep silent; if you have lost, to protect the honour of a lady; if you have won, to protect my own pride.

PRINCE: Very well – I shall make my enquiries and finally learn the truth. What did you want with me?

KEAN: Sir, what am I to you? A protégé or a friend?

PRINCE: But . . . Devil take it! How can I answer? My purse is yours – my palace is open to you day and night – when you require my influence, it is yours to command. Isn't that enough?

KEAN: All those favours are given by the prince to the subject. Supposing I asked you for one of the sacrifices granted between equals . . .

PRINCE: Well?

KEAN: Would the goodwill of the patron stretch as far as the devotion of a friend?

PRINCE: Let us try.

KEAN: Sir . . . do not go to her box.

PRINCE: Her box? [*Understanding*] Ah . . .

KEAN: You are young – handsome – and a prince. To amuse you, distract you, love you, you have London, the whole kingdom. Pay your court to the others . . .

PRINCE [*imitating him*]: 'But leave me Elena.' Is that it? [KEAN *bows*.] Then I see, she did come. You confess.

KEAN: No!

PRINCE: If I leave her, another will take my place . . .

KEAN: What do I care for the others! The others are so many sheep . . . [*Pause.*] Do not go to her box, sir. Do not go to her tonight.

PRINCE: So this is the sacrifice?

KEAN: Yes.

PRINCE: Very well – I will not go. [*He takes a paper from his pocket.*] On condition that you sign this.

KEAN: What is it?

PRINCE: The receipt for your debts you were to have signed yesterday.

KEAN: Swearing I would never see her again?

PRINCE: Yes. Against six thousand pounds.

KEAN [*quickly*]: But I do not wish to sign.

PRINCE: You have betrayed yourself, Kean! If you do not wish to sign, then you have seen her again!

KEAN: No, sir, no, but . . . if you wish to avoid a scandal . . . that I shall regret . . .

PRINCE: Confess you are her lover?

KEAN: I cannot confess what isn't true!

PRINCE: Then sign.

KEAN: No, sir, I cannot sign.

PRINCE: Good-bye, Kean.

KEAN: Sir . . . where are you going?

PRINCE: To applaud you.

KEAN: From your own box?

PRINCE: No half-confidences, Mr Kean, or I will only give you a half-promise.

KEAN [*bowing*]: Do as you please, sir.

PRINCE: Thank you, Mr Kean. [*He goes out angrily, banging the door.*]
   [SOLOMON *appears, carrying the Othello belt and dagger.*]

SOLOMON: Sir! Sir. . . . We must hurry . . .

KEAN: I'm ready.
   [*There is a knock at the secret door.*]
   Solomon – someone knocked at the secret door. See who it is.
   [SOLOMON *opens the door, and* GIDSA, *Elena's maid, enters.*]

KEAN [*making up*]: You, Gidsa? What has happened?

GIDSA: My mistress left her fan behind. I have come to fetch it.

KEAN: Her fan? Have you seen it, Solomon?

SOLOMON: No, sir.

KEAN: See if you can find it.

GIDSA [*searching*]: Oh, how could she have lost it? My mistress is devoted to it. It was a present from the Prince of Wales.

KEAN: Indeed! I had forgotten. Look carefully, Gidsa, look carefully. The gift of a prince should not go astray in the dressing-room of an actor. [*Pause.*] Look in the carriage. She may have dropped it there.

GIDSA: You're right . . . I will see. [*She turns as she is about to go through the secret door, seeing the royal costumes.*] Oh – what lovely clothes!
   [*She disappears, and the door closes.*]

KEAN [*bitterly, as he continues to make up*]: A royal fan! . . . That must look very fine. [*He imitates* ELENA *with her fan. Shouting*] Darius! [*To* SOLOMON] Fetch that ridiculous girl!

SOLOMON [*opening the door*]: Darius!

[*We hear the voice of the Stage Manager calling* 'Beginners, please.' *There are impatient sounds from the invisible audience.*]

KEAN: Where is he?

SOLOMON: Just coming, sir.

DARIUS (*off*): Just coming . . . just coming . . . Othello's wig . . . all quite ready . . .

[*He enters, mincing, with the wig and comb.*]

Curled to perfection, sir – you'll be delighted.

KEAN [*imitating him*]: Hair-style No. 1. I know, I know . . .

DARIUS: No, no, it's No. 3. Much more suitable for a general.

KEAN: Come – put it on!

DARIUS [*to* SOLOMON]: Why is he so nervous today? He'll have another triumph, you'll see. Ah, we're in a bad mood. [*He helps* KEAN *to put on the wig.*]

STAGE MANAGER [*opening the door*]: May we ring the curtain bell, sir?

KEAN: Yes. I'm ready.

S.M.: Thank you, sir. [*He bows and goes.*]

KEAN: Solomon – see who's in the theatre, then come back and tell me who is in Count de Koefeld's box.

[SOLOMON *goes.* ANNA *enters dressed as Desdemona, so badly made up that she looks like a painted doll.* KEAN *roars with laughter.*]

ANNA [*entirely at ease*]: Here I am.

KEAN: What on earth do you look like! Who made you up?

ANNA: I did.

KEAN: You'd make a cat laugh. Come here. Kneel down – I'll try and fix you up.

[*He alters her make-up and combs her hair while* DARIUS *continues to arrange his own wig.*]

Are you nervous?

ANNA: No.

KEAN: Amateur – I'm not surprised. Don't worry. If you hesitate, I will cut in. If you don't know where to move, I'll take your arm. If you forget your words, you need only say, 'I love you.' In a love scene, that always fits. [*Pause.*] I have no one to take my arm or whisper me my lines. That's why I'm always nervous. You, you have me, but I am alone. Darius – give me that bottle.

DARIUS [*aside, fetching the hidden bottle*]: He's off!

KEAN [*drinking*]: This is the finest cure for nerves. [*He drinks.*] I'm exhausted.

[SOLOMON *returns.*]

Well?

SOLOMON: The theatre is full, with a queue as far as the river.

KEAN: What do I care. Is Madam de Koefeld in her box?

SOLOMON: Not yet, but the Count is there with the Prince of Wales and another lady.

KEAN: The Prince of Wales! I was sure! [*To* ANNA] If I asked you not to appear tonight, would you be very upset?

ANNA: Very.

KEAN: But if I asked you – for my sake?

ANNA: I would do anything.

KEAN: Thank you. [*He kisses her forehead. To* DARIUS] Go and ask Miss Gish if she knows the part. She must still be in the theatre. If not – ask Miss Pritchett. Hurry. [DARIUS *runs out.*]

DARIUS: I fly, sir.

ANNA: She doesn't want me to appear, does she?

KEAN [*gently*]: No.

ANNA: And it makes you happy to sacrifice me to her?

KEAN: Not particularly.

ANNA: That's what I thought: you don't look very pleased.

S.M. [*at the door*]: Your call, Mr Kean.

KEAN: I'm not ready.

S.M.: You told me we could begin!

KEAN: Go to the devil!

S.M. [*shouting*]: Hold the curtain! Hold the curtain!

[*The invisible audience becomes more vociferous.*]

DARIUS [*running in*]: Miss Gish doesn't know the part. She says she can do Cordelia – would that help?

KEAN: No, it would not. What about Miss Pritchett?

DARIUS: Miss Gish reminds you that Miss Pritchett has been ill since last Thursday.

KEAN: Very well – then I won't appear. [*But he continues to make up and get ready.*]

SOLOMON [*coming from behind the screen*]: Sir – sir – what are you saying?

KEAN [*firmly*]: That I won't appear – that's what I'm saying.

[*Through the open door, the* STAGE MANAGER *appears.*]

S.M.: Sir – you will be compelled!

KEAN: By whom – if you please?

S.M. [*in uncertain tones, recoiling slightly*]: The constable.

KEAN: Send for him – he is my best friend.

SOLOMON: In the name of heaven – you'll be thrown into prison!

[STAGE HANDS *and* ACTORS *begin to cluster in the doorway.*]

KEAN: In prison – in prison – there, at least I shall be free! I shan't have to act!

SOLOMON [*imploringly*]: Can nothing make you change your mind?

KEAN: Nothing.

S.M.: The house is sold out!

KEAN: Give back the money!

FIREMAN [*appearing from behind the* STAGE MANAGER, *with a* STAGE CARPENTER]: Mr Kean . . . to please us!

CARPENTER: It's our favourite part!

KEAN: I refuse . . . I refuse . . . I refuse . . .

[ANNA *kneels beside him.* SOLOMON *drops back, signing to the others that everything will be all right.* DARIUS, *frightened, has taken refuge behind the screen.*

Prolonged whistles and cat-calls from the invisible audience.]

ANNA [*gently, beside* KEAN]: Kean, what about Bob? It isn't his fault if you are unhappy. You aren't happy now, but if you don't play tonight, you will be even less happy. You gave them your word, you know. It will be the first time you've broken a promise.

KEAN [*after a pause, smiles and kisses her hand*]: Where is Darius?

DARIUS [*popping his head out from behind the screen*]: Here I am!

KEAN [*rising*]: My cloak!

DARIUS [*holding it out*]: I pressed it myself!

KEAN: My belt!

SOLOMON [*holding it out*]: Here it is! Here it is!

S.M. [*who has been standing in the doorway with the others, all smiles*]: Thank you, thank you, Mr Kean!

KEAN: My dagger! [*Everyone hurries round.*]

DARIUS: His dagger! His dagger! Here it is – no, over there . . . [*The* STAGE MANAGER *holds out the dagger.*]

KEAN: Well – what are you standing there for? Go and tell them I am going on.

[*The* CARPENTER, *the* FIREMAN *and the* STAGE MANAGER *rush off to the stage, crying:* 'He's going on – he's going on – he's going on.']

[*Going to the door and calling after them.*] Make an announcement. Say I am ill – nervous – anything you like . . .

S.M.: Yes, yes – Guv'nor – leave it to me . . .

KEAN [*surveying himself in the mirror*]: Well – you great cart horse – harnessed and ready – go and plough through your Shakespeare!

[*The noise of the audience increases.* KEAN *goes to the door and exits.* ANNA, *knowing she is going to play, picks up the book and reads through her part. She follows* KEAN *with great dignity. The noise from the audience diminishes.*]

BLACK OUT

ACT FOUR

SCENE TWO

Scene: The gas jets of the footlights appear, as well as the prompter's box in the centre of the stage. The curtain of the real theatre rises on the curtain of Drury Lane. The whole scene is lit entirely from below. In the real theatre the COUNT DE KOEFELD *is half asleep in the stage box on the dress circle level. The audience continues to show impatience. A theatre* ATTENDANT *walks up and down, trying to quieten them down. A* DRESSER *runs across to the* ATTENDANT, *crying:* 'He's going to appear.' *The* ATTENDANT *shouts up at the gallery:* 'Quiet – quiet! He's going to appear.'

ATTENDANT [*catching up with the* DRESSER, *pointing to* LORD NEVILLE *who has come into the stage box left, followed by a* DANDY]: Keep your eye on that one! He's the man Kean insulted last night . . .

DRESSER: He doesn't look as if he means to make trouble!

ATTENDANT: Keep your eye on him all the same. . . . The Prince of Wales will be here tonight . . .

[*The* STAGE MANAGER *appears in front of the curtain and bows. The* ATTENDANT *and* DRESSER *say:* 'Sh! Sh!']

DRESSER: What's he going to say?

ATTENDANT: Maybe the Guv'nor won't play after all . . . [*He taps his forehead significantly.*]

S.M.: Quiet . . . quiet, please. . . . My lords, ladies and gentlemen . . . Mr Kean is very tired and fearing not to be worthy of your kind attentions, asks me to request your indulgence.

[*Applause from the audience and cries of* 'Bravo!']

Mr Kean will not be playing in his own scenery, since that has been lent to Mr Macready for a Provincial tour.

['Oh!' *of disappointment from the gallery.*]

But we have done our best. . . . Lastly, the part of Desdemona will be taken by a young lady making her first appearance on any stage. ['Ah!' *of satisfaction from the audience. The* STAGE MANAGER *goes, as the* PRINCE OF WALES *enters the box with* ELENA *and* AMY. *He nods to* LORD NEVILLE, *who bows. The orchestra plays the National Anthem.* LORD NEVILLE, *the* DANDY, ELENA, AMY *and the* COUNT *rise. The house lights go down.* SOLOMON *enters and takes his place in the prompter's box.*]

PRINCE [*to* ELENA]: Who is playing Desdemona?

ELENA [*drily*]: I hope it is Miss MacLeish.

PRINCE: Why?

ELENA [*recovering herself*]: Because he is used to her. With anyone else, he would be quite ridiculous.

AMY [*very excited*]: Did you see?

ELENA: Who?

AMY: Over there, in the box opposite. It's Lord Neville. There's sure to be trouble. Kean struck him last night, apparently because of some girl.

ELENA: That story must be greatly exaggerated.

[*The* COUNT *has gone to sleep.*]

PRINCE: Madam, I am full of admiration for your husband. How can he sleep in this din?

ELENA [*furiously, shaking her husband*]: Sir!

COUNT [*waking with a start*]: Eh?

ELENA: Sir, we have his Royal Highness with us tonight, and you promised me not to go to sleep.

PRINCE [*amicably*]: Please, madam. The Count is not asleep – he is practising diplomatic impenetrability. [*The* COUNT *smiles and drops off to sleep again.*]

[*The curtain of the inner stage rises.* ANNA, *as Desdemona, is asleep in bed.*]

ELENA [*between her teeth*]: He shall pay for this!

AMY: What was that, dear?

ELENA: Nothing.

[*Desdemona sleeps on. There is a torch burning on either side of the bed.* KEAN, *as Othello, enters.*]

KEAN: 'It is the cause, it is the cause, my soul:
  Let me not name it to you, you chaste stars!
  It is the cause. Yet I'll not shed her blood,
  Nor scar that whiter skin of hers than snow
  And smooth as monumental alabaster.
  Yet she must die, else she'll betray more men.
  Put out the light, and then put out the light:
  If I quench thee, thou flaming minister,
  I can again thy former light restore,
  Should I repent me: but once put out thy light,
  Thou cunning'st pattern of excelling nature,
  I know not where is that Promethean heat
  That can thy light relume. When I have pluck'd the rose,
  I cannot give it vital growth again,
  It must needs wither: I'll smell it on the tree.
    [Kissing her.]
  Ah, balmy breath, that dost almost persuade
  Justice to break her sword! One more, one more:
  Be thus when thou art dead, and I will kill thee,
  And love thee after: one more, and this the last:
  So sweet was ne'er so fatal. I must weep,
  But they are cruel tears: this sorrow's heavenly;
  It strikes where it doth love. She wakes.'
    [Applause.]
PRINCE [to AMY]: Well, what do you think?
AMY: I prefer Kemble!
    [Applause continues.]
ANNA [as Desdemona]: 'Who's there?'
KEAN [spoken]: Be quiet – let them applaud till the end. [He bows.]
ANNA [after a suitable pause]: 'Who's there, Othello?'
KEAN: 'Ay, Desdemona.'
ANNA: 'Will you come to bed, my lord?'
KEAN: 'Have you pray'd tonight, Desdemona?'
ANNA: 'Ay, my lord.'
KEAN: 'If you bethink yourself of any crime

Unreconciled as yet to heaven and grace,
Solicit for it straight.'

ANNA: 'Alas, my lord, what may you mean by that?'

KEAN: 'Well, do it and be brief: I will walk by.'

[*She prays. He walks round the bed.*]

PRINCE: Who is the girl?

ELENA: How should I know?

[KEAN *stops and stares at them. They are quiet.*]

KEAN: 'I would not kill thy unprepared spirit;
No, heaven forfend! I would not kill thy soul.'

ANNA: 'Talk you of killing?'

KEAN: 'Ay, I do.'

ANNA: 'Then . . .' [*She hesitates*] 'Then . . .'

SOLOMON [*prompting*]: 'Heaven have mercy on me.'

[*She doesn't understand. He repeats*]
'Then heaven have mercy on me!'

ANNA [*desperately, as Desdemona*]: I love you.

SOLOMON [*prompting*]: 'Then heaven have mercy on me . . .'

ANNA [*losing her head*]: I love you, I love you, I love you.

KEAN [*improvising*]: You love me not, and the hour is unfit for your
lies. You should pray, at this fatal moment, saying: 'Then heaven
have mercy on me.'

ANNA [*getting it*]: Oh yes. Thank you. 'Then heaven have mercy on
me.'

KEAN: 'Amen, with all my heart.'

ELENA [*to the Prince*]: On top of everything, she doesn't know her
lines.

COUNT [*waking with a start*]: Who doesn't know her lines?

ELENA: That girl.

COUNT: Which one? Ophelia?

ELENA: Yes, that's right. Go to sleep.

[*The* COUNT *goes to sleep.* KEAN *has deliberately turned towards the
box.*]

ANNA: 'If you say so, I hope you will not kill me.'

KEAN [*absently*]: Yes, yes, in a minute.

T – T.P. – D

NEVILLE: He's dried. [*He brings a whistle from his pocket and blows it.*
  KEAN *shivers, and turns back to* ANNA.]

KEAN: 'Think on thy sins.'

ANNA: 'They are loves I bear to you.'

KEAN: 'Ay, and for that thou diest.'

ANNA: 'That death's unnatural that kills for loving.
  Alas, why gnaw you so your nether lip? . . .
  Why gnaw you so your nether lip?'

SOLOMON: 'Some bloody passion . . .'

ANNA: 'Some bloody passion frames your shake . . .'
  [*Murmur of surprise from the audience.*]

KEAN [*spoken*]: Idiot – get on with it.

ANNA [*spoken*]: I can't!

KEAN [*spoken*]: Very well. [*As Othello, superbly carrying it off.*] And
  why should I not shake, since thou hast shaken my soul? The
  courage that has never quailed, thou hast blasted with inconstancy.
  Sorceress, 'tis thou who hast transformed Othello!
  [*Applause.* KEAN *bows.*]

AMY [*to the* PRINCE]: Is that Shakespeare?

PRINCE [*indifferently*]: Probably.

KEAN [*to* ANNA]: Quickly – carry on.

ANNA: How can I, when you're making it up!

KEAN [*to* SOLOMON]: Give her the line!

SOLOMON: I can't find the place.

ANNA [*making up her mind suddenly, hurling herself half out of bed and
  clinging to* KEAN.] I love you! I love you!
  [*He tries to free himself. They struggle, she crying:* 'I love you', *until
  he finally manages to throw her back on the bed.*]

KEAN: 'That handkerchief which I so loved and gave thee
  Thou gavest to Cassio.'

ANNA: 'No, by my life and soul!
  Send for the man and ask him.'

KEAN: 'Sweet soul, take heed,
  Take heed of perjury, thou art on thy death-bed.'

ANNA: 'Ay, but not yet to die.'

KEAN: 'Yes, presently.'

ANNA: 'Then Lord have mercy on me!'

KEAN: 'I say amen.'

ANNA: 'O, banish me, my lord, but kill me not!'

KEAN: 'Down, strumpet!'

ANNA: 'Kill me tomorrow; let me live tonight!'

KEAN: 'Nay, if you strive . . .'

ANNA: 'But half an hour!'

ELENA: Good heavens! Why on earth doesn't he kill her? Have you ever seen such a bad performance?

[*The* PRINCE *laughs.* AMY *and* ELENA *laugh with him.* KEAN *turns to the box and folds his arms.*]

PRINCE: Everything is possible, madam, except that anyone could be as beautiful as you.

KEAN [*in a voice of thunder*]: Silence!

[*The* PRINCE, *momentarily startled, recovers.*]

PRINCE [*to* ELENA]: Good heavens. I believe he's speaking to me.

ELENA: Sir, sir, I implore you – watch the stage and don't look at me again.

KEAN: May I ask your Royal Highness to be quiet.

PRINCE [*slightly raising his voice*]: Madam . . .

ELENA [*speaking without looking at him*]: Not another word, if you love me. If there is a scandal, I shall be the first victim.

PRINCE [*scowling at* KEAN]: Very well, let us hear Mr Kean. I am curious to know just how far he will go.

KEAN: Where do you think you are? At court? In a boudoir? Everywhere else you are a prince, but here I am king, and I ask you to be quiet, or we will stop the performance. We are working, sir, and if there is one thing the idle should respect, it is the labour of others.

PRINCE [*between his teeth*]: Mr Kean! You are ruining yourself.

KEAN: And if I want to be ruined?

PRINCE [*shrugging his shoulders*]: Fool!

KEAN [*threateningly*]: What did you say?

[*The audience begins to murmur – he turns on them.*]

Are you still there? I had forgotten you. You paid to see blood and now you demand blood. Isn't that so? But only stage blood, of course. [*Pause. The* PRINCE *laughs again.*] What would you say if I showed you real blood?

[*He comes down to the stage box and tries to draw his sword. The hilt comes away in his hand with a short piece of the broken blade. The* PRINCE *bursts out laughing. The audience laughs and jeers. We hear:* 'Throw him in jail! Arrest him!' *etc.*

The CONSTABLE *appears and begins to make his way towards the stage. The* PRINCE *sees him.* KEAN *remains motionless, his head hanging, overcome.*]

PRINCE: Officer! [*The* CONSTABLE *looks up.*] Where are you going?

CONSTABLE: To arrest him, Sir.

PRINCE: Go back to your place, and wait for your orders.

[*The* CONSTABLE *retires.* ANNA, *meanwhile, has picked up a cushion and tries to make* KEAN *go on with the scene.*]

ANNA: Othello . . .

[*He doesn't reply.*]

Othello!

KEAN [*shivering*]: Who calls me Othello? Who thinks I am Othello? [*Pointing to himself.*] Is this Othello? He was a killer . . . I – I am nothing but a fool. Ah, God, make me Othello – give me his strength and passion – for a moment – a single moment. I have played the part so often, it should be possible. Only for a moment – the time to pull down the pillars of the theatre. [*He makes a violent effort, as if he were trying to transform himself into Othello.*] What do I lack? I wear the Moor's garments – I stand here in his shoes – I am a character who has found himself in the wrong part. Ah, Prince, Prince, you are in luck's way. If it were real, you would not escape me this time.

[*Cries and* 'oh's' *of shocked surprise.*]

Ladies and gentlemen – there will be no execution tonight. We are pardoning all the guilty. [ANNA *comes to him, pillow in hand.*] Get out of here – you don't know your part. [*He takes the pillow.*] Give me that.

[SOLOMON *catches* ANNA *by the arm and drags her off stage.*]

KEAN [*turning to* ELENA]: You, madam – why not play Desdemona? I should stifle you with this very lovingly. [*He raises the pillow above his head.*] Ladies and gentlemen – the instrument of the crime. See how I treat it. [*He hurls the cushion into the box at* ELENA'*s feet.*] To the loveliest in the land. That cushion was my heart – my coward's heart – for her to rest her feet upon. [*Beating his breast.*] This man isn't dangerous. You were wrong to take Othello for a tragic cuckold. He . . . I . . . am a co-co-comic cuckold.

[*Laughter, followed by cries of* 'Oh!']

[*To the* PRINCE OF WALES, *familiarly*] You see, sir, I was right. Now I am in a real rage, I can only stammer.

[*The cat-calls redouble.* 'Down with Kean! Down with the actor Kean!' *He takes a step towards the audience and stares at them. The whistles stop.*]

All against me? All? What an honour! But why! Ladies and gentlemen, will you allow me a question? What have I done to you? I know you all – but this is the first time I see you with murderous faces. Are these your real aspects? You come here each night and throw bouquets at my feet, crying bravo. I thought you really loved me . . . But who were you applauding? Eh? Othello? Impossible – he was a sanguinary villain. It must have been Kean. 'Our great Kean – our dear Kean – our national idol.' Well, here he is – your beloved Kean. [*He drags his hands over his face, smearing the make-up.*] Behold the man! Look at him. Why don't you applaud? Isn't it strange! You only care for illusion.

NEVILLE [*from his box*]: Mountebank!

KEAN: Who is that? Why, it's Lord Neville. [*He crosses to the other box.*] I hesitated a moment ago because I am afraid of princes, but I warn you that black beetles cannot frighten me. If you don't keep your mouth shut, I will take you between two fingers and crush you. Like that. [NEVILLE *is silent. The audience waits.*] Good night, ladies – good night, sweet ladies. Romeo, Lear and Macbeth make you their adieus. I must rejoin them, and give them your regards. I return to the imaginary world where my real fury awaits me.

Tonight, kind ladies, I shall be Othello, in my own home, sold out,
house full, and commit my murders in my own fashion. Of course,
if you had really loved me.... But we must not ask too much, must
we? By the way, I was wrong just now to mention Kean. Kean the
actor died very young. [*Laughter.*] Be quiet, murderers, it was you
who killed him. It was you who took an infant and turned him
into a monster. [*The audience is silent.*] That's right. Silence – a
silence of death. Why were you booing just now? There was
nobody on stage. No one. Or perhaps an actor playing the part of
Kean playing the part of Othello. Listen – I am going to tell you
something. I am not alive – I only pretend. Ladies and gentlemen –
your humble servant. I . . . [*He hesitates, then shrugs.*] The rest is
silence.

[*He turns, and marches upstage in silence, kicking over one of the
canvas flats and disappearing into the back of the stage.*]

COUNT: It's over. Well, sir, what did you think of Kean?

PRINCE: He was magnificent.

[*The* PRINCE *rises, and the orchestra in the inner theatre plays the
National Anthem.*]

CURTAIN

Scene: KEAN's *house. Ten o'clock next morning.* SOLOMON, *looking very glum, pours out and swallows two or three quick glasses of brandy. The* STAGE MANAGER *and* DARIUS *tiptoe in.*

SOLOMON: What do you want?

S.M.: To see him!

SOLOMON: He is in his room – with the doctor. Sign here . . . on this list.

    [*He shows them a long list on the table. They both sign their names.*]

S.M.: How did he spend the night?

SOLOMON: On all fours – on top of the cupboard.

DARIUS: Is he really mad?

SOLOMON: Bedlam!

DARIUS: Is the doctor bleeding him?

SOLOMON: For the fourth time.

DARIUS [*a little scream*]: Ah!

S.M.: What is his madness like?

SOLOMON: Very dangerous!

S.M.: What does he do?

SOLOMON: He strikes everyone.

S.M.: Everyone?

SOLOMON: Everyone, but preferably his friends.

DARIUS: He must have been bitten by a mad dog!

SOLOMON: I fear so. [*A pause. Pretending to listen*] Sh!

DARIUS [*frightened*]: Is it . . .

S.M.: Kean? [SOLOMON *nods.*]

BOTH [*hurrying for the door*]: Good-bye. Good-bye. Poor Solomon.

    [*They have gone.*]

    [KEAN *enters, very preoccupied, without seeing* SOLOMON.]

SOLOMON: Guv'nor . . .

KEAN [*startled*]: What? [*He sees* SOLOMON.] I'm not the Guv'nor any

more. Call me Mr Edmund. [*Pause.*] Was someone here? I heard
you talking.

SOLOMON: Actors, Guv'nor.

KEAN: Actors? Then there was no one. [*He laughs.*] No one. What did
you say to them?

SOLOMON: I tell everyone you are raving mad.

KEAN: That the great Kean is mad? Idiot, the opposite has happened.
Cry from the housetops that a shopkeeper called Edmund has
recovered his senses. [*He takes him by the chin.*] Now I know:
Shakespeare is a cheese.

SOLOMON [*frightened*]: What . . . ?

KEAN: And I sell him by the pound. Why didn't you tell me?

SOLOMON [*frightened*]: Why didn't I tell you what?

KEAN: That I was a cheesemonger. [*Calming down*] You see I am in
my right mind? Well – go and proclaim it from the housetops.

SOLOMON: No.

KEAN [*springing at him*]: What's that?

SOLOMON: If I tell them you're in your right mind, they will put
you in prison.

KEAN: Prison? Because I'm in my right mind? What a strange world!
Very well – I shall go to prison.

SOLOMON: If you go to prison, you will never act again.

KEAN [*going to him*]: What a fate!

SOLOMON [*gently*]: Guv'nor, you mustn't let them.

KEAN: What do you want me to do?

SOLOMON: If you would only . . . just for a day or two . . .

KEAN: What?

SOLOMON: Pretend . . .

KEAN [*tapping his forehead*]: To . . . ?

SOLOMON: Yes. [KEAN *starts to protest. Hurriedly*] You were so
magnificent in Lear.

KEAN [*slowly*]: Lear? [*To* SOLOMON, *affectionately*] My dear fellow,
even if I wanted to, it would be impossible. I can never act
again.

SOLOMON [*startled*]: You can never . . . Since when?

KEAN: Since last night. I've been thinking. To act you must take yourself for someone else. I thought I was Kean, who thought he was Hamlet, who thought he was Fortinbras . . .

SOLOMON: But Hamlet . . .

KEAN: Yes. Hamlet does think he is Fortinbras. Sh! It's a secret. What a series of misunderstandings! [*Pause.*] Fortinbras doesn't think he is anyone. Fortinbras and Mr Edmund are alike. They know who they are and they say only what is. You can ask them about the weather, the time of day and the price of bread. But never try to make them act on a stage. You're an old fool – you understand nothing. What's the weather like?

SOLOMON: Can't you see? The sun is shining.

KEAN [*going to the window*]: Is that your sun? I shall have to grow accustomed to it. Kean's sun was painted on a stage canvas. Solomon, the London sky is a painted cloth; every morning, you drew the curtains, I opened my eyes, and I saw . . . Ah, I don't know what I saw. When the man himself is a sham, everything is a sham around him. Under a sham sun, the sham Kean cried the tale of his sham sufferings to his sham heart. Today, the sun is real. How flat real light is. Truth should be blinding, dazzling. It's true – it's true I am a ruined man. I tell you, I can't believe it. There are moments when I believe I am going to understand, and then it eludes me. [*Pause. He brings a purse from his pocket.*] There are a hundred florins in this purse. Divide the rest between the servants and dismiss them all. I shall wait for the police here. [*He installs himself in a regal attitude.*]

SOLOMON: That is Richard III's chair.

KEAN [*sharply*]: In this very chair. When you go, leave the main door wide open. I want the police to have free access.

SOLOMON: Like the Gauls invading the Roman Senate?

KEAN: Who told you I was thinking of that?

SOLOMON: It was in *Brenius* – the new play you gave me to read.

KEAN: My God, you are right. I am making a gesture. D'you know, my whole life is made up of gestures: there is one for every hour, every season, every period of my entire life. I learnt to walk, to breathe, to die. Now at last those gestures are dead. Like so many dead branches. I killed them all last night, at one blow. If I try and repeat one, it breaks in my hand. You never make gestures, do you? No, of course not. I will root them out, and if I cannot, I will cut off my arms. [*He laughs.*] D'you hear? D'you hear? Ah, mountebank – you're going to have a hard life. You must learn to be simple – perfectly simple. [*With sudden violence, addressing the chair*] Out of my sight! Out of my sight, or I will kill you. [*Calming*] No, stay. You do not incommode me. [*He sits down.*] No. [*He rises.*] You see: the man in the armchair wasn't me, it was Richard III. And that one is Shylock, the Jew of Venice. Oh well – it will have to happen by degrees. I will imitate the natural until it becomes second nature. [*Pause.*] Tell me – you saw me last night?

SOLOMON: Alas!

KEAN: Well – what did I do?

SOLOMON: You insulted the Prince of Wales, a peer of the realm, and seven hundred and eighty-two people.

KEAN: Yes, yes, I know. But what was it?

SOLOMON: They say it was a crime. Lese-majesty.

KEAN: That's not what I asked you, fool. Was it a gesture or an act?

SOLOMON: I couldn't say.

KEAN: It was a gesture, d'you hear? The last. I took myself for Othello, and that woman, laughing in her box – I took her for Desdemona. A meaningless gesture, for which I need account to no one. Sleep-walkers are innocent of their crimes.

SOLOMON: That's exactly what I said; you can't be guilty and that's why you must defend yourself.

KEAN [*loudly*]: You lie! It was an act. It was an act since it has ruined my life. Seven hundred and eighty-two people saw me commit a crime. A deliberate act. But I? Did I intend to commit that crime? Or did I dream it? It was only an imaginary suicide. But the pistol was loaded and the great Kean killed himself in earnest. [*He takes his head in his hands.*] If only I could put back the clock! Fool! If I could live my life again, it would be to do deliberately what I have done in spite of myself. If you must ruin your life, let it be in the sight of the world. Ah, Solomon – prison frightens me. [*Pause.*] You know the story of the frog who wished to be as big as the ox. The ox was the Prince of Wales. An ox? Say rather a bull. I was sick with pride. Pride is the opposite of shame. A bubble – it fills and fills, and then it bursts. Last night, I pricked the bubble myself. [*Pause.*] When I come out of jail, I shall sell cheese. How fortunate I am – the end of pride, the end of shame. At last I can become a nobody. [SOLOMON *has picked up the list and holds it carelessly.*] What's that?

SOLOMON: Nothing interesting. The list of fools who have called on the nobody this morning.

KEAN: Let me see. [*He reads.*] All the names – except the one I want. If she didn't come – it may be because she couldn't. Solomon, let no one enter, except . . .

SOLOMON: Except her. [*He laughs.*]

KEAN: Why do you laugh?

SOLOMON: Because you have come to yourself. Mr Edmund isn't capable of passion.

KEAN: No, he is not. [*Pause.*] That is all that remains of Kean, a mad and hopeless passion. If this fire dies out in my heart, there will be nothing left but cinders. It must burn. It must. Go, go . . . and if she comes, bring her in immediately.

SOLOMON: Yes, Guv'nor. [*He goes.*]

KEAN [*alone*]: Ten o'clock and not a word from her. Ah, you were more concerned for your fan than for my safety, madam. [*Pause.*] Supposing it were the count who found the fan? But . . . but it's obvious! Of course he did. He found it when he came to my room. And when I think that at this moment she is suspected, accused, humiliated, perhaps, and calling to me for help . . . Solomon! Solomon!

SOLOMON [*appearing*]: Sir . . .

KEAN: Order the horses!

SOLOMON: Horses?

KEAN: Unless you want to pull my carriage yourself?

SOLOMON: Your carriage!

KEAN: Yes – I'm going out.

SOLOMON: Out?

KEAN: Can't you see I have a fever? That my head is burning? Besides, I can lower the blinds – I will only drive beneath her windows.

[Knock at the door.]

SOLOMON: Someone knocked ... Do you still want the carriage?

KEAN: Go and see.

SOLOMON: At once ...

[ANNA enters timidly.]

KEAN: Oh, good heavens! [Aloud] Solomon! I told you not to admit anyone.

SOLOMON [smiling]: Do you call Miss Anna someone? She will only stay for a moment ... she wants to say good-bye.

KEAN [going to ANNA]: Good-bye? You are going away?

ANNA: Yes.

[SOLOMON smiles as he looks at them and goes out discreetly.]

KEAN: You are leaving London?

ANNA: And England.

KEAN: Oh ... Oh, well that's good. You're quite right, child. The rats must leave the sinking ship. Well, what are you waiting for? Can't you see my ship has struck?

ANNA: If you really had been mad, I would have stayed to nurse you.

KEAN: I wasn't lucky enough; I am merely a man dishonoured, ruined – whose career is finished, and on top of everything, threatened with prison. There's nothing here to attract a woman.

ANNA: Oh, Kean – why did you do it?

KEAN: Do what?

ANNA: Last night.

KEAN: The improvisation at the end? Oh well, to amuse myself. Don't you ever want to break things?

ANNA: No. Why?

KEAN: I don't know why. To see what will happen. Supposing your life were only a dream – you pinch yourself, and you wake up. Last night, I pinched myself. A pretty suicide, wasn't it? Fame and fortune, that was all a game, but prison, you see, will be very real. Brr . . . how real it must be – particularly in winter. Where are you going?

ANNA: To America.

KEAN: America? What will you do there?

ANNA: A manager from a New York theatre saw me last night. He thought I was very good.

KEAN: He had the effrontery to think you good while I was dying on the stage! The man has no heart.

ANNA: All the same, he has given me a contract.

KEAN: He's mad – completely mad. And you – you're a fool. You aren't ready yet! I would have made you work.

ANNA: You wouldn't have been able to – you would have been in prison.

KEAN: Good heavens, you're right. And your guardian – is he allowing you to go? He lacks authority.

ANNA: After last night, he only has one thought – to send me to the antipodes.

KEAN: In a sense, I understand. Oh well, it's all over.

ANNA: All over.

KEAN: But why are you going?

ANNA [surprised]: Why? Because you don't love me.

KEAN: Oh, yes . . . I see.

ANNA: Have you forgotten?

KEAN: Today my head is hardly my own. In fact, your plan didn't succeed?

ANNA: No.

KEAN: I thought you always got what you wanted.

ANNA: I thought so too.

KEAN: You see, it was only a bluff. I said to myself: 'That child always gets what she wants: one of these days, I shall find myself madly in love with her.' It promised to be very amusing. And then, no; it was only more theatre. I'm afraid I'm disappointed in you.

But you need have no regrets. I should have been a very bad husband.

ANNA: That was what I hoped.

KEAN: If I do marry, you can be sure it will be to have someone I can talk to about myself.

ANNA: I'm a very good listener.

KEAN: So much the better for you. You can listen to one of those Puritans in New Scotland. I think you would make a very good minister's wife. When do you go?

ANNA: In two hours' time.

KEAN [*startled*]: What?

ANNA: A cabin has been booked for me on the *Washington*.

KEAN [*furiously*]: I see. Good luck and good-bye.

ANNA: Good luck.

KEAN: Will you write to me while I'm in prison?

ANNA: I'll send you some food parcels.

KEAN [*sarcastic*]: They'll be rotten before they arrive. [*Pause.*] I could order you to stay . . .

ANNA: Order me?

KEAN: Exactly. Don't be afraid; I shall do no such thing. But it would be my right. [*He begins to be angry.*] After all, it's your fault that all this happened. If you hadn't appeared on the stage, Elena would never have defied me, and I shouldn't have caused the scandal. Yes, yes, all things considered you are the only one responsible. And I know what a great many men would say in my place. They would say that it is too easy to enter a man's life, to ruin it, and fly away with a flick of your wings. Yes, viewing events clearly, that is exactly what they'd say. Without mentioning your scandalous devotion, you provoke a scandal, break my heart and my career – get yourself a contract in New York and I have to be thrown into prison. In brief, the good are punished and the wicked get their reward. I don't mean I want to keep you. You can imagine there is no room for you in my life. But it is certain that if you had had a little feeling – that is perhaps too much to ask – let us say a little tact, or merely a touch of politeness, the idea of deserting me would never have entered your head. You really are deserting me. Abandoning me – betraying me . . .

ANNA: But since you don't love me . . .

KEAN: Fortunately! It would be charming if I were to fall in love with an irresponsible child who destroys a man's life as an evening's entertainment!

ANNA: You're talking nonsense: if you loved me, of course I would stay.

KEAN: That's right – for you to deign to stay, I must fall on my knees, put on a pair of white gloves, and ask your guardian for your hand in marriage. Have you ever seen a man of forty on his knees before a child? Do you know what I should do if I weren't an honourable man? [*He rises and marches on her.*] I should give you a sound thrashing! Yes – a thrashing. None of this would have happened if you had been thrashed every time you deserved it.

SOLOMON [*running in*]: Sir – sir – she's here!

KEAN [*off balance – without thinking*]: Send her to the devil! Eh? What? D'you mean . . .

ANNA [*moving to go*]: Is it Elena?

KEAN: Yes, but you needn't imagine I've finished with you. Go in there – little fool – and to pass the time think of the good hiding you are going to get from me in a moment. [*He pushes her into his room. To* SOLOMON] Ask her to come in.

[SOLOMON *goes.* ELENA *enters.*]

Ah, Elena! Is it you? You have come, in spite of the risks . . . If you knew how I have wanted you! Will you forgive me?

ELENA: A woman must always pardon the follies committed for her sake.

KEAN: Let me look at you! How pale you are, and how lovely. How happy I am! I cannot regret my madness, even if it has ruined me, if I owe it the honour of your visit.

ELENA [*sitting down*]: I hesitated for a long time. But our common danger . . .

KEAN: Danger?

ELENA: A letter could be intercepted . . . I feared that you were already arrested.

KEAN: Ah! has it come to that?

ELENA: Alas! Kean, you must fly!

KEAN: Fly? I – leave England like a coward? You know me very ill.

ELENA: If not for your sake, then for mine . . .

KEAN: On one condition, one only . . . Do you love me, Elena?

ELENA [lowering her eyes]: Can you ask?

KEAN: Yes. The fan you left behind on my table . . .

ELENA: Well?

KEAN: Has been found.

ELENA: By whom?

KEAN: I fear it was your husband.

ELENA: Great heavens! [Pause.]

KEAN [softly]: Elena – must I fly alone?

ELENA: Kean – you are mad . . . no, no, it's impossible.

KEAN: My carriage is ready.

ELENA: Cruel! And my honour?

KEAN: What could be more honourable than to leave England with the king of London? Here you are only a countess – in exile you would be a queen.

ELENA [a pause]: And my husband?

KEAN: I bow before his future grief.

ELENA: It will kill him.

KEAN: It is he or I. We must save the younger man.

ELENA: Later, when we have recovered our senses, how shall we endure the guilt of his death?

KEAN: Very easily.

ELENA: And if he kills you first?

KEAN: Highly improbable.

ELENA: Ah! How do you know?

KEAN: Too short-sighted.

ELENA: Kean! And my children?

KEAN [very surprised]: Children? Surely, madam, you have none?

ELENA: I have sworn to have children.

KEAN: Sworn? To whom?

ELENA: To my husband – before God.

KEAN: Is that all? Before God, you shall have them – I'll see to that.

ELENA: You don't understand. I promised my husband to give him a son and heir.

KEAN: God has not taken note of your vows. He is only concerned with the preservation of the race, not of a particular family.

ELENA: But I adore him already – my unborn son! If I go with you, I must strangle him in my bosom. Ah, Kean, I have loved you as far as adultery, do not drive me as far as infanticide!

KEAN: In a word, you refuse?

ELENA: Did I say that? Accept, refuse – whichever way, I choose despair. Ah, my friend, I can see it too clearly. If you want to ruin my life, you must make me mad.

KEAN [*tenderly*]: Elena, my love! [*He takes her in his arms.*]

ELENA [*freeing herself*]: Not like that! Talk to me – intoxicate me with your words: you must use your whole genius. I can feel that the fight will be terrible. I shall resist with my whole strength, and only give way on the edge of the precipice. Show me that I am the world to you, and that you will be the world to me . . . [KEAN *does not reply. She repeats, astonished*] . . . and that you will be the world to me.

KEAN [*annoyed*]: Don't prompt me.

ELENA [*astounded*]: What?

KEAN [*startled*]: Don't . . . [*He stops.*]

ELENA: What did you say?

KEAN: You were standing there, repeating the last words of your speech. It reminded me . . . [*He begins to laugh.*] Madam, you were giving me my cue.

ELENA: How dare you . . . ? [*She rises.*]

KEAN: Oh, I dare nothing. I will never act again. Curtain!

ELENA: Look at me. I see.

KEAN: What?

ELENA: You are suffering the tortures of the damned.

KEAN: Not as much as that, I assure you.

ELENA: You are tortured by your love, and you are trying to debase it out of revenge. It's horrible, Kean, and very wonderful. Here, my dear, take my hand, press it to your lips. Well? How long must I wait? Kiss my hand.

KEAN [*without taking it*]: Elena – I told you it was over. You aren't going to try and act the comedy alone?

ELENA [*suddenly*]: Take me away!

KEAN: What?

ELENA: You told me your carriage was ready? Very well, take me with you. You think I'm acting. You can spend the rest of your life repaying me for that word. I am full of passion, jealous, real, terrible – I can be angel or tiger. For the man I loved, I should lay modesty and reputation at his feet – I should go with him everywhere, to the galleys, to the very scaffold. [*She looks at him with sparkling eyes.*] Ha!

KEAN [*without moving*]: And it is I you love?

ELENA: You? I hate you. Well, what are you waiting for? Abduct me! Carry me off. [*He does not move. Long silence.*] So, I see. You were speaking the truth. Your love was only another act. I confess, when you made that . . . confession . . . just now, I gazed at you with all my strength, but I couldn't believe you. Now I have driven you into the open. I said: Take me away, and you stand there like a fool, ashamed of your lack of feeling, and too cowardly to have even a surge of pride. A woman ready to ruin herself for you? Good heavens, what have you to do with her? The ones whose happiness you deign to make, others must clothe, feed and protect. You play the lover every evening at Drury Lane, and sometimes in the afternoon in a lady's boudoir. Don't be afraid, sir, I give you back your liberty. You will fly alone. But don't believe I bear you any ill will; it is I who should ask your forgiveness. I was fool enough to take you for a man. It isn't your fault you are only an actor.

KEAN: Is an actor not a man?

ELENA: No, my friend. The Prince of Wales was quite right. He is only a reflection.

KEAN: Oh, he said I was a reflection! [*He catches her up in his arms.*] Very well, let us go!

ELENA [*frightened*]: What are you doing?

KEAN: Abducting you. [*He starts for the door, still carrying her in his arms.*]

ELENA: Wait! Wait!

KEAN: What for?

ELENA: I . . . I want to get my breath. Put me down. Please – just for a moment, and I will come with you gladly. [*He puts her down.*] So, we go together?

KEAN: Yes, together.

ELENA: Will you regret nothing?

KEAN: Nothing. And you?

ELENA: Nothing. Where are we going? Madrid? Rome? Paris?

KEAN: Amsterdam.

ELENA: Oh. [*Pause.*] I don't like Amsterdam.

KEAN: Neither do I. It can't be helped. [*He starts to pick her up again.*]

ELENA: One more word. [*He stops.*] How long will you give me to learn my parts?

KEAN: Which parts?

ELENA: All of them. Desdemona – Juliet – Ophelia . . .

KEAN: Oh! You expect to act?

ELENA: What else am I to do all day? Wait for you?

KEAN: You won't go on the stage, Elena. Neither will I. That's over. You are eloping with Mr Edmund, the jeweller. I have some very fine jewels – the gifts of admirers. I am planning to start a business. Don't be afraid. You will have everything. Except perhaps friends. But we will be enough for each other. On working days, I will go to the shop, and you will lie on the sofa and read novels. Three times a week we will go to the theatre to replenish our provision of love-words. Come! [*He moves towards her, but she runs round the other side of the table.*]

ELENA: Let me go! Let me go! Help!

[KEAN *begins to laugh.*]

KEAN [*imitating her*]: To the galleys! To the scaffold! To the ends of the earth! [*He laughs.*] You see, you were only acting.

ELENA [*looks at him, disconcerted, then begins to laugh*]: That sounds a little severe: say rather, coquetting.

KEAN: Be frank. You came to ask me for your letters.

ELENA [*indignant*]: No!

KEAN: No? Very well, I will keep them.

ELENA [*weakly*]: I didn't want to ask for them . . . immediately.

KEAN: Not immediately, of course, you would have observed the conventions. Only time is short; they are coming to arrest me. [*He fetches the letters.*] Here they are. Count them.

ELENA: I trust you.

KEAN: No, you don't trust me at all. [*He counts.*] One, two, three, four, five, six, seven.

ELENA [*carelessly*]: There were eight.

KEAN: Don't you remember – I tore up the eighth in front of you. Here, take them. [*She doesn't move.*] What? Not yet? [*He lays them on the table.*] I leave them within reach; you can take them when you judge the time has come.

ELENA: Kean!

KEAN: What is it? Am I going too fast? I confess that in a modern play I should have refused to give them to you at first. But I have cut a few lines. Do you know where we went wrong; we started two or three tones too high. [*Smiling*] Why on earth did we both decide to be noble?

ELENA: Oh, Kean, it's so amusing to live above the level of your strength. [*Dreaming*] A real passion must be very wonderful.

KEAN [*doubtfully*]: Do you think so?

ELENA: With your genius, you could do anything. I haven't your powers, so I should rely on love. Love is the genius of the poor. [*She laughs. Without malice.*] If I had gone away with you, you would have been finely caught.

KEAN: Not in the least. All I risked was that you would have come as far as Dover.

ELENA: In other words, you were only attacking the ambassadress?

KEAN: Say rather the ambassador. I am a bastard. For a bastard, it's flattering to supplant an Excellency. And you? Was it the king of London you wanted to attract?

ELENA: I want to attract all men. Because I am ugly.

KEAN: You? Ugly?

ELENA: My poor friend, all women are ugly. Beauty is very hard work; if you knew how tiring it is to have to paint and perfume a long white animal every day!

KEAN [smiling]: So it has to be made worth while?

ELENA: Of course. [They both laugh.] Enough! Enough! Let us keep to the sentimental comedy; we women very rarely adventure on the terrain of farce. Come – talk to me – say anything. I dislike being left unprotected.

KEAN: Good luck, Elena.

ELENA [surprised]: Good luck?

KEAN: Yes. I'm not on in the last act, and I won't stay for the calls. But you still have your best scenes to play.

ELENA: My best scenes?

KEAN: With the Prince of Wales.

ELENA: Ah, yes. Perhaps.

KEAN: So I wish you luck. That's all.

ELENA: Aren't you jealous any more? [KEAN shakes his head.] How strange.

KEAN: No. Not in the least. Do you know why? The Prince of Wales, was I. Listen – we are three victims. You, because you were born a woman – he, because he was too highly born, and I, because I was a bastard. The result is you enjoy your beauty through the eyes of others, and I discover my genius through their applause. As for him, he is a flower. For him to feel he is a prince, he has to be admired. Beauty, royalty, genius; a single and same mirage. We live all three on the love of others, and we are all three incapable of loving ourselves. You wanted my love – I yours, he ours. What a mix-up. You were right. Three reflections, each of the three believing in the existence of the other two; that was the comedy. Jealous? Oh, no, it is you who will be jealous. The Prince only cares for me, my women, and my dressing-gowns. Why do you laugh?

ELENA: Because I was thinking of Shakespeare.

KEAN: Is that amusing?

ELENA: Yes. Because if this were Shakespeare, we should all have been dead by now. You would have killed the prince in a duel.

KEAN: Your husband would have had me murdered.

ELENA: The king would have had his head cut off.

KEAN: And you would have stabbed yourself on our triple tomb.

ELENA [laughing]: What a massacre!

KEAN: Regret nothing. You managed brilliantly, and God knows the scene wasn't easy to play. Spite, passion, anger – you did them all, even sincerity. You are the one with genius. Good-bye, Juliet – farewell, Desdemona – au revoir, Beatrice.

ELENA: Au revoir, Falstaff!

KEAN: That was unkind. Are you angry with me?

ELENA: No one can be angry with Mr Edmund. As for the great Kean . . .

KEAN: Well?

ELENA: I shall never forget he killed himself for me.

KEAN: For you? Hm!

ELENA: Sh! Sh! Of course he killed himself for my sake. Besides, jeweller, how do you know? What do you know about love?

KEAN: He breathed his last in my arms.

ELENA: And what did he say before he died?

KEAN [softly]: That he was dying for your sake.

ELENA: You see!

KEAN: He also asked me to return your letters. [He holds them out.] Will you take them?

ELENA: Yes. To gratify the last wish of a dying man. Thank you. [She slips them into her dress.] What should I wish Mr Edmund? A passionate love?

KEAN: A jeweller is incapable of inspiring passion. Wish rather that I may fall in love – it will be a change. [He kisses her hand.]

COUNT [off]: I tell you I shall go in.

SOLOMON [off]: And I say that you shan't.

[ELENA *and* KEAN *look at each other and begin to laugh.*]

ELENA [*laughing*]: Heavens – my husband! I am lost!

KEAN: Can you hear that? He isn't playing in the same production as we are. Listen to those intonations! Pure tragedy!

ELENA: He thinks he is still in Shakespeare.

KEAN: Nobody told him. [*Laughing.*] He has come to kill me.

ELENA [*laughing*]: How horrible – I couldn't bear it. [*Going towards the room where* ANNA *is hiding.*] I shall wait in here until you have finished.

KEAN: No, not in there. [*He points to the other room.*] In here.

ELENA: Naturally, I forbid you to fight: the count isn't a young man, and accidents happen so easily.

KEAN: Poor man! Don't be afraid. Yesterday I should have provoked him in a dream, killed him in a dream, and he would have been dead in good earnest. Good-bye, Elena.

ELENA [*closing the door*]: Good-bye.

COUNT [*off*]: I tell you I must see him.

KEAN [*opening the door*]: What's the matter, Solomon? Why didn't you show the Count in?

SOLOMON: But you told me . . .

    [*The* COUNT *enters, followed by* SOLOMON.]

KEAN: That I could see no one? It's true – but I couldn't expect the honour of receiving the Danish Ambassador.

COUNT: Sir – you remember what I told you yesterday?

KEAN: Yes, indeed. What was it?

    [SOLOMON *goes.*]

COUNT: I told you that if we Danes are insulted, we fight the whole world.

KEAN: Ah, yes, I remember. What a fine saying, and what pleasure it gave me.

COUNT: Thank you. I . . .

KEAN: What breadth of vision, especially. Ah, we English, we're unaccustomed to such language.

COUNT: Well – I have been insulted and I intend to fight.

KEAN: Insulted? You amaze me. A soul like yours cannot be offended.

It must understand everything. Whoever the wretch may be who has had the temerity to displease you – I am sure at this moment he is more wretched than you.

COUNT: I tell you I want to fight.

KEAN: Very well. If nothing can make you change your mind – I should be delighted to be your second.

COUNT: My second! Sir – I came here to challenge you.

KEAN: Me? Oh, no, sir.

COUNT: What?

KEAN: I regret. It's impossible.

COUNT: Why not?

KEAN: Because I never fight. To begin with, I haven't insulted you.

COUNT: Yes. Mortally.

KEAN [*gentle reproach*]: Sir – surely I should know.

COUNT: I understand your delicacy, but it is only a further insult.

KEAN: I have offended you? After all – because you say so . . . Very well, I apologize.

COUNT: Apologize?

KEAN: Most abjectly.

COUNT: I won't accept.

KEAN: Allow me to insist. I swear to you it is offered with all my heart. No? Well, you cannot leave here without some gift – a snuff-box, some flowers. Since I cannot make you amends by force of arms, I must at least offer you some compensation.

COUNT: That's where you are mistaken, sir. You will make me amends.

KEAN: Alas, no. No question. Since you have been insulted, I find it natural that you wish to fight. But for the same reason, I hope you will find it just that I do not wish to fight, since you have not insulted me.

COUNT: What's that got to do with it?

KEAN: What will you wager that it won't happen? I am very good-natured, and I don't lose my temper easily.

COUNT: You are a liar, sir.

KEAN [*beaming*]: How true – of course, a professional liar.

COUNT: A coward!

KEAN: Sincerely – I don't think so. I will search my conscience.

COUNT: A dog!

KEAN: No, no, a dog is a quadruped. [*Friendly*] Come, you don't believe a word you're saying.

COUNT: Sir, I have insulted you irreparably. My intention was to sting you to the quick.

KEAN: But sir, since you say so, how could I be angry with you?

COUNT [*raising his hand*]: Coward!

KEAN [*catching his hand*]: Fear nothing, sir – I have already forgotten this moment of madness. [*He bows.*] No, definitely, sir, it's no good, I cannot fight you. It is only children who fight. Children and lords. You see – last night I realized I wasn't the one any longer and I could never be the other. Yes, I have given a few sword-thrusts in my time – but I was still living in my comedy. I risked death because of my lack of breeding. Besides, I hated all lords. Because their blood didn't flow in my veins, I wanted to let it out of their own. That is all over – Mr Edmund never fights. Sir, isn't it enough to have had the misfortune to wound you – must I go so far as to kill you?

COUNT: Very well – I cannot force your hand. But I must spend my rage.

KEAN: Spend it – spend it – my carpets are thick. They will soak up your fury.

COUNT: Remember, if not on you, it will fall on your accomplice.

KEAN [*interested*]: Have I an accomplice?

COUNT: You know quite well. You are afraid of my vengeance, and you have taken refuge behind a woman.

KEAN: Is there a woman in this affair? Do I know her? Let me guess. Is she young or old?

COUNT: I will show you. Do you know this fan?

KEAN: A fan?

COUNT: It belongs to the countess.

KEAN: Indeed!

COUNT [*losing his temper again*]: Well, sir – I found that fan last
  night . . .
    [SOLOMON *enters precipitately.*]

SOLOMON: An urgent note from the Prince of Wales.

KEAN: Later.

SOLOMON: No, at once.

KEAN [*to the* COUNT]: Will you excuse me?

COUNT [*sneering*]: Read it – but I shall not move a step.

KEAN [*he reads the note rapidly*]: Count – do you know the Prince of
  Wales's handwriting?

COUNT: I don't see what . . .

COUNT [*reading*]: 'Er . . . er . . . er . . . Will you please search your
  room. I believe I left the countess' fan there last night. I had borrowed it in order to have it copied for a friend . . . I shall come and
  ask you this afternoon for an explanation of the stupid quarrel you
  tried to fasten on me at the theatre last night because of the little
  ballet dancer. I should never have believed a friendship of such long
  standing . . . er . . . er . . . Your affectionate George.' Perfect.
  Well – this is a very convenient letter, Mr Kean.

KEAN: Can you deny it is the Prince's writing?

COUNT: I deny nothing. That is why I only half believe you.

KEAN: What must I do to reassure you?

COUNT: Only one thing – allow me to see the veiled lady who came
  in here a little while ago.

KEAN: No lady has been here this morning.

COUNT [*furiously*]: You are lying. [*Calming down*] Come, Mr Kean
  – don't spoil the effect of this letter. I am half convinced – persuade
  me altogether.

KEAN: There is no lady here.

COUNT: I tell you I saw her come in with my own eyes.

KEAN: I . . .
    [ANNA *enters.*]

ANNA: Well, Kean – what about my thrashing? Oh, forgive me,
  I didn't know you had a guest.

COUNT: Well, sir, you see?

KEAN: You said, 'A lady'. How could I think you meant this child?

COUNT: To me she is a lady – and a very lovely one. I am grateful. [*He bows, takes a step, then turns.*] Do not forget that consulates are inviolable, and that the Danish embassy is a consular palace.

KEAN: Thank you, sir.

COUNT: Good-bye. [*He bows.*] Madam.

ANNA: Oh, not yet, sir.

COUNT: You will be soon, young lady; I am quite sure. [*He goes.*]

KEAN: Thank you.

ANNA: Why didn't you fetch me in yourself?

KEAN: You were listening? Oh, well, I did think of it – but I didn't want to compromise you.

ANNA: Bah! I am already – a little more or less . . .

KEAN: In other words, you have made me a present of your reputation.

ANNA: It would seem so.

KEAN: Without even knowing if I would marry you? Do you know that yesterday that would have made me wild with joy?

ANNA: Why not today?

KEAN: Yesterday I wanted a woman – any woman – to ruin herself for my sake . . .

ANNA: And today?

KEAN [*looking at her*]: I am conscious of more concrete advantages. [*Pause.*] Now we must deal with the other. [*He takes a step towards the other door.*] Go back to your room. No – stay. What does it matter now? Elena? [*He opens the door.*] Eh?

ANNA: What? [*He goes into the room and returns at once.*]

KEAN: Gone – flown away – disappeared. And the window's open. It's miraculous. [*He laughs.*]

ANNA: How can you laugh? That window overlooks the river. She may perhaps . . .

KEAN: Have killed herself? Don't worry. Women like Elena never kill themselves. But I should very much like to know . . .

SOLOMON [*entering*]: Two visitors are waiting downstairs. Which one shall I bring up first?

KEAN: Who are they?

SOLOMON: One is the constable – the other is the Prince of Wales.

KEAN: What does the constable want?

SOLOMON: To arrest you. He is in tears – he admires you so much.

ANNA: Oh!

KEAN: And the Prince? What does he want?

PRINCE [*entering*]: To stop you being arrested.

KEAN: Thank you, sir. And thank you for your letter. Unhappily, Elena . . . [*He waves towards the window.*]

PRINCE: Don't worry. She is safe.

KEAN: How?

PRINCE: A friend watches over you. Foreseeing your danger, he had a boat under your window, and a carriage at your door.

KEAN: Where is she now?

PRINCE: At home, where I had her taken.

KEAN: Sir, you have saved me twice over. How can I expiate my sins towards you?

PRINCE: By forgiving me those I committed against you. I have obtained from the King that your six months in prison shall be changed to a year of exile.

KEAN: Where is your Royal Highness sending me?

PRINCE: Where you please. Provided you leave England. Paris – Berlin – New York . . .

KEAN [*looking at* ANNA]: I choose New York.

ANNA [*going to him*]: What did you say?

KEAN: We leave in an hour. Have you chosen a boat?

PRINCE: Choose yourself.

KEAN: Then I settle for the *Washington*. [*He calls.*] Solomon, send someone to book me a berth.

ANNA: We shall need two.

KEAN: Why two?

ANNA: Because I need one as well!

KEAN: But I thought . . . So you lied?

ANNA: Yes.

KEAN: What for?

ANNA: To make you marry me.

PRINCE [*who has not been listening*]: I hope America suits you.

KEAN: I expect to marry there, sir. Miss Anna Danby looks unimportant, but she always gets what she wants.

ANNA: Your Royal Highness. [*Curtsy.*]

PRINCE [*surprised*]: What's this, Mr Kean? Taking a lady with you?

KEAN: Unless His Majesty objects?

PRINCE [*serious*]: No, of course not; if your intentions are honourable . . .

KEAN: Your Royal Highness seems disappointed.

PRINCE: I? Not at all. At your age, it's high time to settle down. Only, you – you surprise me. I thought you had fire in your veins, passion in your soul – I attributed your taste for exaggeration to the profundity of your feelings . . . And I'm afraid I may have been wrong. Tell me frankly: isn't your heart broken?

KEAN: Not at all.

PRINCE [*persisting*]: Just a little? Merely cracked?

KEAN: Not even cracked.

PRINCE: How strange. In your place I . . . and I who was feeling guilty; good heavens, what a fool I was. You don't love her any more?

KEAN: Who?

PRINCE: Elena, of course!

KEAN: Did I ever love her?

PRINCE [*furiously*]: Then allow me to tell you that I find you unpardonable. You rushed into the affair with your eyes closed, and naturally, I followed you. Now you tell me . . . [*He turns to* ANNA.] Particularly as she wasn't at all my type. And without my blind confidence in your fiancé's taste . . . I sometimes wondered what he saw in her? I believed she must have hidden charms. [*Turning to* KEAN, *furiously*] But if you don't love her, what am I to do with her? [*He looks at* ANNA.] You, at least, madam – one need only look at you to see that our great Kean has remained the most subtle of connoisseurs. [*To* KEAN] Fascinating, dear fellow. Fascinating!

KEAN: Sir, you say that of every woman I have the honour to present to you.

PRINCE: This time it's different. Your fiancée would have been fascinating even if I had met her alone. [*He crosses to* ANNA.]

KEAN: Sir, sir! I'm going to marry this one!

ANNA [*softly, to* KEAN]: Don't be afraid, darling. Princes seduce shepherdesses, not the daughters of cheesemongers.

PRINCE: So, young lady. You always get what you want.

ANNA: Yes, sir.

PRINCE: I can believe you. If you decided you wanted to seduce a royal prince, I am sure you would succeed.

ANNA: So am I, sir. So sure I don't even want to try.

[KEAN *begins to laugh, reassured.*]

PRINCE [*to* KEAN]: She's much too good for you. [*Still looking at her*] How bored I shall be without you two. I shouldn't have got the King to forgive you. If you had stayed here in prison, I could have gone to see you. Miss Danby and I could have talked about you.

KEAN: You can talk about me with Elena.

PRINCE [*sharply*]: Elena bores me. I shall arrange for the Count de Koefeld to be recalled to Denmark immediately. As for you, take care. I need only say one word . . .

ANNA [*softly*]: Sir . . .

PRINCE: Well?

ANNA [*sadly*]: I would have wished your Royal Highness to spare me, but since we must tell you everything – Kean still loves her.

PRINCE: He loves Elena?

ANNA: Madly.

PRINCE [*reassured, but still incredulous*]: Why didn't he say so?

ANNA: Can't you see he was trying to save his face?

KEAN [*furious*]: Really!

ANNA [*pinching him to make him keep quiet*]: And because he didn't want to cause me pain.

PRINCE: But he is marrying you.

ANNA: Exactly. Does one marry the woman one loves? Just as you came in, d'you know what he was saying? He said: 'You will be my little nurse.'

KEAN [*furious*]: I never . . .

PRINCE: Kean, is that true?

KEAN: I . . . [ANNA *kicks him. Crossly*] Yes, yes, if you like.

PRINCE [*relaxing*]: My dear Kean, you are yourself again! I knew your heart was as wide as the sea. You love her! Then you find her . . .

ANNA [*quickly*]: Fascinating!

PRINCE: Fascinating, that's right. She has . . .

ANNA: Something. Those were his very words.

PRINCE: 'She has something.' Perfect! Perfect! Kean, I wounded you, didn't I? Forgive me, please. If you knew how penitent I shall be. [*Gay and carefree, to* ANNA] You must look after him, you know. England is entrusting you with her most precious treasure. [*To* KEAN] You aren't angry with me?

KEAN [*exasperated*]: Don't let's discuss it. [*Crying out*] Solomon? What are you doing? Go and book us two berths on the *Washington*.

SOLOMON [*entering with his luggage*]: Three.

KEAN: Why three?

SOLOMON: If you are going to keep up the comedy, you will certainly need a prompter.

KEAN [*to* SOLOMON *and* ANNA, *linking arms with them both*]: My true, my only friends.

PRINCE [*at the door*]: Mr Kean, you are an ungrateful wretch!

KEAN [*going to him*]: Ah, sir, what an exit. With your permission, let it be the last word of our play.

[*The two men embrace, while* SOLOMON *kisses* ANNA *on the forehead.*]

CURTAIN

NEKRASSOV

A FARCE IN EIGHT SCENES

Translated by Sylvia and
George Leeson

CHARACTERS

ROBERT ⎫
IRMA ⎭ *Two down-and-outs*

GEORGES DE VALÉRA

INSPECTOR GOBLET

FIRST POLICEMAN

SECOND POLICEMAN

JULES PALOTIN – *Editor of* Soir à Paris

SECRETARY

SIBILOT

TAVERNIER

PERIGORD

MAYOR OF TRAVAJA

INTERPRETER

MOUTON – *Chairman of* Soir à Paris

VERONIQUE

LERMINIER ⎫
CHARIVET ⎪
         ⎬ *Directors of* Soir à Paris
NERCIAT ⎪
BERGERAT ⎭

MESSENGER

FIRST BODYGUARD

SECOND BODYGUARD

MADAME CASTAGNIÉ

INSPECTOR BAUDOUIN

INSPECTOR CHAPUIS

MADAME BOUNOUMI

PERDRIÈRE

DEMIDOFF

Photographers, Servants, Guests,
Two Male Nurses

SCENE ONE

The bank of the Seine, near a bridge. It is moonlight. Two down-and-outs, a man and a woman, are huddled on the bank. He is asleep. She is sitting and dreaming.

IRMA: Oh!

ROBERT [*only half awake*]: Eh?

IRMA: Isn't it pretty?

ROBERT: What?

IRMA: The moon.

ROBERT: The moon's not pretty, you see it every day.

IRMA: It's pretty because it's round.

ROBERT: In any case it's for the rich. And so are the stars. [*He settles down again and goes to sleep.*]

IRMA: Look! Look! [*She shakes him.*]

ROBERT: Can't you leave me in peace?

IRMA [*very excited*]: Over there! There! There!

ROBERT [*rubbing his eyes*]: Where?

IRMA: On the bridge near the lamp. It's one of them!

ROBERT: Nothing extraordinary in that. It's the season now.

IRMA: He is looking at the moon. That tickles me because just now I too was looking at the moon. He is taking off his jacket. He's folding it up. He's not bad looking.

ROBERT: Anyway, he's a weak character.

IRMA: Why?

ROBERT: Because he wants to drown himself.

IRMA: Still, that would be in my line, drowning. But not to dive in. I would lie on my back, let myself go, and the water would come in everywhere like a little lover.

ROBERT: That's because you're a woman. A real man has to make a splash when he leaves this world. That fellow there, it wouldn't surprise me if he was a bit of a woman. [*He lies down again.*]

IRMA: Aren't you going to wait to see him jump?

ROBERT: Plenty of time. You can wake me up when he's decided. [*Goes to sleep.*]

IRMA [*to herself*]: This is the moment I like best! Just before the plunge. They look so sweet. He is bending down. He is looking at the moon in the water. The water flows on but the moon stands still. [*Shaking* ROBERT.] There he goes! There he goes! Lovely dive.

ROBERT: Bah! [*He gets up.*]

IRMA: Where are you going?

ROBERT: His jacket! It's up there.

IRMA: You're not going to leave me alone with him!

ROBERT: You've nothing to be afraid of. He's at the bottom. [*He starts to go out.*] Blast it, he's not dead.

IRMA: Eh?

ROBERT: It's nothing. His head has come up, just the head. That's usual. [*He sits down again.*] Only I'd better wait a little. While he's alive, I don't touch the jacket. That would be stealing. [*He clicks his tongue in disapproval.*]

IRMA: What's happened?

ROBERT: I don't like it.

IRMA: What?

ROBERT: He's swimming.

IRMA: Oh, you're never satisfied.

ROBERT: I don't like frauds!

IRMA: Fraud or not, he'll do it.

ROBERT: All the same, he's a fraud! Besides, the jacket is lost. At least I'm waiting for him to die. But I bet you the first person who crosses the bridge won't have my delicacy. [*He goes up to a mooring post and unwinds the rope around it.*]

IRMA: Robert, what are you doing?

ROBERT [*unwinding the rope*]: I'm unfastening this rope.

IRMA: What for?

ROBERT [*same action*]: To throw it to him.

IRMA: But why do you want to throw it to him?

ROBERT: For him to catch it.

IRMA: Stop, you old fool! Leave that to those who get paid to do it. We down-and-outs should stick together like flowers in a garden. If you stick your neck out, you'll get into trouble.

ROBERT: You talk like a book, old girl.

IRMA: Then don't throw him the rope.

ROBERT: I have to throw it to him.

IRMA: Why?

ROBERT: Because he's swimming.

IRMA [*going to the edge of the quay*]. Stop, there! Stop! You see, it's too late. He's gone under. Good riddance!!

ROBERT [*having a look himself*]: What a life! [*He lies down again.*]

IRMA: The jacket? Aren't you going to look for it?

ROBERT: I've no heart for the job now. There's a man dead for want of help. Well, it makes me think of myself. If someone had helped me in my life . . . [*He yawns.*]

IRMA: Quick, Robert, quick!

ROBERT: Let me sleep.

IRMA: Quick, I tell you! The rope! He's coming to the surface. [*She pulls* ROBERT *up.*] You dirty dog! You'd leave a man in trouble.

ROBERT [*he gets up, yawning*]: You've changed your mind, then?

IRMA: Yes.

ROBERT [*having unwound the rope*]: Why?

IRMA: Because he's come to the surface again.

ROBERT: Women! I give up! [*Throws the rope.*]

IRMA: Good shot! [*Indignant*] Would you believe it! He's not taking it!

ROBERT [*pulling in the rope*]: You're all the same! There's a man who's just thrown himself into the water and you expect him to let himself be pulled out without protesting! Don't you know the meaning of honour? [*Throwing the rope in again.*]

IRMA: He's caught it! He's caught it!

ROBERT [*disappointed*]: Well, he didn't make much fuss about it. I told you he's a bit of a woman.

IRMA: He's pulled himself up. Saved! Aren't you proud of yourself? I feel proud. It's as if you'd given me a child.

ROBERT: You see! There are not only bad people in life. If only I'd met someone like me to pull me out of the gutter.

[GEORGES *appears, the water running from him.*]

GEORGES [*furious*]: You scum . . .

IRMA [*sadly*]: There you are!

ROBERT: That's man's ingratitude for you!

GEORGES [*taking hold of* ROBERT *and shaking him*]: Why did you interfere, you fleabag? Do you think you're Providence?

ROBERT: We thought . . .

GEORGES: Nothing of the kind! It's as bright as day and you could not mistake my intentions. I wanted to kill myself, do you hear? Have you fallen so low that you no longer respect the last wish of a dying man?

ROBERT: You were not a dying man.

GEORGES: Yes I was, since I was going to die.

ROBERT: But you were not going to die, since you are not dead.

GEORGES: I am not dead because you have violated my last wish.

ROBERT: What was it?

GEORGES: The wish to die.

ROBERT: That wasn't your last wish.

GEORGES: It was.

ROBERT: It wasn't, you were swimming.

GEORGES: A fine thing! I was swimming just a little while waiting to go under. If you hadn't thrown the rope . . .

ROBERT: Eh! If you hadn't taken it . . .

GEORGES: I took it because I was forced to . . .

ROBERT: Forced by what?

GEORGES: By human nature, of course. Suicide is against nature!

ROBERT: You see!

GEORGES: What do I see? So you're a nature-lover? I knew quite well that my nature would protest but I had arranged for it to protest too late – the cold was to have numbed me and the water was to choke me. I foresaw everything, everything, except that an old dotard would speculate on my lower instincts!

ROBERT: We meant no harm.

GEORGES: That's just what I blame you for! Everybody means harm – couldn't you have done the same as everybody? If you had meant harm, you would have waited quietly for me to sink, you would have crept up onto the bridge to pick up the jacket I left there, and you would have made three people happy – I, who would be dead, and you two, who would have gained three thousand francs.

ROBERT: The jacket is worth three thousand francs!

[*He tries to slip away, but* GEORGES *catches him.*]

GEORGES: Three thousand at least! Perhaps four.

[ROBERT *tries to escape but* GEORGES *hangs on to him.*]

Stay here! While I live, my clothes belong to me.

ROBERT: Alas!

GEORGES: A fine jacket, brand new, very warm, in the latest style, silk-lined, with inside pockets! It'll slip from under your nose, I'll die with it on. Do you understand, idiot? It was in your interest for me to die.

ROBERT: I knew it, sir. I thought only of you.

GEORGES [*violently*]: What did you say? Liar!

ROBERT: I wanted to do you a service.

GEORGES: You lie!

[ROBERT *tries to protest.*]

Not a word or I'll clout you.

ROBERT: Clout me as much as you like. I'm telling the truth.

GEORGES: I have lived thirty-five years. I have experienced every kind of meanness and I thought I knew the heart of man. But I had to wait for my last day to hear a human being dare to say to my face [*pointing to the river*] and beside my death bed, that he wanted to do me a service! No one, do you hear, no one has ever done anyone a service. Fortunately. Do you know that I should be under an obligation to you? Me, under obligation to you? You see, it makes me laugh. I choose to laugh at it. [*Seized with suspicion.*] Tell me – do you imagine, by any chance, that I owe my life to you? [*Shaking him.*] Answer!

ROBERT: No, sir, no.

GEORGES: Who does my life belong to?

ROBERT: It is yours, entirely yours.

GEORGES [*releasing* ROBERT]: Yes, it's mine. I owe it to no one, not even to my parents who were the victims of a miscalculation. Who fed me, brought me up? Who consoled my first sorrows? Who protected me from the dangers of the world? I, and I alone. I owe account to no one but myself. I am a self-made man. [*Seizing* ROBERT *by the scruff of the neck.*] Tell me the real reason that drove you! I want to know before I die. Money, eh? You thought I would give you money?

ROBERT: When people kill themselves, sir, it is because they haven't any.

GEORGES: Then is must be something else. [*Struck with an idea.*] Why, of course! It's because you're monsters of vanity.

ROBERT [*stunned*]: Us?

GEORGES: You said to yourselves: 'There's a man of quality, well-dressed, well set up, whose features without being regularly handsome, nevertheless are marked with intelligence and energy. Surely this gentleman knows what he wants. If he has decided to put an end to his days it must be for excellent reasons. But I, the sewer-rat, the wood-louse, the stinking mole with the rotten brain, I see more clearly than that man. I know his interests better than he does, and I decide for him that he shall live!' Isn't that vanity?

ROBERT: Goodness . . .

GEORGES: Nero snatched slaves from their wives to throw them to the fish. And you, more cruel than he, you snatch me from the fish to throw me to Man. Did you even stop to think what Man wanted to do with me? No, you only followed your own whim. Poor France, what is going to become of you if your down-and-outs give themselves the pleasures of a Roman emperor!

ROBERT [*frightened*]: Sir . . .

GEORGES: Of a Roman emperor! Your supreme pleasure is to make those who have failed in life, fail to achieve death. Huddled in the shadows, you lie in wait for those who have lost all hope so that you can pull their strings.

ROBERT: What strings?

GEORGES: Don't play the innocent, Caligula! We all have strings, and we dance when someone knows how to pull them. I've learnt that to my cost. I've played that game for ten years. Only I, unlike you, would not attack deprived children, girls who have gone astray and unemployed fathers of large families. I went to the rich, in their homes, at the height of their power, and I sold them the wind. Ah! Life is a game of poker in which the pair of sevens beats the royal flush, since a Caligula of the down-and-outs can make me dance by moonlight. I who juggled with the great ones of the earth. [*Pause*]. Well, I am going to drown myself. Good night.

ROBERT and IRMA: Good night.

GEORGES [*coming back to them*]: Just one thing – you're not going to do it again?

ROBERT: Do it again?

GEORGES: Yes! The rope, you're not going to . . .

ROBERT: Oh, that! No. I swear to you, you won't catch us at that again.

GEORGES: Even if I struggle?

IRMA: We shall wash our hands of it.

GEORGES: If I call for help?

IRMA: We shall sing to drown your voice.

GEORGES: Splendid. That's splendid! [*He does not move.*]

ROBERT: Good night.

GEORGES: What a waste of time! I should have been dead ten minutes ago.

ROBERT [*timidly*]: Oh, sir, what's ten minutes?

IRMA: When you have all Eternity before you?

GEORGES: I'd like to see you there! Eternity was right there just in front of me, that's a fact. But I let it slip away because of you, and I don't know how to recapture it.

ROBERT: It can't be far away.

GEORGES [*pointing to the river*]: No need to look for it! It is there. The question is how to get back to it. Understand me, I had the rare opportunity of crossing a bridge and of being desperate at the same time. Such coincidences don't often recur. Proof is that I am no longer on the bridge. And I hope, I say *hope*, that I am still desperate. Ah! There they are!

ROBERT [*starting involuntarily*]: Who?

GEORGES: My reasons for dying. [*He counts on his fingers.*] They are all there.

ROBERT [*quickly*]: We don't want to keep you, sir, but since you've found them again . . .

IRMA [*quickly*]: If we're not being indiscreet . . .

ROBERT [*quickly*]: We would be interested to know them.

IRMA [*quickly*]: We see a great many suicides at this time of year.

ROBERT [*quickly*]: But it isn't every day that one has the chance to speak to one.

GEORGES: Hide your faces, O stars! Withdraw thy moon, O sky! It needs a double sun to light up the depth of human stupidity. [*To the tramps.*] Do you dare to ask me my reasons for dying? It is I, poor unfortunates, who should ask you your reasons for living!

ROBERT: Our reasons . . . [*To* IRMA] Do you know them?

IRMA: No.

ROBERT: We live . . . that's how it is . . .

IRMA: Since we've begun, we'll go on . . .

ROBERT: We'll get there, anyway, so why get off on the way?

GEORGES: You will get there, yes, but in what condition? You'll be carrion before you're corpses. Take the chance that I offer you. Give me your hands and let us jump. As a threesome, death becomes a picnic.

IRMA: But why die?

GEORGES: Because you have fallen. Life is like a panic in a theatre on fire. Everyone is looking for the exit, no one finds it, and everyone knocks everyone else down. Bad luck to those who fall. They are immediately trampled on. Can't you feel the weight of forty million Frenchmen treading on your face? They're not going to tread on mine. I have trampled on all my neighbours. Today I am on the ground. Oh, well, good night! I'd rather eat dandelions than old boots. Do you know that for a long time I carried poison in the setting of a ring? What a joke! I was dead already. I soared above human enterprise and viewed it with the detachment of an artist. And what pride! I shall myself have brought about both my death and my birth. A self-made man, I destroy my own creator. Let us jump, friends. The only difference between man and beast is that man can put an end to his life and the beast cannot. [*He tries to pull the tramp with him.*]

ROBERT: You jump first, sir. I want to think about it.

GEORGES: Haven't I convinced you then?

ROBERT: Not quite.

GEORGES: It's high time that I did away with myself. I am losing touch. Previously, I only had to talk to convince. [*To* IRMA] And you?

IRMA: No!

GEORGES: No?

IRMA: Not for anything.

GEORGES: Come on! You will die in the arms of an artist. [*He tries to drag her.*]

ROBERT: My old woman, for God's sake, my old woman. She is mine. She is my wife. Help! Help!

GEORGES [*releasing the old woman*]: Shut up there. They'll hear you. [*Lights on the bridge and in the distance. Whistles.*]

ROBERT [*seeing the electric torches*]: The cops!

GEORGES: They're looking for me.

ROBERT: Are you a burglar?

GEORGES [*hurt*]: Do I look like a burglar, my good man? I am a swindler. [*Whistles off stage.*] [*Thoughtfully*] Death or five years in gaol? That is the question.

ROBERT [*looking over to the bridge*]: They look as if they're coming down.

IRMA: What did I tell you, Robert? They'll take us for his

accomplices and beat us till we're half dead. [*To* GEORGES] I beg
you, sir, if you still intend to kill yourself, don't let us stop you.
We would be very grateful to you if you'd make up your mind
before the cops are on top of us. Please do us this favour, sir.

GEORGES: I have never done anyone a favour and I'm not going to
begin on the day of my death.

[*The two tramps look at each other and then throw themselves on*
GEORGES, *trying to push him into the water.*]

Hey there, what are you doing?

IRMA: We're giving you a hand, sir.

ROBERT: As it's only the first step which comes hard . . .

IRMA: We want to make it easier for you.

GEORGES: Will you let me go!

ROBERT [*pushing*]: Don't forget that you are on the ground, sir.

IRMA: Fallen, finished, a wash-out!

ROBERT: And they're going to tread on your face!

GEORGES: Are you going to drown your own child?

IRMA: Our child?

GEORGES: I am your child. You said it yourself just now. [*He pushes
them over backwards.*] I have rights over you, infanticides! It's your
job to protect the son you have brought into the world against his
will. [*Looking to the right and left.*] Have I time to escape?

ROBERT: They are coming from both sides.

GEORGES: If they take me, they will beat you up, therefore my
interests are yours. That's what I like. In saving me you will be
saving yourselves and I shall owe you nothing. Not even thanks.
What's that? [*He points to something dark on the quayside.*]

ROBERT: It's my spare suit.

GEORGES: Give it to me.

[ROBERT *gives it to him.*]

Splendid! [*He takes off his trousers and puts on* ROBERT's *suit.*] What
filth! It's full of lice. [*He throws his trousers into the Seine.*] Scratch
me!

ROBERT: We're not your servants.

GEORGES: You are my father and mother. Scratch me, or I'll hit you. [*They scratch him.*] Here they come! I'm going to lie down and go to sleep. Say that I'm your son. [*He lies down.*]

ROBERT: They won't believe us.

GEORGES: They will believe you if you let your heart speak.

[*Enter* INSPECTOR GOBLET *and* TWO POLICEMEN.]

INSPECTOR: Good day, my beauties.

ROBERT [*grunting indistinctly*]: Huh!

INSPECTOR: Who shouted?

IRMA: When?

INSPECTOR: Just now.

IRMA [*pointing to her husband*]: It was him.

INSPECTOR: Why did he shout?

IRMA: I was beating him.

INSPECTOR: Is it true, what she says? Answer! [*He shakes him.*]

ROBERT: Don't touch me! This is a free country and I have the right to shout when my wife beats me.

INSPECTOR: Tut, tut. Keep calm, take it easy; I'm a police officer.

ROBERT: I'm not afraid of the police.

INSPECTOR: That's a bad thing.

ROBERT: Why? I haven't done anything wrong.

INSPECTOR: Prove it.

ROBERT: It's up to you to prove that I am guilty.

INSPECTOR: That would suit me fine, but the police force is poor. We prefer confessions which cost nothing to proofs which cost a fortune.

ROBERT: I have not made a confession.

INSPECTOR: Be calm, you will. Everything will be done legally. [*To the* TWO POLICEMEN] Take them away.

FIRST POLICEMAN: What do we make them confess, chief?

INSPECTOR: Well, the Pontoise murder and the Charenton burglary.

[*They are taking the tramps away.*]

Stop! [*He goes towards them. Gently*] Couldn't we come to a friendly arrangement, we three? I should hate anything to happen to you.

IRMA: That would suit us, Inspector.

INSPECTOR: I am looking for a man. Thirty-five years of age, five foot ten, black hair, grey eyes, tweed suit, very smart. Have you seen him?

ROBERT: When?

INSPECTOR: Tonight.

ROBERT: Goodness, no. [*To* IRMA] Have you?

IRMA: Oh no! Such a fine man, you can be sure I would have noticed him!

[GEORGES *sneezes.*]

INSPECTOR: Who's that?

IRMA: It's our big son.

INSPECTOR: Why are his teeth chattering?

IRMA: Because he's sleeping.

ROBERT: His teeth always chatter when he sleeps. Ever since he was a baby.

INSPECTOR [*to* POLICEMEN]: Shake him.

[*They shake* GEORGES *who gets up rubbing his eyes.*]

GEORGES: People with mugs like yours shouldn't be allowed to wake people up suddenly.

INSPECTOR [*introducing himself*]: Inspector Goblet. Be civil.

GEORGES: Civil? I've done nothing; too honest to be civil. [*To the tramps*] I was dreaming, mum.

INSPECTOR: Didn't your father's shouting wake you?

GEORGES: Did he shout?

INSPECTOR: Like a stuck pig.

GEORGES: He's always shouting. I'm used to it.

INSPECTOR: Always? Why?

GEORGES: Because mum's always beating him.

INSPECTOR: She beats him and you don't stop her? Why?

GEORGES: Because I'm on mum's side.

INSPECTOR: Have you seen a tall, dark man with grey eyes in a tweed suit?

GEORGES: Did I see him, the swine! He's the one who wanted to push me into the water.

INSPECTOR: When? Where?

GEORGES: In my dream.

INSPECTOR: Idiot!

[*A* POLICEMAN *comes running in.*]

SECOND POLICEMAN: We've found his jacket on the bridge.

INSPECTOR: There! He's jumped in, or wants us to think he did. [*To the tramps*] You heard nothing?

IRMA: No.

INSPECTOR [*to* POLICEMAN]: Do *you* believe he's drowned himself?

FIRST POLICEMAN: I'd be surprised.

INSPECTOR: Me too. He's a lion, that fellow. He'll fight to his last breath. [*He sits down by the edge of the water.*] Sit down, lads. Yes, go on, sit down. We are all equal in the face of defeat.

[*The* POLICEMEN *sit down.*]

Let us draw comfort from the sights of nature. What a moon! Do you see the Great Bear? Oh, and the little one! On such a wonderful night a man-hunt should be a pleasure.

FIRST POLICEMAN: Alas!

INSPECTOR: I told the chief, you know. I said to him: 'Chief, I might as well tell you that I shan't catch him.' I'm second-rate and I'm not ashamed of it. The second-rate are the salt of the earth. Give me a second-rate murderer and I'll pick him up in no time. We second-raters understand each other and know what to expect. But that man, well, I just don't sense him. He is the crook of the century, the man without a face, a hundred and two swindles and not one conviction. What can I do? Genius makes me uneasy. I don't know what to expect. [*To the* POLICEMEN.] Where is he? What is he doing? What are his reactions? How do you expect me to know? Such men are not made like us. [*He bends over.*] Here, what's this? [*He picks up the trousers.*] His trousers!

FIRST POLICEMAN: He must have taken them off to swim.

INSPECTOR: Impossible: I found them on the third step, above the water.

[GEORGES *crawls out left and disappears.*]

Wait a bit . . . he got undressed here. He must have found clothes to change into. And those clothes . . . why, of course! [*He turns towards the place* GEORGES *has left.*] Stop him! Stop him!

[*The* POLICE *start running.*]

ROBERT: Irma?

IRMA: Robert?

ROBERT: You understand?

IRMA: I understand. Give me your hand.

ROBERT: Good-bye, Irma.

IRMA: Robert, good-bye.

INSPECTOR [*turning to them*]: As for you, you dirty tramps . . .

[*The two down-and-outs jump into the water holding each other by the hand.*]

Pull them out! Pull them out! Stop them! Stop them!

[*The* TWO POLICEMEN *run up and throw themselves into the water. The* INSPECTOR *wipes his forehead.*]

Well, didn't I say I wouldn't catch him!

CURTAIN

SCENE TWO

The office of the Editor of Soir à Paris. *A large desk for Palotin. A small one for his Secretary. Chairs, telephone, etc.* Soir à Paris *posters. A mirror.*

JULES [*looking at photos of himself*]: They're a good likeness of me. What do you think?

SECRETARY: I like that one best.

JULES: Get some drawing-pins. We'll put them on the wall.

[*He pins the photos on the wall while speaking.*]

SECRETARY: The Board of Directors has met.

JULES: When?

SECRETARY: Yesterday.

JULES: Without letting me know? That's not so good. What did they say?

SECRETARY: Lucien tried to listen in but they spoke too softly. On his way out, the Chairman said he would come and see you today.

JULES: That stinks, Fifi! That stinks! That old miser wants my scalp.

[*Telephone.*]

SECRETARY: Hello, yes. Very good, sir. [*To* JULES] What did I tell you? It's him. He asks if you can see him in an hour.

JULES: Of course, since I can't stop him.

SECRETARY: Yes, sir. Very good, sir. [*She hangs up.*]

JULES: Miser! Skinflint! Screw!

[*There is a knock at the door.*]

What is it?

[*The door opens and* SIBILOT *appears.*]

Oh, it's you, Sibilot. Come in. What do you want? I can spare you three minutes.

[SIBILOT *enters.*]

Sit down.

[JULES *never sits down. He walks up and down the room.*]

Well? Speak!

SIBILOT: Seven years ago, chief, you decided to devote page five to the fight against Communist propaganda and you did me the honour of confiding it entirely to me. Since then, I have worn myself out on the job. I count as nothing the fact that I have lost my health, my hair, my good humour, and if, to serve you, it were necessary to become even sadder and more crotchety, I wouldn't hesitate for a moment. But there is one thing I cannot renounce without making the paper suffer and that is material security. The fight against the separatists demands invention, tact, and sensibility. To make an impact on people's minds, I'll even go so far as to say it is necessary to be a bit of a visionary. These qualities have not been denied me, but how shall I retain them, if I am tormented by external cares? How can I find the avenging epigram, the vitriolic remark, the damning word? How can I paint the apocalypse which threatens us, and prophesy the end of the world, if my shoes let in water and I cannot afford to have them resoled?

JULES: How much do you earn?

SIBILOT [*pointing to the typist*]: Ask her to go out.

[JULES *looks at him with surprise.*]

Please, just for a moment.

JULES [*to the* SECRETARY]: Go and get the front page proof.

[*She goes out.*]

What stops you speaking in front of her?

SIBILOT: I'm ashamed to admit what I earn.

JULES: Is it too much?

SIBILOT: Too little.

JULES: Let's have it.

SIBILOT: Seventy thousand.

JULES: A year?

SIBILOT: A month.

JULES: But that's a very fair salary and I don't see what you're ashamed of.

SIBILOT: I tell everybody that I get a hundred thousand.

JULES: Well go on telling them. Wait, I'll allow you to go up to a hundred and twenty. People will then believe you get ninety.

SIBILOT: Thank you, chief . . . [*Pause.*] You couldn't actually give it to me?

JULES [*stunned*]: The hundred and twenty?

SIBILOT: Oh no! the ninety. For the last five years my wife has been in a clinic and I can no longer afford to pay for her upkeep.

JULES [*touching his forehead*]: She is . . . [SIBILOT *nods.*] Incurable? [*Another nod.*] Poor old chap . . . [*Pause.*] What about your daughter? I thought she helped you.

SIBILOT: She does what she can but she's not rich. And she hasn't the same ideas as I have.

JULES: Money has no ideas.

SIBILOT: The fact is . . . she is progressive.

JULES: Oh, that's nothing. She'll grow out of it.

SIBILOT: In the meantime I bolster up my budget with Moscow gold. For a professional anti-communist it's embarrassing.

JULES: On the contrary, you are doing your duty. While that gold is in our hands, it can do no harm.

SIBILOT: Even with Moscow gold, the end of the month is a nightmare!

JULES [*with suspicion*]: Look at me, Sibilot. In the eye. Right in the eye. Do you love your work?

SIBILOT: Yes, chief.

JULES: Hm! And me, my boy, do you love me?

SIBILOT: Yes, chief.

JULES: Well, say it!

SIBILOT: Chief, I love you.

JULES: Say it better than that.

SIBILOT: I love you.

JULES: Flabby, flabby, flabby! Sibilot, our paper is an act of love, the link between the classes, and I want my colleagues to work here for love. I would not keep you on another minute if I suspected you of doing your work for what you can get out of it.

SIBILOT: You know, chief, love, on page five. I don't often have the chance . . .

JULES: What a mistake, Sibilot! On page five love is between the lines. You are fighting for the sake of love against the scoundrels who want to impede fraternization of the classes by preventing the bourgeoisie from integrating its proletariat. It's a splendid task. I know some who would consider it a duty to do it for nothing. And you, you, who are lucky enough to serve the noblest of causes and to be paid for it into the bargain, you dare to ask me for a rise?

[*The* SECRETARY *returns with the newspaper.*]

Leave us now. I shall give your case my benevolent consideration.

SIBILOT: Thank you, chief.

JULES: I promise you nothing.

SIBILOT: Thank you, chief.

JULES: I shall call you when I have come to a decision. Good-bye, my friend.

SIBILOT: Good-bye, chief. And thank you.

[*He goes out.*]

JULES [*to* SECRETARY]: He earns seventy thousand a month and he wants me to give him a rise. What do you say to that?

SECRETARY [*indignant*]: Oh!

JULES: See that he doesn't set foot in here again. [*He takes the newspaper and looks it over.*] Oh! Oh! Oh! [*He opens the door of his office.*] Tavernier! Perigord! Front Page Conference!

[*Enter* TAVERNIER *and* PERIGORD. *The* SECRETARY *goes out.*]

JULES: What's wrong, boys? Cares of the heart? Health worries?

TAVERNIER [*astonished*]: Goodness, no . . .

PERIGORD [*astonished*]: I don't think . . .

JULES: Then you don't love me any more?

TAVERNIER: Oh Jules!

PERIGORD: You know very well that everyone adores you.

JULES: No, you do not adore me. You love me a little, because I am lovable, but you do not adore me. It isn't zeal you lack, but ardour. That's my greatest misfortune. I have fire in my veins and I am surrounded by lukewarm people!

TAVERNIER: What have we done, Jules?

JULES: You have botched up the front page for me by giving it headlines that would make the South Sea Islanders laugh.

PERIGORD: What should we have put, chief?

JULES: I am asking you, boys. Suggest something!

  [*Silence.*]

  Think hard, I want a stirring headline, an atomic headline! For the past week we've been stagnating.

TAVERNIER: There's Morocco, of course.

JULES: How many deaths?

PERIGORD: Seventeen.

JULES: There! Two more than yesterday. Put it on page two. And you'll headline: 'Marrakesh: moving demonstrations of loyalty.' Sub-heading: 'Healthy elements of population reject trouble-makers.' Have we a photo of the ex-Sultan playing bowls?

TAVERNIER: It's in the library.

JULES: Front page. Middle. Caption: 'Ex-Sultan of Morocco settles down in his new residence.'

PERIGORD: All that doesn't make the big headline.

JULES: Exactly. [*He thinks.*] Adenauer?

TAVERNIER: He slanged us yesterday.

JULES: Take no notice, not a word. The war? How is it today? Cold? Hot?

PERIGORD: Good.

JULES: Lukewarm, in fact. It's like you.

  [PERIGORD *raises his finger.*]

  You have a headline?

PERIGORD: 'War danger recedes.'

JULES: No, boys, no. Let war recede as much as it likes but not on the front page. On the front page the danger of war increases. What about Washington? No one spilt anything? Ike? Dulles?

PERIGORD: Not a word.

JULES: What are they up to?

  [TAVERNIER *raises his finger.*]

  Go on.

TAVERNIER: 'America's Disturbing Silence.'

JULES: No.

TAVERNIER: But . . .

JULES: America does not disturb; she reassures.

PERIGORD: 'America's Reassuring Silence.'

JULES: *Reassuring!* My dear fellow, I am not alone. I have my duties to the shareholders. You think I am going to amuse myself by splashing 'reassuring' in big type so that people can see it from a distance. If they are reassured in advance, why should they buy my newspaper?

TAVERNIER [*raising a finger*]: 'Disturbing Silence of USSR.'

JULES: Disturbing? The USSR disturbs you now? And what about the H Bomb? What is it? Chickweed for the birds?

PERIGORD: I propose a lead-in: 'America is not worried by the' and underneath: 'Disturbing Silence of the USSR'.

JULES: You're teasing America, son. Finding fleas.

PERIGORD: Me?

JULES: Of course! If this silence is disturbing, America is wrong not to be disturbed by it.

PERIGORD: 'Washington is neither worried nor unconcerned about the DISTURBING SILENCE OF THE USSR.'

JULES: Now what do you call that? A newspaper headline or a charge of wild elephants. Rhythm, good God, rhythm. It has to go quickly, quickly, quickly! A newspaper is not written, it has to dance. Do you know how the Yanks would write your headline? 'USSR: SILENCE; USA: SMILES'. It has swing! Oh! If only I had Americans working with me!

[SECRETARY *enters.*]

What is it?

SECRETARY: The Mayor of Travaja.

JULES [*to* PERIGORD]: Are the photographers here?

PERIGORD: No.

JULES: What! You haven't called the photographers?

PERIGORD: But I didn't know . . .

JULES: Keep him waiting and get hold of all the photographers in the building. [*To* PERIGORD] How many times have I told you that I want a human newspaper.

[*The* SECRETARY *goes out.*]

We are much too far away from our readers. *Soir à Paris* must be associated in everybody's mind with a familiar, smiling and compassionate face. Whose face, Tavernier?

TAVERNIER: Yours, Jules.

JULES [*to* PERIGORD]: Travaja has been destroyed by an avalanche, and its mayor is coming to receive the proceeds of the collection we organized. How is it you didn't understand, Perigord, that this was an occasion for me to appear for the first time to our readers and to be the reflection of their own generosity?

[*The* SECRETARY *enters.*]

SECRETARY: The photographers are here.

JULES: Bring the Mayor in.

[*She goes out.*]

Where is Travaja? Quick!

PERIGORD: Peru.

JULES: Are you sure? I thought it was in Chile.

PERIGORD: You should know better than I do.

JULES: And you? What do you think?

TAVERNIER: I would have leaned towards Peru but you must be right; it's . . .

JULES: No soft-soap! I'm not ashamed of being self-taught! Bring the map of the world!

[*They bring it.* JULES *kneels in front of it.*]

I can't find Peru.

TAVERNIER: Near the top on the left. Not so high. There!

JULES: Why, it's a pocket handkerchief. Where's Travaja?

TAVERNIER: It's the black dot on the right.

JULES [*dryly*]: You see better than I do, Tavernier.

TAVERNIER: I beg your pardon, Jules.

[*The* MAYOR *of Travaja and his* INTERPRETER *enter, followed by* PHOTOGRAPHERS *and* SECRETARY.]

JULES: Good God, where's the cheque? [*He goes through his pockets.*]

TAVERNIER: In your jacket.

JULES: But where is my jacket?

MAYOR [*as if to commence an oration*]: Na . . .

JULES [*hurriedly*]: Good day, sir! Sit down here! [*To the* PHOTO-GRAPHERS] He's all yŏurs. Keep him busy.

MAYOR: Na . . .

[*The* PHOTOGRAPHERS *surround him. Flashlights.*]

JULES: Tavernier, Perigord! Help me. [*On hands and knees under the desks.*]

MAYOR: Na . . . [*Photos.*] Na . . . [*Photos.*]

JULES [*pulling his jacket from under a table and drawing out the cheque. Cry of victory*]: I've got it!

MAYOR: Na . . . [*Photos.*] Ouj ja! . . . [*He bursts into tears.*]

JULES [*to* PHOTOGRAPHERS]: Take it! For God's sake, take it! [*To* SECRETARY] Take the caption: 'Mayor of Travaja weeps with gratitude before our editor.'

[*The* PHOTOGRAPHERS *have taken their photos.* THE MAYOR *is still weeping. To* INTERPRETER]

Tell him to stop. The photos have been taken.

INTERPRETER: O ca ri.

MAYOR: Ou pe ca mi neu.

INTERPRETER: He prepared a speech on the plane. He is crying because he's been prevented from giving it.

JULES: You'll translate it and we'll publish it in full.

INTERPRETER: Ra ca cha pou!

MAYOR: Paim pon!

INTERPRETER: He insists on making it. Permit me to observe that the city of Travaja is situated 12,380 feet above sea-level and the air is rarefied. Because they easily become breathless, speakers have learnt to be concise.

JULES: Quick, then. Quick!

MAYOR [*slowly*]: Na vo ki. No vo ka. Kay ko ray.

INTERPRETER: The children of Travaja will never forget the generosity of the French people. [*Pause.*]

JULES: Go on.

INTERPRETER: That is all.

JULES [*giving the signal for applause*]: Marvellous speech! [*To* PERI-GORD] All the same it will be just as well to pad it out. [*To the* MAYOR] Just we two, Travaja.

[*He hands him the cheque. The* MAYOR *takes it.*]

Take it back from him, quick! It's for the photographers. [*The cheque is taken from the* MAYOR.]

A PHOTOGRAPHER [*placing a telephone directory on the floor*]: Julot.

JULES: Eh!

PHOTOGRAPHER: If you'd be so good as to stand on the directory.

JULES: Why?

PHOTOGRAPHER: Generosity comes from above.

JULES: Then give me two directories.

[*He stands on the directories and hands the cheque over. The* MAYOR *takes the cheque. Flash.*]

PHOTOGRAPHER: Again!

[*He takes the cheque from the* MAYOR *and hands it back to* JULES. *Same action.*]

Again!

[*Same action. The* MAYOR *begins to cry.*]

JULES: Enough, for God's sake, enough!

[*He puts the cheque into the* MAYOR'S *hand. To* INTERPRETER]

How do you say good-bye?

INTERPRETER: La pi da.

JULES [*to the* MAYOR]: Lapida!

MAYOR: La pi da. [*They kiss.*]

JULES [*taking the* MAYOR *in his arms*]: Boys, I believe I am crying. Picture, quick!

[*Photos.* JULES *wipes a tear and smilingly shows his wet fingers to the* MAYOR. *The* MAYOR *does likewise and touches* JULES'S *finger with his own. Photo.*]

JULES [*to* PHOTOGRAPHERS]: Show him around. Sacré-Coeur, the Unknown Soldier, the Folies-Bergères. [*To the* MAYOR] Lapida!

MAYOR [*goes out backwards, bowing*]: La pi da, la pi da.

[PHOTOGRAPHERS *and* INTERPRETER *go out.*]

JULES: Boys, is there any greater pleasure than doing good? [*Abruptly*] Oh! Oh! Oh!

PERIGORD [*worried*]: Jules . . .

JULES: Silence, boys. I feel an idea coming.

PERIGORD [*to typist*]: Stop, Fifi, stop. Here's *the* Idea!

[*Silence.* JULES *paces up and down.*]

JULES: What day is it today?

PERIGORD: Tuesday.

JULES: Splendid. I want a weekly day of kindness. It will be Wednesday. I am counting on you, Roger. On Fridays, find refugees, escapees, survivors, ragged orphans. On Saturdays you open the fund and on Wednesdays, you announce the results. Understand, son? What are you going to prepare for us for next Wednesday?

PERIGORD: Well, I . . . Why not the homeless?

JULES: Homeless? Excellent. Where do they live, your homeless? In Caracas? Puerto-Rico?

PERIGORD: I was thinking of those in France.

JULES: You're crazy! The objects of our compassion must be victims of strictly natural catastrophes. Otherwise you'll sully love with sordid stories of social injustice. Do you remember our campaign: 'Everyone is happy'? We didn't quite convince everybody at the time. Well, this year we shall launch a new campaign: 'Everyone is good', and you'll see everybody'll believe us. That's what I call the best propaganda against communism. The headline, boys, the headline! What did you propose?

TAVERNIER: Nothing was proposed, Jules. We were in the soup.

PERIGORD: Apart from the seventeen dead Moroccans . . .

TAVERNIER [*taking him up*]: . . . two suicides, a miracle at Trouville, exchanges of dipomatic notes, a jewel robbery . . .

PERIGORD [*taking him up*]: . . . four road accidents and two frontier incidents . . .

TAVERNIER [*taking him up*]: . . . nothing at all has happened.

JULES: Nothing new! And you complain? What do you want? The storming of the Bastille? The 1879 Oath of the Tennis Court? Boys, I am a government newspaper, and it isn't up to me to write history since the government refuses to make it and the public doesn't want it. Everyone to his trade. Let historians write history, and daily papers, everyday news. And everyday news is anything but new. It is what has been going on every day since the beginning of the world. Homicides, robberies, abduction of minors, fine exploits and the reward of virtue.

[*Telephone.*]

What is it?

SECRETARY [*who has lifted the receiver*]: It is Lancelot, chief.

JULES: Hello? Oh! Ah! At what time? Good, good, good. [*He hangs up.*] Your headline is found, boys. Georges de Valéra has just escaped.

PERIGORD: The crook?

TAVERNIER: The fifty million man?

JULES: That's the one. The genius of the century. You will put his photo on the front page beside mine.

TAVERNIER: The good and evil, chief.

JULES: Compassion and indignation are sentiments which aid digestion. Don't forget our paper comes out in the afternoon.

[*Telephone.*]

What? What? What? No! No! No details? Oh! Oh! Oh! Good!

[*He hangs up.*]

Oh, God, oh God, oh God!

TAVERNIER: Have they caught him?

JULES: No, but headlines never come singly. A little while ago I had none, now I have one too many.

TAVERNIER: What's happened?

JULES: The Soviet Minister of the Interior has disappeared.

PERIGORD: Nekrassov? Is he in gaol?

JULES: Even better, he's chosen freedom.

PERIGORD: What do we know about it?

JULES: Practically nothing. That's what gets me. He didn't appear at the Opera last Tuesday and no one has seen him since.

TAVERNIER: Where does the news come from?

JULES: From Reuter and A.F.P.

TAVERNIER: What about Tass?

JULES: Not a word.

TAVERNIER: Hm!

JULES: Yes. Hm!

TAVERNIER: Well? What's it to be? Nekrassov or Valéra?

JULES: Nekrassov. We'll put 'NEKRASSOV DISAPPEARS' and as sub-heading, 'Soviet Minister of the Interior chooses freedom.' Have you a photo?

PERIGORD: You know it, Jules. Looks like a pirate. He wears a patch over his right eye.

JULES: You'll put it next to mine to keep the contrast between Good and Evil.

PERIGORD: And Valéra's?

JULES: On page four.

[Telephone.]

If this is another headline, I'll shoot somebody!

SECRETARY: Hello. Yes. Yes, sir. [To JULES] It's the Chairman of the Board of Directors.

JULES: Tell him to come up, the skinflint!

SECRETARY [into telephone]: Yes, sir. Right away, sir.

[She hangs up.]

JULES [to TAVERNIER and PERIGORD]: Disappear, boys. So long.

[PERIGORD and TAVERNIER go out. JULES regards his jacket with perplexity then, after an instant's hesitation, puts it on. Enter MOUTON.]

JULES: Good-day, Mr Chairman.

MOUTON: Good day, my dear Palotin. [He sits down.] Sit down.

JULES: If you don't mind, I'd rather stand.

MOUTON: I do mind. How do you expect me to talk to you if I have constantly to look all round the office for you?

JULES: As you wish. [Sits down.]

MOUTON: I have brought you some excellent news. The Minister of the Interior phoned me yesterday and he gave me to understand that he was thinking of granting us the exclusive rights to advertise Public Appointments.

JULES: Public Appointments? It's . . . it's unexpected! . . .

MOUTON: Isn't it? Following that telephone conversation I took it upon myself to call a meeting of the Board and all our friends agree that this decision is of the utmost importance. We could improve the quality of the paper while reducing costs.

JULES: We shall appear in twenty pages. We'll knock out *Paris-Presse* and *France-Soir*!

MOUTON: We shall be the first daily to publish colour photos!

JULES: And what does the Minister ask in return?

MOUTON: Nothing, my dear chap. Nothing. Nothing at all. We accept favours when they are a recognition of merit and we reject them when they are an attempt to buy our consciences. The Minister is young, go-ahead, a sportsman. He wants to galvanize his colleagues, to make the government really modern. And as *Soir à Paris* is a government paper, it is being given the means to modernize itself. The Minister even coined this charming phrase: 'Let the daily rag become the daily flag.'

JULES [*bursts out laughing, then suddenly becomes serious*]: He called my paper a rag?

MOUTON: It was a joke. But I must tell you that some of my colleagues have pointed out to me that *Soir à Paris* is tending to go to sleep. The general layout of the paper is perfect, but we no longer find in it that bite, that style which caught the public imagination.

JULES: We must take into consideration the relaxation of international tension. Perigord was just telling me quite correctly that nothing is happening.

MOUTON: Of course, of course! You know that I always defend you. But I understand the Minister. 'Virulence,' he said to me, 'will be the New Look of French politics.' He will do more for us than for our colleagues when we have shown our mettle. And now, the occasion arises for us to show that we have the requisite 'virulence'. In substance, this is what the Minister told me. A by-election is going to take place in Seine-et-Marne. It's the constituency the Communists have chosen for a trial of strength. The Cabinet accepts the challenge; the election will be fought on the question of for or against German rearmament. You know Mme Bounoumi; she's the government candidate. This Christian housewife, mother of twelve children, knows how to reach the hearts of the French masses. Her simple and touching propaganda could serve as an example to our politicians and to the editors of our big daily papers. Look at this poster!

[*He takes out a poster from his brief-case and unrolls it. It reads:* 'BROTHERHOOD THROUGH REARMAMENT' *and lower down,* 'TO PRESERVE PEACE, ALL MEANS ARE GOOD, EVEN WAR'.]

How direct it is! I would like to see it on your wall.

JULES [*to* SECRETARY]: Fifi! Drawing-pins!

[SECRETARY *puts the poster on the wall.*]

MOUTON: If merit were rewarded, Mme Bounoumi would easily win. Unfortunately, the situation is not very bright. To start with we can only count on three hundred thousand votes. The Communists have as many, perhaps a little more. A good half of the electors will abstain as usual. There remain about another hundred thousand votes which are bound to go to the Radical deputy, Perdrière. That means there will be a second ballot with the risk that the Communist will get in the second time.

JULES [*who doesn't understand*]: Ah! Ah!

MOUTON: The Minister sees only one way to avoid what he doesn't hesitate to call a disaster, that is, to get Perdrière to stand down in favour of Mme Bounoumi. Only – Perdrière won't stand down.

JULES: Perdrière? But I know him. He's an avowed enemy of the Soviets. We've dined together.

MOUTON: I know him ever better. He is my neighbour in the country.

JULES: He said some very sensible things.

MOUTON: You mean he condemned the policy of the USSR?

JULES: Exactly.

MOUTON: There's a man for you! He detests the Communists and doesn't want to rearm Germany.

JULES: Astonishing contradiction!

MOUTON: His attitude is purely sentimental. Do you know what's at the bottom of it? The Germans plundered his estate in 1940, and deported him in 1944.

JULES: So?

MOUTON: That's all. He won't learn anything and he won't forget anything.

JULES: Oh!

MOUTON: And mark you, it was nothing much. He was only deported for eight or ten months.

JULES: Proof of that is that he returned.

MOUTON [*shrugging his shoulders*]: Well, there you are. He obstinately sticks to his memories. He has Germanophobia. What is even more absurd is that history does not repeat itself. In the next war, it will be Russia that the Germans will plunder and Russians whom they will deport.

JULES: Why, of course!

MOUTON: You can be sure he knows all that!

JULES: And that doesn't shake his convictions?

MOUTON: On the contrary! He maintains he would not allow Russians to be put into Buchenwald. [*Light smile.*] There's no mistake about it, when you talk to him about the Germans, he sees red.

[*Polite laugh from* JULES.]

Well, there you are! You know it all. Perdrière fears the Germans more than the Russians. He will stand down if you make him fear the Russians more than the Germans.

JULES: If *you* make him ... Who is that *you*?

MOUTON: You.

JULES: Me? How do you expect me to set about it? I have no influence over him.

MOUTON: You'll have to acquire it.

JULES: By what means?

MOUTON: His hundred thousand voters read *Soir à Paris*.

JULES: Well?

MOUTON: Be virulent. Create fear.

T – T.P. – F

JULES: Fear? But that's all I do. My entire fifth page is devoted to the red peril.

MOUTON: Exactly. [*Short silence.*] My dear Palotin, the Board directed me to tell you that your fifth page is no longer worth anything.

[JULES *gets up.*]

My dear chap, I beg you to remain seated. [*Urging*] Do me the favour.

[JULES *sits down again.*]

We used to gain something from reading page five. I remember your fine series 'War tomorrow'. People trembled with fear. And your photo montages: Stalin on horseback entering Notre Dame in flames! Real masterpieces. But for more than a year I've noted a suspicious slackening off, criminal oversights. You used to speak of famine in the USSR and you don't mention it any more. Why? Do you claim the Russians have enough to eat?

JULES: Me? I'd watch it.

MOUTON: The other day, I saw your photo: 'Soviet Housewives queueing in front of a food store' and I was stunned to note that some of those women were smiling and that all of them were wearing shoes. Shoes in Moscow! It was obviously a Soviet propaganda photo that you took for an A.F.P. photo by mistake. Shoes! But for the love of God, you might at least have cut off the feet. Smiles! In the USSR! Smiles!

JULES: I couldn't cut off their heads.

MOUTON: Why not? Shall I tell you something? I began to wonder whether you hadn't changed your opinions.

JULES [*proudly*]: My paper is an objective one, a government paper, and my opinions don't change unless the government changes its opinions.

MOUTON: Good. Very good. And you're not worried?

JULES: Why should I be?

MOUTON: Because people are beginning to feel reassured.

JULES: To be reassured? My dear Mr Chairman, don't you think you're exaggerating?

MOUTON: I never exaggerate. Two years ago, there was an open-air dance in Rocamodour. Lightning struck suddenly a hundred yards away. Panic. A hundred deaths. The survivors declared at the inquest that they had thought they were being bombed by a Soviet plane. There's your proof that the objective press did its work well. Good. Yesterday, the Institute of French Public Opinion published the results of its latest gallup poll. Do you know what they are?

JULES: Not yet.

MOUTON: The investigators interrogated ten thousand persons from all walks and conditions of life. To the question: 'Where will you die?' ten per cent replied that they hadn't any idea, and the others – that is, almost all – that they would die in their beds.

JULES: In their beds?

MOUTON: In their beds. And those were average Frenchmen, readers of our paper. Ah! How far away Rocamadour is, and what a setback in two years!

JULES: There wasn't a single one of them who replied that he would die burnt to ashes, pulverized, or dissolved into vapour?

MOUTON: In their beds.

JULES: What? Not one who mentioned the H bomb, the death-ray, radioactive clouds, death-ash or poisoned rains?

MOUTON: In their beds. In the middle of the twentieth century, with the astounding advances in technique, they believe they will die in their beds. As in the Middle Ages! Ah! my dear Palotin, let me tell you in all friendliness, that you are very guilty.

JULES [getting up]: But I had nothing to do with it!

MOUTON [also getting up]: Your paper's flabby! Lukewarm! Insipid! Maudlin! Yesterday again, you spoke of peace. [He advances on JULES.]

JULES [retreating]: No.

MOUTON [advancing]: Yes. On the front page!

JULES [still retreating]: It wasn't me. It was Molotov. I only printed his speech.

MOUTON [advancing]: You printed it in full. You should have given extracts.

JULES: The requirements of a news service . . .

MOUTON: Does that count when the Universe is in danger? The Western Powers are united by terror. If you restore their feeling of security, where will they find the strength to prepare for war?

JULES [*cornered against the desk*]: War? What war?

MOUTON: The next one.

JULES: But I don't want war.

MOUTON: You don't want it? But tell me, Palotin, where do you think you will die?

JULES: In my . . .

MOUTON: In your . . .

JULES: In a . . . How do I know?

MOUTON: You are a neutralist who won't face facts, a shameless pacifist, a merchant of illusions.

JULES [*jumping up on the directories and shouting*]: Leave me alone. Peace! Peace! Peace! Peace!

MOUTON: Peace! You see, that's what you want.

    [*Pause.* JULES *jumps down.*]

Come, let us sit down again and keep calm.

    [JULES *sits down again.*]

Nothing prevents me recognizing your great qualities. I was telling the Board again yesterday: 'You are the Napoleon of objective news.' But will you be the Napoleon of virulence?

JULES: I will be that as well.

MOUTON: Prove it.

JULES: How?

MOUTON: Get Perdrière to stand down. Launch a terrible, a gigantic campaign. Shatter the morbid dreams of your readers. Show that the material survival of France depends on the German army and American supremacy. Make yourself fear life more than you fear death.

JULES: I . . . I will do it.

MOUTON: If the task frightens you, there is still time to withdraw.

JULES: It doesn't frighten me. [*To* SECRETARY] Get Sibilot right away.

SECRETARY [*on telephone*]: Send Sibilot.

JULES: Ah! The poor sods, the poor sods!

MOUTON: Who?

JULES: The readers! They are quietly fishing, playing cards every evening and making love twice a week expecting to die in their beds and I am going to spoil their pleasure.

MOUTON: Don't weaken, my friend. Think of the dangerous situation you are in, and of how I continually defend you. Think above all of the country! Tomorrow at ten o'clock, the Board of Directors will be meeting. It would be very desirable if you could submit your new plans to us. No, no, remain seated. Don't bother to see me out.

[MOUTON *goes out.* JULES *jumps to his feet and paces the room almost at a run.*]

JULES: Oh God, oh God, oh God!

[*Enter* SIBILOT.]

JULES: Come here!

SIBILOT: I thank you, chief.

JULES: Don't thank me, Sibilot, don't thank me yet.

SIBILOT: Ah! I want to do it in advance no matter what your decision. I didn't think you would call me so quickly.

JULES: You were mistaken.

SIBILOT: I was mistaken. I was mistaken through my want of love. Through denouncing Evil, I had come to see it everywhere and I no longer believed in human generosity. To be quite frank, chief, I had become suspicious of Man, of Man himself.

JULES: And you are reassured?

SIBILOT: Completely. From this moment I love Man and I believe in him.

JULES: You are lucky. [*He paces the room.*] My friend, our conversation has opened my eyes. Didn't you tell me that your work required invention?

SIBILOT: Yes, it does.

JULES: Sensibility, tact and even poetry?

SIBILOT: Absolutely!

JULES: In fact – don't let us be afraid of words – a kind of genius?

SIBILOT: I wouldn't have dared . . .

JULES: Don't be shy!

SIBILOT: Well, in a certain way . . .

JULES: Splendid. [*Pause.*] That proves that you are not at all the man I need.

    [SIBILOT *gets up, disconcerted.*]

Sit still! I'm the boss here. I'm the one that does the walking around here. And I shall walk until tomorrow if I want to.

SIBILOT: Didn't you say? . . .

JULES: Sit down!

    [SIBILOT *sits down again.*]

I said that you are an incompetent, a muddlehead and a saboteur. Tact? Finesse? You? You allow photos through, which show Soviet women in fur coats, shod like queens and smiling from ear to ear! The truth is, Sibilot, that you have found a haven, a job, a retreat for your old age! You take page five of *Soir à Paris* for an old folks' home. And from the height of your seventy thousands you despise your comrades who are killing themselves at the job. [*To* SECRETARY] For he earns . . .

SIBILOT [*with a heartrending cry*]: Chief, don't say it!

JULES [*pitless*]: Seventy thousand a month in order to boost up Soviet Russia in my paper!

SIBILOT: It's not true!

JULES: I sometimes wonder whether you aren't an undercover man!

SIBILOT: I swear . . .

JULES: An undercover man, a crypto, a fellow-traveller!

SIBILOT: Stop, chief! I think I am going mad!

JULES: Didn't you yourself confess to me that you received Moscow gold?

SIBILOT: But it's my daughter . . .

JULES: Oh, yes, it's your daughter! So? Someone has to give it to you.

    [SIBILOT *tries to get up.*]

Sit down! And choose: either you've sold out or you're an incompetent!

SIBILOT: I give you my word that I am neither one nor the other!

JULES: Prove it!

SIBILOT: But how?

JULES: Tomorrow I am launching a campaign against the Communist Party. I want to have them on their knees in a fortnight from now. I need a first-class demolition man, a bruiser, a woodcutter. Will it be you?

SIBILOT: Yes, chief.

JULES: I'll believe you if you give me an idea right away!

SIBILOT: An idea . . . for the campaign . . .

JULES: You have thirty seconds.

SIBILOT: Thirty seconds for an idea?

JULES: You have only fifteen left. Ah! We shall see if you have genius.

SIBILOT: I . . . the life of Stalin in pictures!

JULES: The life of Stalin in pictures? Why not Mahomet? Sibilot, the thirty seconds are up, you are fired!

SIBILOT: Chief, I beg of you, you can't do . . . [Pause.] I have a wife, I have a daughter.

JULES: A daughter! Why, of course, it's she who keeps you.

SIBILOT: Listen to me, chief. If you sack me, I shall go home and gas myself.

JULES: Wouldn't be much of a loss! [Pause.] I'll give you until tomorrow. But unless you come into my office tomorrow morning at ten o'clock with a shattering idea, you can pack your bags.

SIBILOT: Tomorrow morning? . . .

JULES: You have the whole night before you. Get going!

SIBILOT: You shall have your idea, chief. But I should like to tell you that I no longer believe in Man.

JULES: For the job you have to do, that will be an advantage.

[SIBILOT goes out, crushed.]

CURTAIN

SCENE THREE

A room – Night

[GEORGES *enters through the window, almost knocks over a vase, but catches it in time. Whistles blow off stage. He flattens himself against the wall. A* POLICEMAN *puts his head through the open window and shines his torch into the room.* GEORGES *holds his breath. The* POLICEMAN *disappears.* GEORGES *breathes again. He is seen to be fighting against a desire to sneeze. He holds his nose, opens his mouth, and ends up by sneezing noisily.*]

VERONIQUE [*off stage*]: What's that?

[GEORGES *sneezes again. He rushes to the window and puts his leg over the sill. Whistles quite close. He hurriedly climbs back into the room. At that moment* VERONIQUE *enters and puts on the light.* GEORGES *draws back and stands against the wall.*]

GEORGES [*with his hands up*]: It's all up!

VERONIQUE: What's all up? [*She looks at* GEORGES.] Well! A thief?

GEORGES: A thief? Where?

VERONIQUE: Aren't you a thief?

GEORGES: Not in the least. I'm paying you a visit.

VERONIQUE: At this time of night?

GEORGES: Yes.

VERONIQUE: And why have you got your hands up?

GEORGES: Because it is night time. A nocturnal visitor puts his hands up when he's surprised. It's customary.

VERONIQUE: Well, you've done the polite thing; now put them down.

GEORGES: It wouldn't be wise.

VERONIQUE: In that case, keep them well up. Make yourself at home. [*She sits down.*] Take a seat. You can put your elbows on the arm-rest. It's more comfortable. [*He sits down with his hands up. She watches him.*] You're right. I ought never to have taken you for a thief.

GEORGES: Thank you.

VERONIQUE: Not at all.

GEORGES: Still, appearances are against me, and I'm glad that you've been good enough to believe me.

VERONIQUE: I believe your hands. Look how ghastly they are. You've never done anything with your hands.

GEORGES [*under his breath*]: I work with my tongue.

VERONIQUE [*continuing*]: Whereas a thief's hands are quick, lively, sensitive ...

GEORGES [*annoyed*]: What do you know about it?

VERONIQUE: I've covered the courts.

GEORGES: You've covered them? That's nothing to boast about.

VERONIQUE: I covered them for two years. Now I'm on foreign affairs.

GEORGES: A journalist?

VERONIQUE: That's right. And you?

GEORGES: An artistic career is more in my line.

VERONIQUE: What do you do?

GEORGES: For my living? I talk.

VERONIQUE: And what are you doing in this room?

GEORGES: Just that.

VERONIQUE: Good. Then talk.

GEORGES: What about?

VERONIQUE: You should know. Say what you have to say.

GEORGES: To you? Oh, no. Call your husband.

VERONIQUE: I am divorced.

GEORGES [*pointing to a pipe on the table*]: Is it you who smokes the pipe?

VERONIQUE: It's my father's.

GEORGES: You live with him?

VERONIQUE: I share his flat.

GEORGES: Call him.

VERONIQUE: He's at his paper.

GEORGES: Ah, so you're both journalists?

VERONIQUE: Yes, but on different papers.

GEORGES: That means we're alone in this flat.

VERONIQUE: Does that shock you?

GEORGES: It's a bad situation; compromising for you, and unpleasant for me.

VERONIQUE: I don't find it compromising.

GEORGES: All the more reason why I find it unpleasant.

VERONIQUE: Good night, then. You can come back when my father is home.

GEORGES: Good night, good night.
[*He gets up slowly. Whistles sound outside. He sits down again.*]
If you don't mind, I prefer to wait for him here.

VERONIQUE: I don't mind, but I was just going out. I'm quite willing to leave you alone in the flat, but I'd still like to know why you came here.

GEORGES: That's fair enough. [*Pause.*] There! [*Pause.*]

VERONIQUE: Well?
[GEORGES *sneezes and stamps his feet.*]

GEORGES: A cold. A cold. The one ridiculous remnant of a flop. I wanted to cool off, and I've caught a cold.

VERONIQUE [*giving him a handkerchief*]: Blow your nose.

GEORGES [*still with his hands up*]: Impossible.

VERONIQUE: Why?

GEORGES: I can't lower my hands.

VERONIQUE: Stand up.
[*He stands up. She pulls at his arms, but cannot pull them down.*]
Are you paralysed?

GEORGES: It's the effect of distrust.

VERONIQUE: Do you distrust me?

GEORGES: I distrust women.

VERONIQUE [*dryly*]: Very well. [*She takes the handkerchief from him.*] Blow! Harder! There you are. [*She folds the handkerchief, and puts it in his pocket.*]

GEORGES [*furious*]: How unpleasant! God, how unpleasant!

VERONIQUE: Relax.

GEORGES: Easy to say.

VERONIQUE: Throw your head back, close your eyes and count up to a thousand.

GEORGES: And what will you do while my eyes are closed? You'll slip out to call the police or you'll go and get a pistol . . .

VERONIQUE: Do you want me to put my hands up?

[*She raises her hands and* GEORGES *slowly lowers his.*]

At last. Do you feel better?

GEORGES: Yes. More comfortable.

VERONIQUE: Then you'll be able to tell me.

GEORGES: Naturally. What?

VERONIQUE: For the past hour I've been asking you what you're doing here.

GEORGES: What I'm doing here? Nothing simpler. But put your hands down. I can't stand it. I can't talk to you while you have your hands above your head.

[VERONIQUE *lowers her hands.*]

Good.

VERONIQUE: I'm listening.

GEORGES: How I wish your father were here! I like women; I adore covering them with jewels and caresses. I'd gladly give them anything – except explanations.

VERONIQUE: How curious. Why?

GEORGES: Because they don't understand them, madam. Let us suppose, just by way of example, of course, that I were to say to you: 'I am a crook, the police were chasing me, your window was open, I came in.' That would appear simple and clear. Well, what does that suggest to you?

VERONIQUE: What does it suggest to me? I don't know . . .

GEORGES: There, you see. You don't even know.

VERONIQUE: It suggests to me that you were a crook . . .

GEORGES: Is that all?

VERONIQUE: Isn't that the main point? [*A brief silence.*] I think it's a pity.

GEORGES: You prefer thieves?

VERONIQUE: Yes, because they work with their hands.

GEORGES: All for the workers, eh? [*Pause.*] In any case, the experiment has succeeded. You've got everything wrong.

VERONIQUE: Then you're not a crook.

GEORGES: No. That's not the point. The point is that I have the cops at my tail. A man wouldn't fail to understand. [*Shouting suddenly*] I've got the cops on my tail, don't you understand?

VERONIQUE: All right. Don't shout. [*Pause.*]

GEORGES: Well? What are you going to do with me?

VERONIQUE: Draw the curtains. [*She goes to the window and draws the curtains.*]

GEORGES: And what about me?

VERONIQUE: You? What can I do? Are you a guitar that I should pluck you, a mandoline that I should strum you, or a nail that I should bang you on the head?

GEORGES: Well, then?

VERONIQUE: Then nothing. I've nothing to do with you.

GEORGES: Nothing is the most imprecise reply. Nothing can mean anything. Anything can happen. You could burst into tears, or poke my eyes out with your hat-pin. Oh, how I wish I had met your father. Do you know what he would have said?

VERONIQUE: I'm going to hand you over to the police.

GEORGES [*with a start*]: You're going to hand me over to the police?

VERONIQUE: No. I'm telling you what my father would have said.

GEORGES: Quite right. There's a man for you.

VERONIQUE: Perhaps so, but if he'd been here you would already be in handcuffs.

GEORGES: Oh, no.

VERONIQUE: No?

GEORGES: No. I know how to persuade men. They have logical minds. I control their thoughts by logic. But you, madam, where's your logic. Where's your common sense? If I've understood you, you *don't* intend to hand me over.

VERONIQUE: You've understood rightly.

GEORGES: And that's just why you will hand me over. Don't protest. You're like all women; impulsive and hysterical. You

will smile at me, cajole me, and then you will take fright at
my ears or at a hair sticking out of my nose and you'll start
screaming.

VERONIQUE: Did I scream when I discovered you?

GEORGES: Of course not. But you will. I know women. Whenever
they feel like screaming, they let you have it. You're still holding
yours in. But just let the police knock at the door, and you'll
enjoy yourself by letting it go. What a pity you're not a man.
You might have been my luck. As a woman, by your very nature
you're my fate.

VERONIQUE: I'm your fate?

GEORGES: What else? A door which shuts, a noose which tightens,
an axe which falls – that's woman.

VERONIQUE [irritated]: You've come to the wrong floor. For fate
call on the lady on the second floor, who has ruined two family
men. As for me, I leave all doors open, and I [She stops and bursts
into laughter.] You nearly made me . . .

GEORGES: I beg your pardon.

VERONIQUE: You have two strings to your bow; logic for men and
challenge for women. You pretend to think that we are all alike,
while really believing that each of us wishes to be unique. 'You
are a woman, therefore you'll hand me over.' You thought to
lead me on so that I would have to prove to you that I'm not like
anyone else. My poor chap, you've wasted your time, for I've no
desire to be unique. I'm like all women, and I am content to be
like them.

[There is a ring at the doorbell.]

GEORGES: Is it? . . .

VERONIQUE: I'm afraid it is.

[He raises his hands.]

GEORGES: Are you going to give me up?

VERONIQUE: What do you think? [She sees his raised hands.] Put
your hands down. You'll make me lose my head.

[He lowers his hands and puts them in his pockets.]

GEORGES: What are you going to do?

VERONIQUE: What any woman would do in my place. [*Pause.*] What would they do?

GEORGES: I don't know.

VERONIQUE: Don't you think they'd scream?

GEORGES: I tell you, I've no idea.

VERONIQUE: You were more confident just now.

[*Another ring at the door.*]

You've only to say one word, and I'll become impulsive, hysterical.

GEORGES: Have I fallen so low that my fate is in a woman's hands?

VERONIQUE: Give the sign, and I'll put it back into the hands of men.

[*There is a knock at the door, and someone says* 'Police'.)

GEORGES [*making his decision*]: It's understood that I'm under no obligation to you.

VERONIQUE: Understood.

GEORGES: That you won't expect any gratitude from me . . .

VERONIQUE: I'm not so foolish.

GEORGES: And that I'll repay evil for good.

VERONIQUE: Of course.

GEORGES: Then hide me. [*Suddenly nervous*] Quick! What are you waiting for?

VERONIQUE: Go in there.

[*He disappears. She opens the door, and the* INSPECTOR *pokes his head through the doorway.*]

INSPECTOR: Naturally, madam, you haven't seen a dark man about five feet ten in height . . .

VERONIQUE [*quickly*]: Naturally, I haven't.

INSPECTOR: I was sure of it.

[*He bows and disappears. She closes the door.*]

VERONIQUE: You can come back.

[GEORGES *comes in, wrapped in a red blanket. She laughs.*]

GEORGES [*with dignity*]: There's nothing to laugh at. I'm trying to warm myself up. [*He sits down.*] You lied.

VERONIQUE: Well I never!

GEORGES: That's rich!

VERONIQUE: I lied for you.

GEORGES: That won't solve anything.

VERONIQUE: This is too much! Perhaps you don't tell lies?

GEORGES: It's different with me. I'm dishonest. But if all honest people behaved like you . . .

VERONIQUE: Well?

GEORGES: What would happen to the social order?

VERONIQUE: Bah!

GEORGES: Bah what? What do you mean, bah?

VERONIQUE: This social order of yours . . .

GEORGES: Do you know a better one?

VERONIQUE: Yes.

GEORGES: Which one? Where is it?

VERONIQUE: Take too long to explain. Let's just say that I lied to the cops because I don't like them.

GEORGES: What are you? A pickpocket, a kleptomaniac?

VERONIQUE: I've told you that I'm a journalist, and I'm honest.

GEORGES: Then you like them. Honest people like the cops. That goes without saying.

VERONIQUE: Why should I like them?

GEORGES: Because they protect you.

VERONIQUE: They protect me so much that they set on me last week. [Pulling up her sleeves.] Look at these bruises.

GEORGES: Oh!

VERONIQUE: That's what they did.

GEORGES [surprised]: Was it a mistake?

VERONIQUE: No.

GEORGES: You were guilty, then?

VERONIQUE: We were demonstrating.

GEORGES: Who's we?

VERONIQUE: I – and other demonstrators.

GEORGES: What were you demonstrating?

VERONIQUE: Our discontent.

GEORGES: Incredible! Look at yourself and look at me, and tell me which of us has the right to be discontented. Well, I'm not discontented. Not at all. I've never complained. I've never demonstrated in all my life. On the threshold of prison, on the brink of death, I accept the world. You're twenty, you're free, and you reject it. [*Suspicious*] In fact, you're a red.

VERONIQUE: Pink.

GEORGES: This is getting interesting. What about your father? What does he say to all this?

VERONIQUE: It worries him to death, poor man.

GEORGES: Is he on the other side?

VERONIQUE: He writes for *Soir à Paris*.

GEORGES: You thrill me. That's my paper. A great and honest man, your father, with only one weakness – you. [*He shivers, sneezes and wraps himself more tightly in his blanket.*] Delightful evening! I owe my life to a down-and-out with a taste for doing unnecessary favours and my freedom to a revolutionary who makes a cult of mankind. It must be kindness week. [*Pause.*] You ought to be happy; you've sown disorder, betrayed your class, lied to your natural protectors, humiliated a man . . .

VERONIQUE: Humiliated!

GEORGES: Of course! You have made me into a mere object – the unfortunate object of your philanthropy.

VERONIQUE: Would you be any less an object in the Black Maria?

GEORGES: No, but I'd be able to hate you and seek refuge in my own soul. Ah, you've done me a bad turn.

VERONIQUE: I?

GEORGES [*vigorously*]: A very bad turn. You see no further than the end of your nose. But I think about things. I think of the future. It's dark, a very dark future. Saving people is not everything, my girl. You must give them the means to live. Have you asked yourself what's to become of me?

VERONIQUE: You'll become a crook again, I suppose.

GEORGES: That's just it – I shan't.

VERONIQUE: What? Are you going to become an honest man?

GEORGES: I don't say that. I say that I no longer have the means to be dishonest. One needs a certain amount of capital to be a crook: a certain outlay, two suits, a dinner suit, a dress suit if possible, twelve shirts, six pairs of underpants, six pairs of socks, three pairs of shoes, a range of ties, a gold tie-pin, a leather briefcase, and a pair of horn-rimmed glasses. All I possess are these rags and I haven't a cent. How do you expect me to manage? Can I present myself to the manager of the Bank of France in this get-up? I've been brought very low. Much too low for me to be able to climb up again; and it's all your fault. You've saved me from gaol only to plunge me into destitution. In prison I could save my face. As a down-and-out I lose face. I, a down-and-out? I've nothing to thank you for, madam.

VERONIQUE: Suppose I were to get you a job?

GEORGES: A job? Thirty thousand francs a month, work and an employer? Keep it. I'm not selling myself.

VERONIQUE: How much would you need to build up your wardrobe?

GEORGES: I've no idea.

VERONIQUE: I have a little money on me.

GEORGES: Don't say any more. Money is sacred. I never accept money: I take it.

VERONIQUE: Then take it.

GEORGES: I can't take it from you, since you're giving it to me. [*Suddenly*] I'll make you a proposal. It's an honest one of course, but then I have no right to make things difficult. I'll give you an interview, with exclusive world rights.

VERONIQUE: You give me an interview?

GEORGES: Aren't you a journalist? Ask me some questions.

VERONIQUE: What about?

GEORGES: About my art.

VERONIQUE: I've told you, I'm on foreign affairs. Besides, my paper is not interested in crooks.

GEORGES: Of course. A progressive paper! What a bore it must be. [*Pause.*] I am Georges de Valéra.

VERONIQUE [*unable to restrain her interest*]: The . . .

GEORGES: Yes, the great Valéra.

VERONIQUE [*hesitantly*]: Well, of course . . .

GEORGES: I imagine your rag is poor.

VERONIQUE: Yes, fairly poor.

GEORGES: All I ask is two suits, a dozen shirts, three ties and a pair of shoes. You can pay me in kind. [*He stands up.*] In 1917 a blue baby was born in Moscow of a Black Guard and a White Russian.

VERONIQUE: No.

GEORGES: Doesn't that interest you?

VERONIQUE: I haven't the time. I told you I was going out.

GEORGES: What about later?

VERONIQUE: Frankly, no. Crooks, you know, pleasant or otherwise . . .

GEORGES: Go to the devil. [*The door to the flat is heard to open and close.*] What's that?

VERONIQUE: Good heavens! My father!

GEORGES: I'm going . . .

VERONIQUE: If he sees you, he'll give you up. Go in there for the moment. I'll get round him.

[GEORGES *disappears at the moment that the door opens.* SIBILOT *enters.*]

SIBILOT: You still here?

VERONIQUE: I was just going. I didn't think you'd be home so soon.

SIBILOT [*bitterly*]: Nor did I.

VERONIQUE: Listen, Dad, there's something I have to tell you.

SIBILOT: The swine!

VERONIQUE: Who?

SIBILOT: Everybody. I'm ashamed to be a man. Give me a drink.

VERONIQUE [*pouring him a drink*]: Now, just imagine . . .

SIBILOT: Ungrateful wretches, liars, rogues and scoundrels, that's what we are. The sole justification for the human species is the protection of animals.

VERONIQUE: Just now I had . . .

SIBILOT: I'd like to be a dog. They show us an example of love and fidelity. But no, canines are the dupes of man. They are stupid enough to love us. I'd like to be a cat. A cat? No. All mammals are alike. Oh, to be a shark to follow in the wake of ships and devour the sailors.

VERONIQUE: Poor old Dad, what have they done to you now?

SIBILOT: They've kicked me out, my child.

VERONIQUE: They kick you out once a fortnight.

SIBILOT: This time it's the works. Veronique, you're my witness that I've been feeding on Communists for nearly ten years. It's indigestible and monotonous food. How many times have I wanted to change my diet; to feed on priests, for example, or freemasons, millionaires or women. In vain. The menu is fixed for ever. Have I ever jibbed at it? I'd no sooner finished digesting Malenkov when I had to start on Krushchev. Did I complain? Every day I invented a new sauce. Whose idea was the sabotage of the cruiser *Dixmude*? And who thought up the business of the conspiracy against the nation? And the story about the carrier-pigeons? I did. They were all mine. For ten years I've defended Europe, from Berlin to Saigon. I've fed on Viet-Minh, I've fed on the Chinese; I've fed on the Soviet Army, with its planes and tanks. Now, my girl, see the extent of human ingratitude. The first time my stomach turns, the boss throws me out.

VERONIQUE: Have you really been thrown out?

SIBILOT: Like a dish-rag. Unless I find an idea by tomorrow.

VERONIQUE [*without any sympathy*]: You'll find it, don't worry.

SIBILOT: No; not this time. What do you expect? I'm not a titan. I'm a very ordinary man who has worn out his grey matter for seventy thousand francs a month. It's true that for ten years I shone. I was Pegasus, I had wings. The wings have caught fire, and what's left? An old nag, fit for the knacker's yard. [*He walks up and down.*] Ten years of loyal service. You'd expect a human word, a gesture of gratitude. Nothing. Reprimands and threats, that's all. I shall end up by hating your Communists. [*Timidly*] My dear girl? . . .

VERONIQUE: Yes, Dad?

SIBILOT: You wouldn't have any ... now I'm saying it just in the air – you wouldn't have an idea? You don't know anything against them?

VERONIQUE: Oh, Dad!

SIBILOT: Listen, my dear, I've never objected to the company you keep, even though it has been awkward for me, and might perhaps be the reason for my bad luck. I've always left you free, ever since your poor mother's illness, only asking that you save me from the worst when your friends take power. Won't you reward my tolerance? Are you going to leave your poor old father in the lurch? I'm asking you to make a little effort, my child, just a little one. You see the Communists at close quarters. You must have a lot on your mind.

VERONIQUE: No, Dad.

SIBILOT: Come on!

VERONIQUE: They're my friends.

SIBILOT: All the more reason. Who are the people whose seamy side you know, if not your friends? The only friends I have are at the paper, and, I tell you, if I wanted to speak out. ... Here! I'll make an exchange with you. You tell me what you know about Duclos, and I'll give you the lowdown on 'Braces' Julot. You'll have a terrific story. Will you do it?

VERONIQUE: No, Dad.

SIBILOT: I'm Job. My own daughter abandons me on the dung-heap. Go, then.

VERONIQUE: I'm going. I'm going. But I wanted to tell you ...

SIBILOT: Veronique, do you know who is dying? Man. Work, Family, Fatherland. All finished. There, that's a story. The Twilight of Man. What do you say to that?

VERONIQUE: You can read that every month in *Preuves*.

SIBILOT: You're right. To hell with him.

VERONIQUE: Who?

SIBILOT: Man. I'm a fool to wear myself out for seventy thousand francs a month. After all, the Communists haven't done me any harm. For seventy thousand francs a month, it would even be justifiable for me to be on their side.

VERONIQUE: I didn't make you say that.

SIBILOT: No, my girl, no. You won't tempt me. I'm an old-fashioned man. I love freedom too much. I have too much respect for human dignity. [*He pulls himself together.*] Respect for human dignity is proper, beautiful. Thrown out like a dish-rag. An old employee, a family man. Thrown into the street with a month's wages and no pension. Here! That's an idea perhaps. Old workers get no pensions in the USSR. [*He looks at himself in the mirror.*] There'd have to be something about their grey hairs.

VERONIQUE: They have pensions, Dad.

SIBILOT: Be quiet. Let me think. [*Pause.*] It's no good. The readers would be right in saying 'Maybe the Russian workers don't have pensions, but that's no reason for rearming Germany.' [*Pause.*] Veronique, Germany *must* be rearmed. But why, eh? For what reason?

VERONIQUE: There's no reason.

SIBILOT: Yes, my girl, there is one; and this is it. All my life I've been as furious as any Russian about it, and I've had enough. Let the others get worked up about it for a change. And they will, if Germany rearms, I tell you. Rearm, then! Rearm Germany! Rearm Japan! Set fire to the four corners of the globe! Seventy thousand francs to defend Man. Think of that. At that price Man can damned well go under.

VERONIQUE: You'll go under as well.

SIBILOT: So much the better. My life has been one long funeral, and no mourners following the coffin. But my death will make some stir. What an apotheosis! I'd like to go out like a rocket, if only I could see old Julot spinning above my head. Seventy thousand francs a month. Seventy thousand kicks in the pants daily. We'll all go under together, and long live war! [*He splutters and coughs.*]

VERONIQUE: Here, have a drink.

[*He does so.*]

SIBILOT: Ooh!

VERONIQUE: There's a down-and-out in my room.

SIBILOT: Is he a Communist?

VERONIQUE: Not at all.

SIBILOT: Well, what am I supposed to do about it?

VERONIQUE: The police are after him.

SIBILOT: Then phone the police station and ask them to come and get him.

VERONIQUE: But, Dad, I want to save him.

SIBILOT: What's he done, this pal of yours? If he has stolen, he must be punished.

VERONIQUE: He hasn't stolen. Be a sport. Don't worry about him. Go on quietly looking for your idea. In the morning he will go without making any noise, and we shan't see him again.

SIBILOT: Very well. If he keeps perfectly quiet I'll close my eyes to his presence. But if the police come, don't bank on my telling lies.

VERONIQUE [half-opening the door of her room.]: I'm going. You can stay the night here, but don't leave my room. Good-bye. [She closes the door.] See you tomorrow, Dad. And don't worry about your idea. Your people use the same idea every time, and you'll just have to dig it up again.

SIBILOT: Go to the devil! [She goes out.] The same idea. Of course it's the same idea. And what next? I've got to have something good if I have to dress it up again every time. [He puts his head between his hands.] The life of Stalin in pictures. They don't want that, the idiots. I wonder why. [GEORGE sneezes. SIBILOT listens, then returns to his meditations.] Sabotage . . . conspiracy . . . treason . . . terror. [At each word he thinks and shakes his head.] Famine . . . famine, eh? [Pause.] No. Done to death. Used ever since 1918. [He looks through his newspapers.] What have these Russians done? [Looking through the papers] Nothing? Impossible. It is incredible that in a country of 200 million inhabitants a day should pass without an injustice or some foul crime being committed. I've got it! The Iron Curtain. [He thinks awhile.] Sabotage . . . conspiracy . . .

   [GEORGES sneezes. Irritated]

If only I could work in peace. Treason ... conspiracy ... Let's start from the other end. Western culture. The mission of Europe. The right to think.

[GEORGES *sneezes*.]

Stop it! Stop it! [*He starts to dream again*.] The life of Stalin in pictures. [*Whistles sound in the street. He is in torment, and buries his head in his hands*.] Oh! The life of Stalin without pictures.

[GEORGES *sneezes*.]

I'll kill that fellow.

GEORGES [*offstage*]: Oh, my God! Oh, my God!

SIBILOT: God help me! God help me! [*He goes to the telephone and dials a number*.] Hallo! Police? This is René Sibilot, journalist, 13 rue Goulden, ground floor, the door on the left. Someone has broken into my flat. It seems that the police are looking for him. That's right. Send someone over.

[*During the last few words, the door opens and* GEORGES *enters*.]

GEORGES: A healthy reaction at last. Sir, you are a normal man. Allow me to shake your hand. [*He comes forward with his hand held out*.]

SIBILOT [*jumping back*]: Help!

GEORGES [*throwing himself on* SIBILOT]: Ssh! [*He puts a hand over* SIBILOT's *mouth*.] Do I look like a murderer? What a misunderstanding! I admire you, and you think that I want to cut your throat. Yes, I admire you. Your phone call was sublime. It should serve as an example to all good people who have been misled by a false liberalism into surrendering their rights. Don't be afraid that I may escape. I want to contribute to your glory. Tomorrow the papers will report that I was arrested at your place. You believe me, don't you? Do you believe me?

[SIBILOT, *still gagged, signs assent*.]

Good. [*He releases* SIBILOT *and steps back a pace*.] Let me look at the honest man in his full and splendid majesty. [*Pause*.] Suppose I were to tell you that I tried to kill myself just now in order to escape my pursuers?

SIBILOT: Don't try to get round me.

GEORGES: Splendid. And suppose I were to take a packet of powder from my rags, swallow the contents and fall dead at your feet?

SIBILOT: Well?

GEORGES: What would you say?

SIBILOT: I'd say 'The rogue has saved the law a job'.

GEORGES: The quiet certitude of an irreproachable conscience. It is easy to see, sir, that you have never entertained any doubts about what is right . . .

SIBILOT: Of course!

GEORGES . . . and that you don't listen to those subversive doctrines which make the criminal a product of society.

SIBILOT: A criminal is a criminal.

GEORGES: Splendid! A criminal is a criminal. That's well said. Ah, there's no danger that I'd touch your heart by telling the story of my unfortunate childhood.

SIBILOT: It would do you no good. I had a tough childhood myself.

GEORGES: And little you'd care that I'm a victim of the first World War, the Russian Revolution and the capitalist system?

SIBILOT: There are others who are victims of all that – me, for example – and who don't stoop to thieving.

GEORGES: You have an answer for everything. Nothing saps your convictions. Ah, sir, with that bronze forehead, those enamel eyes and that heart of stone, you must be an anti-Semite.

SIBILOT: I should have known it. Are you a Jew?

GEORGES: No, sir, no. And I'll admit to you that I share your anti-Semitism. [At a gesture from SIBILOT] Don't be offended. Share is going too far, let's say that I pick up the crumbs. Not having the good fortune to be honest, I don't enjoy your assurance. I have doubts, sir, I have doubts. That is the prerogative of troubled souls. I am, if you like, a probabilist anti-Semite. [Confidentially] What about the Arabs? You hate them, don't you?

SIBILOT: That's enough. I have neither the time nor the inclination to listen to your nonsense. I ask you to go back into that room immediately and to wait there quietly until the police arrive.

GEORGES: I'll go. I'll go back into the other room. But just tell me that you hate the Arabs.

SIBILOT: Er, yes.

GEORGES: Say it better than that, just to please me, and I swear to you it's my last question.

SIBILOT: They should stay where they belong.

GEORGES: Wonderful. Allow me, sir, to take off my hat to you. You are honest to the point of ferocity. After this brief tour of the horizon, our identity of views is plain, which doesn't surprise me. What honest people we scoundrels would be if your police would give us the chance.

SIBILOT: Are you going to clear out?

GEORGES: Just one word more, sir, just one, and then I'll go. What! You, a Frenchman, son and grandson of French peasants, and I, a man without a country, provisional guest of France; you honesty itself, and I the criminal; we can shake hands disregarding all vices and virtues, both condemning the Jews, the Communists and subversive ideas? Our agreement is of deep significance. I know its significance, sir, and I'll tell you what it is: we both respect private property.

SIBILOT: You respect property?

GEORGES: I? But I live on it, sir. Why shouldn't I respect it? Come, sir, your daughter wanted to save me. You have given me away, but I feel closer to you than to her. The practical conclusion that I draw from all this is that we have the duty, you and I, to work together.

SIBILOT: Work together? Who? We? You're mad.

GEORGES: I can do you a great service.

SIBILOT: You amaze me.

GEORGES: Just now I had my ear to the door, and I heard everything you said to your daughter. You were looking for an idea, I believe. Well, I'm in a position to give you that idea.

SIBILOT: An idea? About Communism?

GEORGES: Yes.

SIBILOT: You ... you know the subject?

GEORGES: A crook has to know everything.

SIBILOT: All right, give me your idea quickly, and I'll ask the court to be lenient with you.

GEORGES: Impossible.

SIBILOT: Why?

GEORGES: I can only help you if my hands are free.

SIBILOT: The police . . .

GEORGES: Yes, the police. They're coming. They'll be here in a couple of minutes. That just gives me time to introduce myself: an orphan, driven since childhood to choose between dying of starvation or using my wits. There's no credit in my having chosen to use my wits. I have an excess of genius, sir, as you have an excess of honesty. Have you ever thought what an alliance of genius and honesty could do, of inspiration and obstinacy, of light and blindness? We should be masters of the world. I have ideas. I produce dozens every minute. Unfortunately, they convince no one. I don't pursue them enough. You, you have none, but ideas hold you in their grip, they furrow your brow, and you are blinded by them, and that is just why they convince others. They are dreams of stone; they fascinate all who have a nostalgia for petrification. Suppose that now a new thought emanated from me and took possession of you. It would quickly take on your manner, poor thing; it would become so gross and true that it would capture the Universe.

[*A ring at the doorbell.* SIBILOT, *who has been listening fascinated, starts with surprise.*]

SIBILOT: It's the . . .

GEORGES: Yes. You must decide. If you hand me over, you'll have a sleepless night and you'll be sacked tomorrow. [*The bell rings again.*] If you save me, my genius will make you rich and famous.

SIBILOT [*tempted*]: What proof have I of your genius?

GEORGES [*going into the other room*]: Ask the inspector.

[*He disappears while* SIBILOT *goes to open the door to admit the* INSPECTOR.]

INSPECTOR: M. Sibilot?

SIBILOT: Yes.

INSPECTOR: Where is he?

SIBILOT: Who?

INSPECTOR: Georges de Valéra.

SIBILOT [*impressed*]: You're looking for Georges de Valéra?

INSPECTOR: Yes. Oh, no hope, of course. He's as slippery as an eel. Do you mind if I sit down? [*He does so.*] I see that you haven't a grand piano. I congratulate you.

SIBILOT: Don't you like grand pianos?

INSPECTOR: I've seen too many.

SIBILOT: Where?

INSPECTOR: Among the rich. [*He introduces himself.*] Inspector Goblet.

SIBILOT: Delighted.

INSPECTOR: I like your place. I'll be sorry to leave it.

SIBILOT: Make yourself at home.

INSPECTOR: You don't know how much at home I am. Your living-room is the exact replica of mine. Nineteen twenty-five?

SIBILOT: Eh?

INSPECTOR [*with a sweep of his hand*]: The furniture: nineteen twenty-five?

SIBILOT: Ah, nineteen twenty-five? Oh, yes.

INSPECTOR: The Decorative Arts Exhibition, our youth ...

SIBILOT: The year of my wedding.

INSPECTOR: And mine. Our wives chose the furniture with their mothers; we weren't even consulted. The in-laws lent the money. Do you like those 1925 chairs?

SIBILOT: You know, in the end one no longer sees them. [*Shaking his head.*] To me, it was a temporary arrangement ...

INSPECTOR: Naturally. What isn't temporary? And then, one fine day, twenty years later ...

SIBILOT: We are aware that we shall soon die, and that the temporary has become permanent.

INSPECTOR: We shall die as we have lived, in 1925. [*He gets up quickly.*] What have you there? An original?

SIBILOT: No, it's a reproduction.

INSPECTOR: So much the better. I hate original paintings and private carriages, because the rich collect them and we're forced to know all the hallmarks.

SIBILOT: Who is?

INSPECTOR: We of the Society Branch.

SIBILOT: What for?

INSPECTOR: So that we can keep up a conversation. [*Going to the picture.*] This is a Constable. I wouldn't have thought that you liked Constables.

SIBILOT: I prefer them to the mildew.

INSPECTOR [*looking behind the picture*]: Ah, because *behind* the Constable . . .

SIBILOT: That's right.

INSPECTOR: The damp, eh?

SIBILOT: It's being near the Seine.

INSPECTOR: Don't tell me. I live at Gennevilliers.

[GEORGES *sneezes several times and starts to swear.*]

What's that?

SIBILOT: The neighbour. He can't stand the damp. It gives him colds.

INSPECTOR: You're lucky it's the neighbour. At Gennevilliers I'm the one who catches cold. [*He sits down again.*] Man is a strange animal, my dear sir. I'm enraptured by your flat because it reminds me of my own, which gives me the horrors.

SIBILOT: How do you explain that?

INSPECTOR: Well, it's because my job takes me into the fashionable quarters. I was in the Society Branch, and now they've put me on to J.3; murders and swindles, which again leads me to places like Passy. I carry out my investigations above my station, my dear chap, and they make me feel it. I have to go in through the servants' entry, wait between a piano and a big green plant, smile at women in tight-fitting dresses and perfumed men who treat me like a servant. Meanwhile, as they put mirrors everywhere, I see my ugly mug on all the walls.

SIBILOT: Can't you put them in their places?

INSPECTOR: In their places? But that's where they are. I'm the one who isn't in my place. But you must know all about that in your game.

SIBILOT: I? If I were to tell you that I have to kiss my editor's backside every day.

INSPECTOR: It's not possible. Do they make you?

SIBILOT: Figuratively speaking.

INSPECTOR: I know what you mean, and I can tell you that I've kissed the Director of the Sûreté's backside over a thousand times. You know, what I like about your place is the feeling of discomfort and proud humility. At last I'm doing my investigating among equals; at home, so to speak. I'm free. If I felt like taking you inside and giving you the once-over, no one would protest.

SIBILOT: Surely you're not thinking of that?

INSPECTOR: Good God, no. You have far too nice a face. A face like mine. A sixty thousand francs a month face.

SIBILOT: Seventy.

INSPECTOR: Sixty, seventy, it's all the same. It's at a hundred that you start to change. [*Moved*] My poor Sibilot.

SIBILOT: My poor Inspector. [*They shake hands.*]

INSPECTOR: Only we can appreciate our poverty and our greatness. Give me a drink.

SIBILOT: Gladly. [*He fills two glasses.*]

INSPECTOR [*raising his glass*]: To the defenders of Western culture. [*He drinks.*]

SIBILOT: Victory to those who defend the rich without loving them. [*He drinks.*] By the way, you haven't got an idea, have you?

INSPECTOR: Against whom?

SIBILOT: Against the Communists.

INSPECTOR: Ah, you're on propaganda. Well, you won't find your idea; it's much too tricky for you. No more than I'll find my Valéra.

SIBILOT: Is he so smart?

INSPECTOR: He? If I weren't afraid of using fancy words, I'd say he's a genius. By the way, didn't you tell me that he had taken refuge in your flat?

SIBILOT: I . . . I said that someone . . .

INSPECTOR: It's he, without the slightest doubt. If he was here a few minutes ago, he should still be here. All the windows of the building are being watched. I have men in the corridor and on the stairs. Good. Well, that proves the esteem I have for him. I shan't search this room. I shan't even look in the other rooms. Do you know why? Because I know that he has managed to make himself unrecognizable or to get away from the neighbourhood. Who knows where he is? And in what disguise? Perhaps you are he.

SIBILOT: I?

INSPECTOR: Keep calm. Mediocrity can't be counterfeited. Let's close the matter, my dear chap. Give me a couple of lines for my report. You saw him, you rushed to the phone to inform us, and he took advantage of the few minutes your back was turned to disappear. Is that it?

SIBILOT: I . . .

INSPECTOR: Splendid. [*Pause.*] Now I must leave, taking with me the pleasant memory of these brief moments. We shall have to meet again.

SIBILOT: Nothing would please me more.

INSPECTOR: I'll phone you some time. When we're both free, we'll go to the cinema together, like a couple of lads. Don't bother to see me out. [*He goes out.*]

SIBILOT [*opening the door of the other room*]: Give me your idea and clear out.

GEORGES: No.

SIBILOT: Why?

GEORGES: My ideas wither without me. We're inseparable.

SIBILOT: Under those conditions I'll manage without you. Get out!

GEORGES: Didn't you hear what the Inspector said? I'm a genius, Dad.

SIBILOT [*with resignation*]: Well? What do you want?

GEORGES: Very little. I want you to keep me here till the police have evacuated the building.

SIBILOT: And then what? No money?

GEORGES: No, but you can slip me one of your old suits.

SIBILOT: All right. Stay. [*Pause.*] Now, your idea.

GEORGES [*sits down, pours himself a glass of wine and unhurriedly lights one of* SIBILOT'*s pipes*]: Well, here it is . . .

CURTAIN

SCENE FOUR

Jules Palotin's Office. Jules, Tavernier, Perigord and the Secretary are present.

JULES: What's the time?

TAVERNIER: Two minutes to ten.

JULES: And no Sibilot?

TAVERNIER: No.

JULES: He's always been early.

PERIGORD: He's not late yet.

JULES: No, but he's no longer early. He's letting me down.

[*The telephone rings and the* SECRETARY *answers it.*]

SECRETARY: Hallo? Yes. Yes, sir. [*To* JULES] The Board is about to meet and the Chairman asks if there's anything new.

JULES: Anything new? He can go to hell. Say I've gone out.

SECRETARY [*into telephone*]: No, sir, he must have gone to the Composing Room. (*To* JULES) He doesn't seem very pleased.

JULES: Tell him I've got a pleasant surprise for him.

SECRETARY [*into telephone*]: As he left the office he said that he had a pleasant surprise for you. Very good.

JULES: What did he say?

SECRETARY: The Board are expecting you to phone them.

JULES: The old miser. Bandit. I'll give him surprises. [*To* SECRETARY] Ask Sibilot to come right away.

SECRETARY [*into telephone*]: Send Sibilot up to the chief. [*To* JULES] He hasn't come yet.

JULES: What's the time?

SECRETARY: Five past ten.

JULES [*to the others*]: I told you. He begins by not being early, and ends up by being late. [*Pause.*] Well, well, well. We'll wait. [*He sits down and takes up a restful attitude.*] We'll wait calmly. [*He strikes another restful attitude.*] In complete calm. [*To* TAVERNIER *and* PERIGORD] Relax.

[*The* SECRETARY *starts to type. He shouts*]

I said calmly. [*He jumps suddenly to his feet.*] I'm not made for waiting. Someone is being killed.

TAVERNIER: Where, chief?

JULES: How should I know? In Cairo, Hamburg, Valparaiso, Paris. A jet plane explodes over Bordeaux. A peasant discovers the footprint of a Martian in his field. I am news, my boys. News doesn't wait. [*The telephone rings.*] Is it Sibilot?

SECRETARY [*into telephone*]: Hallo? Yes. Yes, sir. [*To* JULES] It's the Minister of the Interior. He asks if there's anything new.

JULES: I'm not here.

SECRETARY: No, sir, the editor isn't here. [*To* JULES] He's furious.

JULES: Say that I've got a surprise for him.

SECRETARY: The editor said just a while ago that he has a surprise for you. Very good, sir. [*She hangs up.*] He'll ring back in an hour.

JULES: An hour! An hour to find that surprise . . .

PERIGORD: You'll find it, Jules.

JULES: I? I'd be the first one to be surprised. [*He stops walking.*] Let's calm down again. Let's try to think of something else. [*Pause.*] Well?

TAVERNIER [*surprised*]: Well?

JULES: Think.

PERIGORD: Yes, chief. What about?

JULES: I've just told you; of something else.

PERIGORD: We're doing so.

JULES: Think out loud.

PERIGORD [*thinking*]: I wonder if the landlord is going to repair the roof. My solicitor advises me to take him to court. He says I'd win, but I'm not so sure . . .

TAVERNIER [*thinking*]: Now where did I put that book of Metro tickets? I've looked in all my pockets. Yet I can remember standing at the booking office this morning. I took out my money with my right hand, and with my left hand . . .

JULES: Thieves!

TAVERNIER [*coming to with a start*]: What's that?

T – T.P. – G

JULES: At last I have seen into your hearts. And what do I find? Roofs and Metro tickets. Your thoughts belong to me. I pay for them, and you steal them from me. [*To the* SECRETARY] I want Sibilot. Phone his home.

SECRETARY: Very good, Jules. [*She dials a number and waits.* JULES *stops walking about and waits.*] No reply.

JULES: I'll throw him out. I won't hear a word from him. I'll throw him out. Whom shall I put in his place?

TAVERNIER: Thierry Maulnier?

JULES: No.

TAVERNIER: He has a noble mind, and a great fear of Communism.

JULES: Yes, but he can't put his fear across to others, and I know of two people who, as a result of reading his articles, rushed straight out and joined the C.P. [*Quickly*] Any news of Nekrassov?

PERIGORD: He's reported in Rome.

JULES: In Rome? That's done it. The Christian Democrats will grab him.

TAVERNIER: Tass has issued a denial, saying he's been in the Crimea for the past fortnight.

JULES: Why not? Let's give him a miss for the moment. Await confirmation, and above all say nothing about him being in Rome. With the crisis in the French hotel industry, this isn't the time to give a boost to the Italian tourist trade. Come, boys, let's take the bull by the horns. Ready?

TAVERNIER ⎫
PERIGORD ⎬ : Ready, Jules.

JULES: What do we need to launch a campaign?

PERIGORD: Headline type.

JULES: We have it. What else.

TAVERNIER: A victim.

JULES: We have that too. What else?

PERIGORD: A theme.

JULES: A theme, that's it. A theme.

TAVERNIER: A striking theme.

PERIGORD: Shattering.

TAVERNIER: Terror and sex appeal.

PERIGORD: Corpses and legs.

JULES: Ah, I see the theme, I see it.

TAVERNIER: So do we, chief, we see it . . .

JULES: I've got it.

PERIGORD: We've got it. We've got it.

JULES: You've got it too?

TAVERNIER: Of course.

JULES: Well, tell me what it is.

PERIGORD: Well, it's, it's a general view . . .

TAVERNIER: An overall picture that it's difficult to . . .

PERIGORD: I think we'll have to find someone for the . . .

TAVERNIER: And then, for the . . .

JULES: So! [*He sits down weakly, then speaks sharply.*] Are you laughing, boys?

TAVERNIER [*indignant*]: Us, Jules, how could you think that?

JULES: You'd better not laugh. If I go under, you go with me.

[*The phone rings and the* SECRETARY *answers it.*]

SECRETARY: Yes? Send him right up. [*To* JULES] It's Sibilot.

JULES: At last.

[JULES *packs* TAVERNIER, PERIGORD *and the* SECRETARY *off
as* SIBILOT *enters with* GEORGES.]

JULES: My dear Sibilot. Do you know I'd almost given you up?

SIBILOT: You must excuse me, chief.

JULES: Oh, forget it. Who's this chap?

SIBILOT: A man.

JULES: I can see that.

SIBILOT: I'll tell you about him in a moment.

JULES: Good morning, sir.

[GEORGES *does not reply.*]
Is he deaf?

SIBILOT: He doesn't understand French.

JULES [*to* GEORGES, *showing him a chair*]: Sit down.

[*He makes a gesture to indicate sitting, but* GEORGES *remains
standing.*]

Doesn't he understand signs, either?

SIBILOT: Not when you make them in French.

[GEORGES *walks away and takes from the desk a newspaper which carries the large headline 'Nekrassov Disappears'.*]

JULES: Does he read?

SIBILOT: No, no, no, he's looking at the pictures.

JULES [*placing his hands on* SIBILOT's *shoulders*]: Well, old chap?

SIBILOT [*not understanding*]: Well?

JULES: Your idea?

SIBILOT: Ah, my idea. [*Pause.*] Chief, I'm so sorry . . .

JULES [*angrily*]: Haven't you an idea?

SIBILOT: I mean . . .

[GEORGES, *behind* JULES, *signs to him to speak.*]

Oh, yes, chief, of course I have.

JULES: You don't seem very proud of it.

SIBILOT: No.

[*Sign from* GEORGES.]

But I . . . I am a modest man.

JULES: Is it good at least?

[*Sign from* GEORGES.]

SIBILOT [*mutters*]: Ah, too good.

JULES: And you complain? Sibilot, you're a card. [*Pause.*] Let's hear it. [*Silence.*] Aren't you going to tell me?

[*Silent exhortations from* GEORGES. SIBILOT *remains silent.*]

I see what it is. You want your rise. Listen, old chap, you shall have it, I promise. You'll have it if your idea pleases me.

SIBILOT: Oh, no! No, no.

JULES: What's the matter?

SIBILOT: I don't want a rise.

JULES: Very well, I won't give you a rise. There. Are you satisfied? [*Exasperated*] Are you going to talk? [SIBILOT *points to* GEORGES.] Well?

SIBILOT: That's it.

JULES: What do you mean . . . it?

SIBILOT: Him.

JULES [*not understanding*]: He is it?

SIBILOT: He's the idea.

JULES: Your idea is him?

SIBILOT: It's not *my* idea. No, no, it's not *my* idea.

JULES: Is it his then?

    [GEORGES *signifies 'No'*.]

SIBILOT [*obeying* GEORGES]: No.

JULES [*pointing to* GEORGES]: Then, who is he?

SIBILOT: A . . . a foreigner.

JULES: What nationality?

SIBILOT: Er . . . [*Closing his eyes.*] Soviet.

JULES [*disappointed*]: I see.

SIBILOT [*taking heart*]: A Soviet official who has broken through the Iron Curtain.

JULES: A high official?

    [GEORGES *signs to* SIBILOT *to say yes.*]

SIBILOT: Yes . . . [*Becomes terrified again.*] That is, no. Just ordinary. Very ordinary. Quite a small official.

JULES : In short, a nobody.

SIBILOT: That's it.

    [*Furious gestures from* GEORGES.]

JULES: And what do you expect me to do with your Soviet official?

SIBILOT: Nothing, chief, absolutely nothing.

JULES: What do you mean, nothing? Why have you brought him?

SIBILOT [*recovering*]: I thought he could supply us with . . .

JULES: What?

SIBILOT: Some information.

JULES: Information! On what? Soviet typewriters? Desk-lamps and ventilators? Sibilot, I instruct you to launch a campaign on a grand scale, and you offer me tittle-tattle that *Paix et Liberté* wouldn't touch. Do you know how many Soviet officials choosing freedom I've had through this office since Kravchenko? A hundred and twenty-two, my friend, genuine and fake. We have had Embassy chauffeurs, children's nurses, a plumber and seventeen hairdressers, and I've got into the habit of sending them to my colleague Robinet of *Figaro*, who doesn't turn his nose up at small stuff. Result – a general slump in Kravchenkos. The latest one, Demidoff, a great administrator, a distinguished economist, hardly ran to four issues and even Bidault no longer invites him to dinner. [*He goes towards* GEORGES.] Ah, sir, so you've broken through the Iron Curtain. You've chosen freedom! Good, give him a bowl of soup and send him to the Salvation Army.

SIBILOT: Bravo, chief.

JULES: Eh?

SIBILOT: You don't know how pleased I am.
   [*Revengefully, to* GEORGES.]
To the Salvation Army, to the Salvation Army.

JULES: Is that all? Have you no other idea?

SIBILOT [*rubbing his hands*]: None, absolutely none.

JULES: Idiot! You're fired.

SIBILOT: Yes, chief, thank you, chief. Good-bye, chief.
   [*He is about to go out, but* GEORGES *stops him and brings him back to the middle of the room.*]

GEORGES: Allow me.

JULES: So you speak French?

GEORGES: My mother was French.

JULES [*to* SIBILOT]: So you lied as well. Clear out!

GEORGES [*holding* SIBILOT]: I kept it from him as a precaution.

JULES: I congratulate you, sir, on your good command of our beautiful language, but in French, as in Russian, you're wasting my time, and I'd be pleased if you'd leave my office at once.

GEORGES: That's what I intend to do. [*To* SIBILOT] To *France-Soir*, quickly.

JULES: To *France-Soir*? Why?

GEORGES [*making to go out*]: Your time is too precious. I shan't bother you any more.

JULES [*standing in front of him*]: I know my colleague Lazareff well and I can assure you he'll do nothing for you.

GEORGES: I don't doubt that. I don't expect anything from any-

one, and no one can help me, but I can do plenty for his paper
and for your country.

JULES: You?

GEORGES: Yes.

JULES: Well, what can you do?

GEORGES: You'll be wasting your time.

SIBILOT: Yes, chief, yes. You'll be wasting your time. [*To* GEORGES]
Let's go.

JULES: Sibilot, keep your place! [*To* GEORGES] I have five minutes
to spare after all, and it shan't be said that I sent anyone away
without giving him a hearing.

GEORGES: Are you asking me to stay?

JULES: Yes, I'm asking you to stay.

GEORGES: Very well. [*He dives under the table and crawls on hands and
knees.*]

JULES: What are you doing?

GEORGES: No hidden tape-recorders? No microphones? Good. [*He
stand up.*] Have you courage?

JULES: I think so.

GEORGES: If I speak your life will be in danger.

JULES: My life in danger? Don't speak. Yes, speak. Speak up.

GEORGES: Look at me. Closer. [*Pause.*] Well?

JULES: Well, what?

GEORGES: You published my photo on your front page.

JULES: Oh, you know how it is with photos. [*Looking at him.*] I
don't see anything.

GEORGES [*putting a black patch over his right eye*]: And like this?

JULES: Nekrassov!

GEORGES: Don't shout, or you're lost. There are seven armed
Communists in your offices.

JULES: Their names.

GEORGES: Later. There's no immediate danger.

JULES: Nekrassov! [*To* SIBILOT] And you didn't tell me!

SIBILOT: I swear I didn't know, chief. I swear it.

JULES: Nekrassov. My dear Sibilot, you're a genius.

SIBILOT: Oh no, chief, that's going too far.

JULES: Nekrassov. Well, I adore you. [*He embraces* SIBILOT.]

SIBILOT [*slumping into an armchair*]: It's all up. [*He faints.*]

GEORGES [*looking at him with contempt*]: Alone at last. [*To* JULES] Let's talk.

JULES: I wouldn't want to hurt your feelings, but . . .

GEORGES: You couldn't, even if you wanted to.

JULES: What proof have I that you're Nekrassov?

GEORGES [*laughing*]: None.

JULES: None?

GEORGES: None at all. Search me.

JULES: I don't . . .

GEORGES [*violently*]: I tell you to search me!

JULES: All right! All right! [*He searches him.*]

GEORGES: What have you found?

JULES: Nothing.

GEORGES: There, that's conclusive proof! What would an impostor do? He would show you his passport, a family allowance book, a Soviet identity card. Now you, Palotin, if you were Nekrassov and if you decided to break through the Iron Curtain, would you be stupid enough to keep your papers on you?

JULES: Good heavens, no!

GEORGES: That's what I had to prove to you.

JULES: I hadn't thought of that! [*Thoughtfully*] But in that case anybody could . . .

GEORGES: Do I look like anybody?

JULES: You've already been reported in Italy . . .

GEORGES: Of course! And tomorrow I'll be reported in Greece, in Spain and in Western Germany. Bring those impostors here. Bring them all here, and the truth will stagger you. The real Nekrassov has lived for thirty-five years in the Red Hell. He has the eyes of a man who has been at death's door. Look at my eyes! The real Nekrassov has killed 118 people with his own hands. Look at my hands! The real Nekrassov has carried on a ten-year reign of terror. Bring here all the impostors who have stolen my name, and you will see which of us is the most terrible. [*Abruptly*] Are you afraid?

JULES: I . . . [*He retreats, and almost knocks the attaché case over.*]

GEORGES: Don't touch the case!

JULES: Oh! [*Looking at the attaché case*] What's inside?

GEORGES: You'll know later. Keep away.

> [JULES *recoils.*]

You see. You're afraid, already. Ah, I'll make you die of fright, all of you. You'll see whether I'm Nekrassov.

JULES: I'm afraid; and yet I hesitate. What if you were deceiving me!

GEORGES: Well?

JULES: The paper would be sunk.

> [*The telephone rings.*]

Hallo? Good morning, my dear Minister. Yes, yes. Of course. Nothing is more important to me than this campaign. Yes, yes. No, I'm not in the least unwilling. I ask you to give me a few hours. Just a few hours. Yes, something new. I can't explain over the phone, but I beg you not to worry . . . He's hung up. [*He puts the receiver back.*]

GEORGES [*ironically*]: You badly need me to be Nekrassov.

JULES: Unfortunately.

GEORGES: Then, I am.

JULES: I beg your pardon.

GEORGES: Have you forgotten your catechism? The proof of God is man's need of Him.

JULES: You know the catechism?

GEORGES: We know everything. Come on, Jules, you heard the Minister. If I'm not Nekrassov, then you're no longer Palotin, the Napoleon of the press. Are you Palotin?

JULES: Yes.

GEORGES: Do you want to remain so?

JULES: Yes.

GEORGES: Then I'm Nekrassov.

SIBILOT [*coming to*]: He's lying, chief; he's lying.

JULES [*throwing himself on* SIBILOT]: Idiot! Blunderer! Fool! Who

asked you to butt in? This man is Nekrassov, and he's just proved
it to me.

SIBILOT: He's proved it to you?

JULES: Conclusively.

SIBILOT: But I swear to you . . .

JULES: Clear out; this moment!

GEORGES: Go, Sibilot, old chap. Wait for me outside. [*They push*
SIBILOT *out.*]

SIBILOT [*going out*]: I'm not responsible for anything. I wash my
hands of the whole affair. [*The door closes behind him.*]

GEORGES: To work.

JULES: You do know everything, don't you?

GEORGES: About what?

JULES: About the Soviet Union?

GEORGES: Of course.

JULES: And it's . . . terrible?

GEORGES [*earnestly*]: Ah!

JULES: Could you tell me . . .

GEORGES: Nothing. Call your Board of Directors, I want to put
forward certain conditions.

JULES: You could make them to me . . .

GEORGES: Nothing, I tell you. Call the Board.

JULES [*taking up the telephone*]: Hallo. My dear chairman, the surprise
is here. It's waiting for you. Yes, yes, yes. Oh, yes. You see that I
always keep my promises. [*He hangs up.*] He's furious, the old
skunk.

GEORGES: Why?

JULES: He was hoping to have my scalp.

GEORGES: What's his name?

JULES: Mouton.

GEORGES: I'll remember that name. [*Pause.*]

JULES: Still, while we're waiting, I would have liked . . .

GEORGES: A sample of what I know. Good. Well, I can reveal
the details of the famous Plan C for the occupation of France in
the event of world war.

JULES: There's a Plan C for the occupation of France?

GEORGES: You mentioned it in your paper last year.

JULES: Did we? Oh, yes, but I was awaiting confirmation.

GEORGES: Didn't you write at that time that Plan C contained the list of people to be shot? Well, you were right.

JULES: They're going to shoot Frenchmen?

GEORGES: A hundred thousand.

JULES: A hundred thousand!

GEORGES: Did you write that? Yes or no.

JULES: You know, one writes without thinking. Have you the list?

GEORGES: I have learned the first twenty thousand names off by heart.

JULES: Let me have some. Who'll be shot? Herriot?

GEORGES: Of course.

JULES: So he's among them; he who has always been so friendly to you. I find that very funny. Who else? All the Ministers, I suppose?

GEORGES: And all former Ministers.

JULES: That is, one out of every four deputies.

GEORGES: Excuse me! One deputy out of four will be shot as a former Minister, but the other three will be executed for other reasons.

JULES: I see, all the Assembly will be shot, except the Communists.

GEORGES: Except the Communists? Why?

JULES: Well, because the Communists, after all . . .

GEORGES: Huh!

JULES: But . . .

GEORGES: You're not yet sufficiently hardened to bear the truth I shall make my revelations gradually.

JULES: Do you know Perdrière?

GEORGES: Perdrière?

JULES: We'd like him to be on the list.

GEORGES: Oh! Why?

JULES: Oh, nothing. Give him something to think about. If he isn't, it's just too bad.

GEORGES: I know of two Perdrières. One is called René . . .

JULES: That's not the one.

GEORGES: Good, for he's not on the list.

JULES: Ours is called Henri. A Radical-Socialist.

GEORGES: Henri, that's it. That's the one I know. A deputy?

JULES: No, he was, but he isn't any longer. He's a candidate in the Seine-et-Marne by-election.

GEORGES: That's the one. You may be sure he won't be spared. As a matter of fact, he's in the first batch.

JULES: You give me great pleasure. And who among the journalists?

GEORGES: Plenty.

JULES: Who, for example?

GEORGES: You!

JULES: Me? [*He rushes to the telephone.*] Perigord, six-column-spread headline: 'Nekrassov in Paris. Our editor on the blacklist.' Funny, eh? Yes, very funny. [*He hangs up. Suddenly*] Me? Shot? It's impermissible.

GEORGES: Huh!

JULES: But I'm a Government paper. There'll still be a government when the Soviets occupy Paris.

GEORGES: No doubt.

JULES: Well?

GEORGES: They'll keep *Soir à Paris*, but liquidate the staff.

JULES: Shot. The funniest thing is that it isn't entirely unpleasing to me. It gives me standing, stature. I'm growing. [*He stands before the mirror.*] Shot. Shot. That man [*pointing to himself in the glass*] will be shot. Heh, I see myself with different eyes. Do you know what it reminds me of? The day I received the Legion of Honour. [*Turning to* GEORGES] What about the Board of Directors?

GEORGES: You have only to name them, and I'll tell you what their fate will be.

JULES: Here they are. [*The members of the Board enter.*]

MOUTON: My dear Palotin.

JULES: Gentlemen, here is my surprise.

ALL: Nekrassov.

JULES: Yes, Nekrassov. Nekrassov, who has supplied me with conclusive proofs of his identity, who speaks French and who is ready to make stupendous revelations. Among other things, he knows by heart the names of twenty thousand people whom the Soviet command is going to shoot when the Russian troops occupy France.

[*Murmurs from the Board* – 'Names', '*Are we on the list?*', '*Am I?*'.]

GEORGES: I would like to know these gentlemen by name.

JULES: Naturally. [*Pointing to the nearest one.*]M. Lerminier.

LERMINIER: Delighted.

GEORGES: Executed.

JULES: M. Charivet.

CHARIVET: Delighted.

GEORGES: Executed.

JULES: M. Nerciat.

NERCIAT: Delighted.

GEORGES: Executed.

NERCIAT: I am honoured, sir.

JULES: M. Bergerat.

BERGERAT: Delighted.

GEORGES: Executed.

BERGERAT: Which proves, sir, that I am a good Frenchman.

JULES: And this is our chairman, M. Mouton.

GEORGES: Mouton?

JULES: Mouton.

GEORGES: Ah.

MOUTON [*coming forward*]: Delighted.

GEORGES: Delighted.

MOUTON: I beg your pardon.

GEORGES: I said delighted.

MOUTON [*laughing*]: You've made a slip?

GEORGES: No.

MOUTON: You meant to say executed.

GEORGES: I meant what I said.

MOUTON: Mouton, m o u t o n.

JULES: M for Mary, O for Oswald . . .

GEORGES: It's no use. M. Mouton is not on the list.

MOUTON: You must have forgotten me.

GEORGES: I forget nothing

MOUTON: And why, if you please, do they not deign to execute me?

GEORGES: I don't know.

MOUTON: Ah, no, that's not good enough. I don't know you, yet you dishonour me, and refuse to give an explanation. I demand . . .

GEORGES: The press black-list was supplied to us by the Ministry of Information without comment.

NERCIAT: My dear Mouton.

MOUTON: It's a joke, gentlemen, merely a joke.

GEORGES: A Soviet Minister never jokes.

MOUTON: This is extremely unpleasant. Friends, tell M. Nekrassov that my position makes me the declared victim of the Soviet Government. Ex-soldier of the 1914 War, Croix de Guerre, chairman of four boards of directors, and I . . . [*He pauses.*] Well, say something! [*Embarrassed silence.*] Palotin, you don't intend to publish this list?

JULES: I shall do what you decide, gentlemen.

BERGERAT: Naturally, it must be published.

MOUTON: Well, see that you put my name in. The public wouldn't understand it if I were left out. You would have protests.

[GEORGES *takes up his hat as if to go.*]

JULES: Where are you going?

GEORGES: To *France-Soir.*

NERCIAT: To *France-Soir*? But . . .

GEORGES: I never lie, that's my strong point. You will publish my statements without altering them, or I shall go elsewhere.

MOUTON: Go to the devil! We'll manage without you.

NERCIAT: You're mad, my dear chap.

CHARIVET: Completely mad.

BERGERAT [*to* GEORGES]: Please excuse us, sir.

LERMINIER: Our chairman is rather upset . . .

CHARIVET: And you can understand how he feels.

NERCIAT: But we want the Truth.

BERGERAT: The whole Truth.

LERMINIER: And nothing but the Truth.

JULES: And we shall print whatever you wish.

MOUTON: I tell you this man is an impostor.

[*Murmurs of disapproval.*]

GEORGES: If I were you, sir, I wouldn't talk of impostors, for it is you who are not on the black-list, not I.

MOUTON [*to the members of the Board*]: Are you going to allow your chairman to be insulted? [*Silence.*] The heart of man is a shell filled with rottenness. You have known me for twenty years, but what does that matter to you? It is enough for an unknown to utter one word, and you turn on me. On me, your friend.

CHARIVET: My dear Mouton.

MOUTON: Away! Your soul is poisoned by greed. You hope to thrill old women with sensational and unfounded revelations. You hope to double the circulation. You sacrifice twenty years of friendship for a golden calf. Well, gentlemen, publish your revelations. I shall leave you, and I am going to find proof that this man is a liar, an impostor, a crook. Pray God that I find it before the whole world laughs at your stupidity. Good-bye. When we meet again you will be in sackcloth and ashes, and you will beat your breasts, begging my forgiveness. [*He goes out.*]

NERCIAT: Well.

CHARIVET: Well, well.

LERMINIER: Well, well, well.

BERGERAT: Well, well, well, well.

GEORGES: Ah, gentlemen, you'll see plenty more like that.

NERCIAT: That will suit us.

BERGERAT: Speak! Quickly!

GEORGES: One moment, gentlemen. I have some explanations to give you, and some conditions to make.

LERMINIER: We're listening.

GEORGES: To avoid any misunderstandings, I must first tell you that I despise you.

NERCIAT: Of course, that goes without saying.

BERGERAT: And we would not expect it to be otherwise.

GEORGES: To me, you are the abject props of capitalism.

CHARIVET: Bravo!

GEORGES: I left my country when I saw that the masters of the Kremlin were betraying the principles of the revolution; but don't deceive yourselves, I remain a Communist, *out and out!*

LERMINIER: That does you credit.

NERCIAT: And we respect your candour.

GEORGES: In providing you with the means to overthrow the Soviet régime, I am not unaware of the fact that I am prolonging bourgeois society for a century.

ALL: Bravo! Very good! Very good!

GEORGES: I resign myself to it with sorrow because my main objective is to purify the revolutionary movement. Let it die, if it must. In a hundred years' time it will rise again from its ashes. Then we shall resume our march forward, and then, I am pleased to tell you, we shall win.

NERCIAT: That's right. In a hundred years' time!

CHARIVET: In a hundred years' time, the deluge!

NERCIAT: For my part I've always said that we're going towards Socialism. The thing is to go slowly.

BERGERAT: Till then, let's have only one aim: down with the Soviet Union!

CHARIVET: Bravo! Down with the Soviet Union!

LERMINIER: Down with the Soviet Union! Down with the Soviet Union! Smash the French Communist Party!

[*The* SECRETARY *brings in glasses of champagne on a tray.*]

NERCIAT [*raising his glass*]: To the health of our dear enemy.

GEORGES: Your health.

[*They clink glasses and drink.*]

Here are my conditions. I want nothing for myself.

LERMINIER: Nothing?

GEORGES: Nothing. A flat in the Avenue Georges V, two body-guards, decent clothes and pocket-money.

NERCIAT: Agreed.

GEORGES: I shall dictate my memoirs and revelations to a reliable journalist.

JULES: Would you like Cartier?

GEORGES: I want Sibilot.

JULES: Splendid.

GEORGES: I understand that he's getting a rise. What does he earn?

JULES: Er . . . seventy thousand a month.

GEORGES: You bloodsucker. You'll treble it.

JULES: It's a promise.

GEORGES: To work, then

JULES: What about the seven Communists?

GEORGES: Which Communists?

JULES: The armed ones in my offices.

GEORGES: Ah . . . er . . .

NERCIAT: There are Communists on *Soir à Paris*?

JULES [*to* GEORGES]: Seven. Isn't that right?

GEORGES: Yes, yes, yes, that's the figure I gave you?

NERCIAT: Unbelievable. How did they slip in?

GEORGES [*laughing*]: You are naïve.

LERMINIER: Armed? What arms?

GEORGES: The usual armament: grenades, plastic bombs, revolvers. And there are probably a few tommy-guns under the floor.

NERCIAT: But it's highly dangerous.

GEORGES: No, not for the moment. Let's get back to our subject.

BERGERAT: But that is our subject.

NERCIAT: Allow me to tell you that your first task must be to prevent the massacre of the Board of Directors.

GEORGES: They are not thinking of massacring you.

NERCIAT: Then why these arms?

GEORGES: Pah!

NERCIAT [*astonished*]: Pah?

GEORGES: You'll know everything in its turn.

JULES: In any case, we must clean up the staff. M. Nekrassov will give us these seven names.

LERMINIER [*laughing*]: Of course he'll give them to us. He will be pleased to do so.

BERGERAT: The swine. The swine. The swine.

LERMINIER: You'll throw them out this very morning.

JULES: And what if they shoot at me?

BERGERAT: Phone the police and get a carload of inspectors.

NERCIAT: Handcuffs on at the first move.

CHARIVET: You can bet they won't dare do a thing.

LERMINIER: In any event, it would be good to give their addresses to the Ministry of the Interior. We mustn't neglect the usual official channels.

NERCIAT: I should think not. Palotin, you'll telephone all our morning and evening colleagues to give them the list. Those scoundrels must be blacklisted out of the profession.

LERMINIER: Away with them!

CHARIVET: Let them starve, the pirates.

BERGERAT: Unfortunately, their Party will feed them.

CHARIVET: Their Party? They'll drop them as soon as it's known that they've been found out.

NERCIAT: You don't think they'll throw bombs in revenge?

CHARIVET: The building will be guarded by Security Guards.

LERMINIER: By the troops if necessary.

CHARIVET: For six months.

LERMINIER: For a year. For two years.

BERGERAT: Ah, they are looking for trouble, those rogues. Well, they'll get it, I assure you.

NERCIAT [*turning to* GEORGES]: We're listening, my dear sir.

GEORGES: I'm afraid I can't remember all the names.

JULES [*to the* SECRETARY]: Fifi, get the staff list.

[FIFI *brings the list. He takes it and speaks to* GEORGES.]

This will refresh your memory. You have only to point them out.

[*He puts the list on his desk and signs to* GEORGES *to sit.* GEORGES *sits at the desk. Long silence.*]

BERGERAT: Well?

GEORGES [*unable to restrain himself*]: I'm not a stool-pigeon.

LERMINIER [*surprised*]: Pardon?

GEORGES [*aware of his slip*]: I meant to say . . .

BERGERAT [*suspicious*]: You refuse to give the names?

GEORGES [*recovering himself*]: You shall have names by the thousand. But you are children. In order to uncover a handful of enemies you are going to give the alarm to all the others. The situation is much more serious than you think. Do you know that the whole world has been tricked, that you have been living in a fool's paradise, and that if fate had not put me on your track you would have died in ignorance?

BERGERAT: In ignorance of what?

GEORGES: Ah, how can I make myself understood? The minds of men are not ready to receive the truth, and I cannot reveal everything at once. [*Suddenly*] Look at this case. [*He takes the attaché case and puts it on* JULES'*s desk.*] Is there anything remarkable about it?

JULES: Nothing.

GEORGES: Pardon me, what is remarkable about it is that it is like all such cases.

NERCIAT: You would swear it was made in France.

GEORGES: It was *not* made in France. But you can get one like it at the Hotel de Ville market for three thousand five hundred francs.

LERMINIER [*amazed*]: Oh.

BERGERAT: Well I never!

GEORGES: Is there anything so terrible about this harmless object, *without any distinguishing mark*? It looks so ordinary that it becomes suspect for that very reason. Shielded from investigations and descriptions by its insignificance, its appearance instantly strikes one with horror, but one immediately forgets its form and even its colour. [*Pause.*] Do you know what they put in it? Fifteen pounds of radio-active powder. In each of your large towns a Communist is stationed with an attaché case just like this one. It may be a churchwarden, an inspector of finances, a teacher of dancing and deportment, or it may be an old maid who lives with her cats and her birds. The case lies in the attic, underneath other cases, amid trunks, old stoves and wicker baskets. Who would think of looking for it there? But on the appointed day the same code message will be delivered in every French town, and all the cases will be opened at the same time. You can guess the result – a hundred thousand deaths a day.

ALL [*in terror*]: Ah!

GEORGES: You see. [*He goes to open the case.*]

BERGERAT [*cries out*]: Don't open it.

GEORGES: Don't be afraid. It's empty. [*He opens it.*] Come closer. Look at the trade mark, see the handles, touch the leather . . .

[*The members of the Board come nearer, one by one, and timidly touch the case.*]

BERGERAT [*touching it*]: It's. It's true, by heavens.

LERMINIER [*also touching it*]: What a nightmare!

CHARIVET: The scoundrels!

NERCIAT: The scoundrels, the scoundrels, the scoundrels.

BERGERAT: Ah, how I hate them.

LERMINIER: All the same, we're not going to die like rats. What shall we do?

GEORGES: Have detection instruments made. We still have a few months. [*Pause.*] Do you understand? Are you convinced that it will be hard going, and that you risk losing all by punishing a few unimportant underlings?

CHARIVET: Give us their names, just the same.

LERMINIER: We promise you that their suspicions won't be aroused.

BERGERAT: But we want to know with whom we have to deal . . .

NERCIAT: And face the danger . . .

GEORGES: Very well. But you must follow my instructions to the letter. I have just thought of a way of rendering them harmless.

BERGERAT: What is it?

GEORGES: Raise their wages. [*Murmurs.*] Announce that you are delighted with their services, and that you are giving them a substantial rise.

BERGERAT: You think we can corrupt them?

GEORGES: No, not that. But you will bring them into disrepute in the eyes of their leaders. This inexplicable favour will make it appear that they have turned traitor.

LERMINIER: Are you sure?

GEORGES: It's obvious. Then you won't have to worry about them any more. The hand of Moscow will see that they are liquidated. [*He goes to the desk, sits down and points to seven names on the list.*]

NERCIAT: No, no, no. I won't give these scoundrels a rise.

LERMINIER: Take it easy, Nerciat.

BERGERAT: You've been told that it's in order to get rid of them more easily.

CHARIVET: We embrace them to strangle them.

NERCIAT: Very well, do as you please.

   [GEORGES *rises and holds out the list.*]

JULES [*reading*]: Samivel? It's not possible.

BERGERAT: Madame Castagnié? Who would have thought it?

GEORGES [*interrupting them with a gesture*]: This is nothing. I shall raise the curtain a little at a time, and you will see the world as it it. When you mistrust your own son, your wife, your father; when you look in the mirror and ask yourself whether you aren't a Communist without knowing it, then you are beginning to get a glimpse of the truth. [*He sits down at* JULES*'s desk and invites them to be seated.*] Be seated, gentlemen, and let's get to work. We haven't much time if we wish to save France.

CURTAIN

The drawing-room of a flat in the Avenue Georges V. Curtains and shutters closed. Three doors. One on the left leads to the bedroom, the second, at the back, to the bathroom, and the third, on the right, to the hall. Enormous bunches of flowers are heaped up in vases against the wall. Roses predominate.

[*A messenger enters carrying a bouquet of roses in a basket, followed by the two bodyguards who have their revolvers thrust into his back. He puts the basket down and hurries out backwards through the door on the right with his hands in the air. The door on the left opens, and* GEORGES *comes in, wearing his dressing-gown and yawning.*]

GEORGES: What is it?

FIRST BODYGUARD: Flowers.

GEORGES [*yawning and coming over to the flowers*]: More roses. Open the window.

FIRST BODYGUARD: No.

GEORGES: No?

FIRST BODYGUARD: Dangerous.

GEORGES: Aren't you aware that these roses stink?

FIRST BODYGUARD: No.

GEORGES: You're lucky. [*He takes the envelope and opens it.*] 'With the passionate admiration of a group of French women.' They admire me, eh?

FIRST BODYGUARD: Yes.

GEORGES: They love me?

FIRST BODYGUARD: Yes.

GEORGES: A little, a lot, passionately?

FIRST BODYGUARD: Passionately.

GEORGES: To love so much, they must hate like hell.

FIRST BODYGUARD: Hate whom?

GEORGES: The others. [*He bends over the flowers.*] Let us breathe the perfume of hate. [*He inhales.*] It is powerful, vague and foul. [*Pointing to the flowers*] There's the danger. [*The guards draw their revolvers and aim at the flowers.*] Don't shoot. It's a thousand-headed hydra. A thousand red angry little heads which throw out their odour and yell themselves hoarse before they die. These roses exhale poison.

SECOND BODYGUARD: Poison?

FIRST BODYGUARD [*to* SECOND BODYGUARD]: Toxicology laboratory, Gutenberg 66–21.

[SECOND BODYGUARD *goes towards the telephone.*]

GEORGES: Too late. Everything is poisoned here because I work in hatred.

FIRST BODYGUARD [*not understanding*]: Hatred?

GEORGES: Ah! It's an evil-smelling passion. But if you want to pull strings, you must pick them up wherever they may be, even from the dung-heap. I have them all in my hands. It is my day of glory, and long live hatred, since it is to hatred that I owe my power. Don't look at me like that. I am a poet. Are you employed to understand me or to protect me?

FIRST BODYGUARD: Protect.

GEORGES: Well then, protect, protect. What time is it?

FIRST BODYGUARD [*with a quick look at his wrist-watch*]: Half past five.

GEORGES: What's the weather like?

SECOND BODYGUARD [*goes to consult the barometer near the window*]: Set fair.

GEORGES: Temperature?

FIRST BODYGUARD [*goes to consult a thermometer, hanging on the wall*]: Seventy.

GEORGES: A fine spring afternoon. A clear sky, the sun flashing on the window panes. A peaceful crowd, dressed in light clothes, is walking up and down the Champs-Elysées, the afternoon sunlight softening their faces. Oh well, I'm glad to know it. [*He yawns.*] What's the time-table?

FIRST BODYGUARD [*consulting a list*]: Five-forty, Sibilot, for memoirs.

GEORGES: Next?

FIRST BODYGUARD: Six-thirty, a woman journalist from *Figaro*.

GEORGES: Search her carefully. You never know. Next?

FIRST BODYGUARD: A dance.

GEORGES: Where?

FIRST BODYGUARD: At Madame Bounoumi's.

GEORGES: *She's* giving a dance?

FIRST BODYGUARD: To celebrate the withdrawal of her rival, M. Perdrière.

GEORGES: I'll celebrate it. It's my doing. Away you go!

[*They go out.* GEORGES *closes the door and yawns.*]

GEORGES [*goes to the mirror, looks at himself and puts out his tongue*]: Disturbed sleep, coated tongue, loss of appetite – too many official banquets. And I'm hardly ever out of doors. [*He yawns.*] A touch of boredom. It's quite natural. One is always alone at the height of one's power. Little transparent men, I see into your hearts, but you can't see into mine. [*Telephone rings.*] Hallo? Speaking. I'm a rat? Ah, it's you, my dear sir; the man who thinks I'm a rat. This is the thirty-seventh time you've been good enough to tell me. Please understand that I'm now fully aware of your sentiments, and don't bother to tell me again. He's hung up. [*He starts to walk about.*] A rat. A traitor to the Party. It's easily said. *Who* is a rat? Not I, Georges de Valéra, who has never been a Communist, and betrayed anyone. Not Nekrassov, who is on a cure in the Crimea and thinking no harm. My unknown caller is thus talking rot. [*He goes towards the mirror.*] Oh, for my childhood! Oh, the pretty painted wooden sledge. My father would sit me on it. Off we go. Bells ringing, whips cracking, the snow . . .

[SIBILOT *has entered during this speech.*]

SIBILOT: What are you doing there?

GEORGES: Practising my scales.

SIBILOT: What scales?

GEORGES: I'm lying to myself.

SIBILOT: To yourself as well?

GEORGES: To myself first. I am much too cynical, and therefore

it is absolutely necessary that I fool myself first. Sibilot, I'm dying.
You find me in my death throes.

SIBILOT: Eh?

GEORGES: I die Valéra to be reborn Nekrassov.

SIBILOT: You are not Nekrassov!

GEORGES: I am he from head to toe, from maturity back to childhood.

SIBILOT: From head to toe you are a miserable crook, who is heading
for disaster and will drag me down with him unless I put things
right.

GEORGES: Ho! Ho! [*Looking at him.*] So you're cooking up some
stupid gesture of honesty which will put paid to us. Well, speak!
What do you want to do?

SIBILOT: Confess the truth!

GEORGES: Idiot! Everything was going so well.

SIBILOT: I made up my mind a little while ago, and I have come
to warn you. Tomorrow morning at eleven o'clock I shall throw
myself at Jules's feet and confess everything. You have seventeen
hours in which to prepare your escape.

GEORGES: Are you mad? Perdrière stands down, *Soir à Paris* has
doubled its circulation, you get 210,000 francs a month, and you
want to give yourself up?

SIBILOT: Yes!

GEORGES: Think of me, you wretch! I have supreme power, I
am the giddy peak of the Atlantic Pact, I hold war and peace
in my hands, I am writing history, Sibilot, I am writing history
and you choose this moment to throw a banana-skin in my path!
Do you know that I have dreamed of this moment all my life?
Take advantage of my power. You will be my Faust. Do you
want money? Beauty? Youth? . . .

SIBILOT [*shrugging his shoulders*]: Youth . . .

GEORGES: Why not? It's a question of money.

    [SIBILOT *goes to leave.*]

Where are you going?

SIBILOT: To give myself up.

GEORGES: You'll give yourself up, don't fear; you'll give yourself up. But there is no hurry. We have time for a chat. [*He brings* SIBILOT *back to the centre of the room.*] You're scared to death, my friend. What's wrong?

SIBILOT: Mouton will have your scalp, and mine too. He's joined up with Demidoff, a real Kravchenko, confirmed by Tass Agency, and he's looking for you. If they find you – and they're bound to – Demidoff will denounce you as a fraud. We'll be done for.

GEORGES: Is that all? Let them bring your Demidoff. I'll take care of him. I'll take them all on – industrialists and bankers, magistrates and ministers, American colonists, Soviet refugees, and I'll make them dance. Is that all?

SIBILOT: Oh, no! There's much worse!

GEORGES: So much the better. I shall enjoy myself.

SIBILOT: Nekrassov has just made a statement on the radio.

GEORGES: I have? I swear to you that I have done nothing of the kind.

SIBILOT: It's not a question of you. I said Nekrassov.

GEORGES: I'm Nekrassov.

SIBILOT: I am talking of the one in the Crimea.

GEORGES: Now why do you want to meddle? You are French, Sibilot. Keep your own doorstep clean, and don't concern yourself with what is happening in the Crimea.

SIBILOT: He claims he is cured, and that he will be back in Moscow towards the end of this week.

GEORGES: So?

SIBILOT: So! We're done for.

GEORGES: Done for? Because a Bolshevik spouts nonsense over the microphone? You, Sibilot, you, the champion of anti-communism, you put trust in those people? Really, I'm disappointed in you.

SIBILOT: You'll be less disappointed on Friday, when all the ambassadors and foreign journalists, invited to the Opera House in Moscow, see Nekrassov in person, in the government box.

GEORGES: On Friday . . .

SIBILOT: Yes.

GEORGES: It's been announced?

SIBILOT: Yes.

GEORGES: Well, they'll be seeing my double. For I have a double over there just like the other ministers. We're so afraid of attempts on our lives that we have doubles to take our places at official ceremonies. Now take that down. It's to be published tomorrow. Wait. I must give it just that amusing little touch of authenticity. I must invent the anecdote that couldn't be invented. Here it is. My double resembled me so much that we couldn't be told apart at ten paces. Unfortunately, when they brought him to me I noticed that he had a glass eye. Imagine my embarrassment! I had to spread the rumour that an incurable disease had destroyed my right eye. That's the origin of this patch. You will captain it, 'Nekrassov wears an eye-patch because his double had a glass eye.' Have you taken it down?

SIBILOT: What good will that do?

GEORGES [*with authority*]: Write!

[SIBILOT *shrugs his shoulders, takes out his pencil and writes some notes.*]

You'll conclude with this challenge. When the alleged Nekrassov takes his place in the Government box, let him take off his eye-patch if he dares. I shall take mine off at the same time in front of oculists and doctors. They will see that I have two perfectly good eyes. As for the other, if he has only one eye, we have the conclusive proof that this man is not me. Are you writing?

SIBILOT: I am writing, but it will do no good.

GEORGES: Why?

SIBILOT: Because I want to give myself up. I am honest, do you understand. Honest! honest! honest!

GEORGES: Who's said anything to the contrary?

SIBILOT: I have, I! I!

GEORGES: You?

SIBILOT: I, who tell myself a hundred times a day that I am a dishonest man! I lie, Georges, I lie as I breathe. I lie to my readers, to my own daughter and to my boss.

GEORGES: Didn't you lie, then, before you knew me?

SIBILOT: I lied, but I had the approval of my superiors. I manufactured lies that were controlled, that bore the official stamp, big news lies, lies in the public interest.

GEORGES: And aren't your present lies in the public interest? They're no different.

SIBILOT: Perhaps not, but I make them without Government guarantee. I am the only one on earth who knows who you are. That's what is suffocating me. My crime is not that I lie but that I'm alone in it.

GEORGES: Well, go on, then! What are you waiting for? Run and give yourself up!

    [SIBILOT *takes a step.*]

One simple question, one only, and I'll let you go. What are you going to tell Jules?

SIBILOT: All.

GEORGES: All what?

SIBILOT: You know very well.

GEORGES: But I don't . . .

SIBILOT: Well, I shall tell him that I have lied and that you are not *really* Nekrassov.

GEORGES: I don't understand.

SIBILOT: It's quite clear.

GEORGES: What do you mean, *really*?

    [SIBILOT *shrugs his shoulders.*]

Are you *really* Sibilot?

SIBILOT: Yes, I am Sibilot, yes. I am that unfortunate father whom you have corrupted, you wretch, and who is bringing shame upon his grey hairs.

GEORGES: Prove it.

SIBILOT: I have papers.

GEORGES: So have I.

SIBILOT: Mine are genuine.

GEORGES: So are mine. Do you want to see the alien's permit issued to me by the Prefecture of Police?

SIBILOT: It's worthless.

GEORGES: Why, if you please?

SIBILOT: Because you're not Nekrassov.

GEORGES: And are your papers valid?

SIBILOT: Yes.

GEORGES: Why?

SIBILOT: Because I am Sibilot.

GEORGES: You see. It's not the papers that prove identity.

SIBILOT: Well, no, it's not the papers.

GEORGES: Well, then? Prove to me that you are Sibilot.

SIBILOT: Everybody will tell you.

GEORGES: Everybody means how many people?

SIBILOT: A hundred, two hundred, I don't know, a thousand . . .

GEORGES: A thousand people take you for Sibilot, you would like
me to accept their word for it, and yet you challenge the evidence
of two million readers who take me for Nekrassov?

SIBILOT: It's not the same . . .

GEORGES: Are you trying to silence this tremendous clamour
which makes me the hero of freedom and the champion of the
West? Do you set your miserable individual conviction against the
collective faith which is stirring those good citizens? It's you whose
identity is not even established. It is you who are heedlessly going
to drive two million men and women to despair. Courage! Ruin
your boss! Go even further! Bring about the downfall of the
government. I know who'll get the biggest laugh out of it.

SIBILOT: Who?

GEORGES: The Communists, of course. Would you work for them?

SIBILOT [anxiously]: Look here, Georges!

GEORGES: You would not be the first one they've paid to demoralize
public opinion.

SIBILOT: I swear to you.

GEORGES: How do you expect me to believe you; you who have
just confessed your profound dishonesty?

SIBILOT [in a panic]: You must believe me. I am a dishonest honest
man, but I am not a dishonest man.

GEORGES: Agreed. But then . . . then . . . Ho, ho! What's happening to you? My poor friend, I wonder if I will be able to get you out of this.

SIBILOT: What is it now?

GEORGES: How can I make you understand? Listen! Put on one side forty million Frenchmen, our contemporaries, sure that they are living right in the middle of the twentieth century, and on the other side one individual, a single one, who obstinately declares that he is the Emperor Charles the Fifth. What would you call that man?

SIBILOT: A lunatic.

GEORGES: And that is exactly what you are; you who are trying to deny the truths founded on universal assent.

SIBILOT: Georges!

GEORGES: Do you know what Jules will do to you when he sees his oldest employee throw himself on his knees and beg him to bury his newspaper with his own hands?

SIBILOT: He'll fire me.

GEORGES: Will he? Nothing of the kind. He'll have you locked up.

SIBILOT [*utterly crushed*]: Oh!

GEORGES: Here, read this telegram. It's from McCarthy, offering me an engagement as a permanent witness. Here are congratulations from Franco, from the Fruit Company, a cordial word from Adenauer, a letter signed by Senator Borgeaud. In New York my revelations have sent shares up on the Stock Exchange. There is a boom everywhere in the war industries. There are great interests at stake. Nekrassov is no longer only me. It is a generic term for the dividends drawn by the shareholders in armament factories. That's objectivity, old chap. There's reality for you. But it will crush you if you try to stop it. Good-bye, my poor chap. I was very fond of you.

    [SIBILOT *does not budge.*]

What are you waiting for?

SIBILOT [*in a choked voice*]: Can I be cured?

GEORGES: Of your madness?

SIBILOT: Yes.

GEORGES: I hope it's not too late.

SIBILOT: But if you were to undertake to cure me, Georges? If you'd be good enough to do it?

GEORGES: Eh! I am not a psychiatrist. [*Pause.*] It's true, it is mainly a question of re-education. Do you wish me to re-educate you?

SIBILOT: Please.

GEORGES: Let us begin. Assume an attitude of honesty.

SIBILOT: I don't know how.

GEORGES: Sink down deeply into this armchair. Put your feet on this pouf. Put this rose in your buttonhole. Take this cigar. [*He hands a mirror to* SIBILOT.]

SIBILOT [*looking at himself*]: Well?

GEORGES: Do you feel more honest now?

SIBILOT: Perhaps a little more.

GEORGES: Good. Leave aside your personal convictions, and tell yourself that they are false because no one shares them. They exile you. Rejoin the flock. Remember that you are a good Frenchman. Look at me with the countless eyes of the Frenchmen who read us. Whom do you see?

SIBILOT: Nekrassov.

GEORGES: Now I shall go out and come in again. Put yourself in a state of sincerity. Collective sincerity, of course. When I open the door, you will say to me: 'Good afternoon, Nikita . . .'

[*He goes out.* SIBILOT *settles down, drinks and smokes.* GEORGES *returns.*]

SIBILOT: Good afternoon, Nikita.

GEORGES: Good afternoon, Sibilot.

SIBILOT: Did I say it well?

GEORGES: Not too bad. [*He walks round* SIBILOT'*s armchair, suddenly bends over him and puts his hands over* SIBILOT'*s eyes.*] Cuckoo!

SIBILOT: Leave me alone . . . Nikita!

GEORGES: You're improving. Get up.

[SIBILOT *gets up with his back to* GEORGES. GEORGES *tickles him.*]

SIBILOT [*wriggling and laughing in spite of himself*]: Stop it . . . Nikita.

GEORGES: I'll cure you all right. [*Pause.*] Enough for today. To work. Chapter eight: 'Tragic interview with Stalin.'

SIBILOT [*writing*]: 'Tragic interview with Stalin.'

[*The telephone rings.*]

GEORGES [*lifting the receiver*]: Hallo! Yes? Madame Castagnié? Just a moment.

[*Turning to* SIBILOT.]

I seem to know that name.

SIBILOT: She's a typist at *Soir à Paris*.

GEORGES: Ah! One of the seven they wanted to sack and that I got a rise for? What does she want with me?

SIBILOT: Jules must have sent her!

GEORGES [*into the telephone*]: Send her up. [*Turning to* SIBILOT *after putting the receiver down.*] 'Tragic Interview with Stalin.' Sub-heading: 'I escape from the Kremlin in a sedan chair.'

SIBILOT: Nikita! Is that possible?

GEORGES: Nothing more natural. I am being chased. I hide in one of the rooms of the museum where the carriages are kept. In a corner is a sedan chair . . .

A BODYGUARD: Madame Castagnié.

GEORGES: Show her in. And don't frighten her with your revolvers.

[*Enter* MME CASTAGNIÉ.]

SIBILOT [*going towards her*]: Good afternoon, Mme Castagnié.

MME CASTAGNIÉ: Good afternoon, M. Sibilot. I didn't expect to find you here. [*Pointing to* GEORGES.] Is he Nekrassov?

SIBILOT: That's him. That's our Nikita.

GEORGES: My compliments, madam.

MME CASTAGNIÉ: I would like to know why you had me dismissed.

GEORGES: What?

SIBILOT: You've been dismissed?

MME CASTAGNIÉ [*to* GEORGES]: You know very well I have, sir. Don't pretend to be surprised.

GEORGES: I swear to you . . .

MME CASTAGNIÉ: M. Palotin sent for me just now. The directors were there, and they didn't look at all pleased.

GEORGES: What happened?

MME CASTAGNIÉ: What happened? They dismissed me.

GEORGES: But why? For what reason?

MME CASTAGNIÉ: When I asked them their reason, I thought they would jump down my throat. They all shouted in my face: 'Ask Nekrassov! Nekrassov will tell you.'

GEORGES: Swine! The swine!

MME CASTAGNIÉ: I don't wish to be rude, but if you have given them bad reports about me, you are an even bigger swine than they are.

GEORGES: But I haven't said anything! I haven't done anything! I don't even know you.

MME CASTAGNIÉ: They told me to ask you so you must know something.

GEORGES: Madam, have you ever seen me before today?

MME CASTAGNIÉ: Never.

GEORGES: There you are, then.

MME CASTAGNIÉ: What does that prove? Perhaps you wanted my job.

GEORGES: What would I do with it? That's a joke, madam, and a joke in bad taste.

MME CASTAGNIÉ: I am a widow with a sick daughter. If I lose my job we shall be unable to live. That is nothing to joke about.

GEORGES: You are right. [*Turning to* SIBILOT] The swine!

MME CASTAGNIÉ: What have you got against me?

GEORGES: Nothing. On the contrary, Sibilot is my witness that I wanted to get you a rise.

MME CASTAGNIÉ: Get me a rise?

GEORGES: Yes.

MME CASTAGNIÉ: You're a liar. Just now you said you didn't know me!

GEORGES: I know you slightly. I know the loyal service you've given for more than twenty years . . .

MME CASTAGNIÉ: I've only been there for five years.

T – T.P. – H

GEORGES: I'll admit everything to you. Important political reasons . . .

MME CASTAGNIÉ: I've never meddled in politics. And my poor husband wouldn't even hear of it. I'm not well educated, sir, but I'm not a complete fool, and I'm not taken in by your fancy talk.

GEORGES [lifting up the receiver]: Give me Soir à Paris. [To MME CASTAGNIÉ] It's a misunderstanding! Just a misunderstanding! [Into the telephone] Hullo, Soir à Paris? I want to talk to the editor. Yes. Nekrassov speaking. [To MME CASTAGNIÉ] You'll get your job back. I'll see to that. And with apologies.

MME CASTAGNIÉ: I don't want apologies. I want my job back.

GEORGES: Hullo? He's not in his office? Is he in the building? Where? Right. Tell him to ring me up as soon as he gets back. [He puts the receiver down.] Everything will be all right, madam, everything will be all right. In the meantime, will you allow me . . . [Taking out his wallet.]

MME CASTAGNIÉ: I don't want charity.

GEORGES: What do you mean? It's not a question of charity, but a friendly gift . . .

MME CASTAGNIÉ: You're no friend of mine.

GEORGES: Not now. But I shall be when you've got your job back. You'll see! You'll see! [Suddenly remembering] Oh! [Pause.] What about the others?

MME CASTAGNIÉ: The others?

GEORGES: Do you know if anyone else has been dismissed?

MME CASTAGNIÉ: So I heard.

GEORGES: Who? How many?

MME CASTAGNIÉ: I don't know. They gave me my notice. I took my things and left.

GEORGES [turning to SIBILOT]: You'll see, they'll have sacked them too. The dirty swine! The bunglers! I thought I had frightened them. Well, Sibilot, old chap, there's a lesson for you. Fear is less powerful than hate. [He picks up his hat.] I must put an end to this nonsense. Come with us, madam. As if I would attack the poor!

It would be the first time in my life. I'm going to take Jules by the throat . . . [*He opens the door. A bodyguard appears.*]

THE BODYGUARD: No!

GEORGES: What do you mean, no! I want to go out.

BODYGUARD: Impossible! It's dangerous!

GEORGES: All right, you come with us.

BODYGUARD: Not allowed.

GEORGES: And suppose I try to get out?

BODYGUARD [*with a short derisive laugh*]: Ha!

GEORGES: Oh! go away. I shan't go out. [*To* SIBILOT] Go with Mme Castagnié, find Jules and tell him that I think this is beyond a joke. Unless all those who have been dismissed are reinstated within twenty-four hours, I shall give the rest of my memoirs to *Figaro*. Please go, madam, I may have wronged you, but it was unintentional, and I give you my word that you will be compensated for it.

    [SIBILOT *and* MME CASTAGNIÉ *go out.*]

Aren't you going to say good-bye to me, Sibilot?

SIBILOT: Good-bye.

GEORGES: Good-bye, whom?

SIBILOT: Good-bye, Nikita.

GEORGES: Ring me as soon as you've seen Jules. Sacked . . . [*He starts walking up and down.*] It's not my fault. Hatred is an emotion which is completely foreign to me. I am obliged to play with terrible forces, of which I know little. But I'll adapt myself, I'll . . . Sacked! . . . And they only had their wages to live on. They may have saved twenty thousand francs . . . I'll shower them with gold. The Board of Directors will meet them at the door with roses, with armfuls of roses . . .

A BODYGUARD [*entering*]: The woman journalist from *Figaro*.

GEORGES: Show her in! Wait, is she pretty?

BODYGUARD: Not bad.

    [GEORGES *goes over to the mirror, puts on his black patch, looks at himself for a moment, takes it off, and puts it in his pocket.*]

GEORGES: Tell her to come in.

[VERONIQUE *comes in.*]

GEORGES [*seeing* VERONIQUE]: Ah! [*He puts up his hands.*]

VERONIQUE: I see you recognize me.

GEORGES [*lowering his hands*]: Yes. Are you on *Figaro* now?

VERONIQUE: Yes.

GEORGES: I thought you were with the Communists.

VERONIQUE: Things change. Where's Nekrassov?

GEORGES: He's . . . he's gone out.

VERONIQUE: I'll wait for him. [*She sits down.*] Are you waiting for him, too?

GEORGES: Me? No.

VERONIQUE: What are you doing here?

GEORGES: Oh, you know, I never do very much. [*Pause.*] [*He gets up.*] I'm beginning to think Nekrassov won't come back this evening. You would do better to call again tomorrow.

VERONIQUE: All right.

[GEORGES *seems relieved. She pulls a notebook out of her bag.*]

But while I have you here, you can tell me what you know about him.

GEORGES: I don't know anything.

VERONIQUE: Go on with you! You must be a close friend of his, or his bodyguards wouldn't leave you in his room while he's out.

GEORGES [*disconcerted*]: A close friend of his? Of course, it's . . . it's quite natural. [*Pause.*] I'm his cousin.

VERONIQUE: Ah, ah!

GEORGES: My mother's sister remained in Russia. Nekrassov is her son. The other morning I found a newspaper on a bench. I picked it up and saw that my cousin had just arrived . . .

VERONIQUE: You managed to contact him, you talked to him about the family, he welcomed you with open arms . . .

GEORGES: And took me on as his secretary.

VERONIQUE: Secretary! Pah!

GEORGES: Wait a minute. I became his secretary for a lark. Within a fortnight I'll make off with the cash.

VERONIQUE: In the meantime you are helping with his filthy work.

GEORGES: Filthy work! Look here, sister, you don't come from *Figaro*.

VERONIQUE: Of course not!

GEORGES: You've lied again.

VERONIQUE: Yes.

GEORGES: Did your progressive paper send you?

VERONIQUE: No. I came on my own. [*Pause.*] Well, tell me about him. What does he do when you're together.

GEORGES: He drinks.

VERONIQUE: What does he say?

GEORGES: He says nothing.

VERONIQUE: Nothing?

GEORGES: Nothing.

VERONIQUE: Does he never talk about his wife? Or the three sons he left over there?

GEORGES: Leave me alone! [*Pause.*] He took me into his confidence, and I don't want to betray him.

VERONIQUE: You don't want to betray him, and yet you're going to rob him.

GEORGES: I'm going to rob him, but that doesn't prevent me from having my feelings. I've always had a liking for my victims. My professions demands it. How can I rob people without being pleasant, and how can I be pleasant to them unless I like them? All my affairs have started off with my victim and I taking a sudden fancy to each other.

VERONIQUE: And you took a sudden fancy to Nekrassov?

GEORGES: Oh, only a very small one.

VERONIQUE: To that skunk?

GEORGES: I forbid you to . . .

VERONIQUE: Are you defending him?

GEORGES: I am not defending him. I am shocked to hear you say such a word.

VERONIQUE: Isn't he a skunk?

GEORGES: Perhaps he is. But you have no right to condemn a man you don't even know.

VERONIQUE: I know him very well.

GEORGES: You know him?

VERONIQUE [*quietly*]: Naturally! Since it's you.

GEORGES [*repeating, without understanding*]: Ah! Since it's me. [*Jumping to his feet.*] It's not me! It's not me! It's not me! [*She looks at him, smiling.*] Where did you get that idea?

VERONIQUE: My father . . .

GEORGES: He told you?

VERONIQUE: No.

GEORGES: Well?

VERONIQUE: Like all those whose speciality is lying in public, he lies very badly in private.

GEORGES: Your father's in his dotage! [*He walks across the room.*] Well! Suppose for a moment, just to please you, that I were Nekrassov.

VERONIQUE: Thank you.

GEORGES: What would you do if I were? Give me away to the cops?

VERONIQUE: Did I give you away the other evening?

GEORGES: Would you publish my real name in your rag?

VERONIQUE: That would be a blunder at this stage. We lack proof, and no one would believe us.

GEORGES [*reassured*]: In fact, I have rendered my enemies powerless?

VERONIQUE: For the moment, yes, we are powerless.

GEORGES [*laughing*]: Left, right, centre, I have you all in my hands. You must be bursting with anger, my beauty! Secret for secret. Yes, I am Nekrassov. Do you remember the miserable tramp you took into your room? What a long way I have come since! What a dizzy leap! [*He stops, and looks at her.*] Come, now, what are you really doing here?

VERONIQUE: I came here to tell you that you're a skunk.

GEORGES: Drop the fine words; I am proof against them. Every morning *l'Humanité* calls me a slimy rat.

VERONIQUE: They are wrong.

GEORGES: I'm glad to hear you say so.

VERONIQUE: You're not a slimy rat. You're a skunk.

GEORGES: Oh, you get on my nerves. [*He takes a few steps and comes back to* VERONIQUE.] Now, if a high Soviet official were to come to Paris with the express purpose of giving weapons to the enemies of his people and his Party, then I agree that he would be a skunk. I would go even further; he'd be a dirty louse. But I've never been a Minister nor a member of the C.P. I was six months old when I left the Soviet Union, and my father was a White Russian. I am under no obligation to anyone. When you knew me, I was a smart crook, working alone; a self-made man. Well, I still am. Yesterday I was selling bogus properties and bogus titles, and today I am selling bogus gen on Russia. Where's the difference? [*She doesn't reply.*] You're not particularly fond of the rich. Is it such a great crime to cheat them?

VERONIQUE: Do you really think you are cheating the rich?

GEORGES: Who's paying my tailor and my hotel bills? Who paid for my Jaguar?

VERONIQUE: Why are they paying?

GEORGES: Because I sell them my concoctions.

VERONIQUE: Why are they buying them?

GEORGES: Because ... Damn it all! That's their business. I don't know.

VERONIQUE: They're buying them in order to palm them off on the poor.

GEORGES: The poor? What have the poor got to do with it?

VERONIQUE: Do you think that the readers of *Soir à Paris* are millionaires? [*Taking a paper from her bag.*] 'Nekrassov states that the Russian worker is the most wretched on earth.' Did you say that?

GEORGES: Yes. Yesterday.

VERONIQUE: For whom did you say it? For the poor or for the rich?

GEORGES: How should I know? For everybody. For nobody. It's a joke of no importance.

VERONIQUE: Here, yes, among the roses. In any case no one in the Avenue Georges V has ever seen any workers. But do you know what that will mean in Billancourt?

GEORGES: I . . .

VERONIQUE: 'Leave capitalism alone, or you will relapse into barbarism. The bourgeois world has its defects but it is the best of all possible worlds. Whatever your poverty, try to make the best of it, for you can be sure you'll never see anything better, and thank heaven that you weren't born in the Soviet Union.'

GEORGES: Don't tell me they think that. They're not so stupid.

VERONIQUE: Luckily they aren't, or they would have no alternative but to drink themselves to death or put their heads in the gas-oven. But even if one in a thousand swallowed your clap-trap, you would be a murderer. You've been well taken in, my poor Georges.

GEORGES: Me?

VERONIQUE: Of course. You thought you were stealing money from the rich, but you are earning it. With what disdain, the other night, you refused the job I offered you: 'Me, work!' Well, you have employers now, and they're making you work hard.

GEORGES: It isn't true.

VERONIQUE: Come, come. You know very well you are being paid to drive the poor to despair.

GEORGES: Listen!

VERONIQUE [taking no notice]: You were an innocent crook with no malice – half dandy, half poet. Do you know what they've made of you? A muck-raker! You will either come to despise yourself or you will have to become vicious.

GEORGES [under his breath]: The rotten swine!

VERONIQUE: Who is pulling the strings this time?

GEORGES: The strings?

VERONIQUE: Yes.

GEORGES: Well . . . [Mastering himself] I am, as usual.

VERONIQUE: So you are setting our deliberately to drive the poor to despair.

GEORGES: No.

VERONIQUE: Then, they're making use of you?

GEORGES: Nobody can make use of me – no one in the world.

VERONIQUE: Nevertheless, you must make the choice; you are either a dupe or a criminal.

GEORGES: The choice is quickly made. Long live crime!

VERONIQUE: Georges!

GEORGES: I drive the poor to despair? So what? Everybody for himself. Let them defend themselves. I slander the Soviet Union? I do it on purpose. I want to destroy Communism in the West. As for your workers, whether they're in Billancourt or in Moscow, I . . .

VERONIQUE: You see, Georges, you see, you're becoming vicious.

GEORGES: Vicious or good, I don't care. Good and evil, I take it all upon myself. I am responsible for everything.

VERONIQUE [*showing him an article in* Soir à Paris]: Even for this article?

GEORGES: Of course! What's it about? [*Reading*] 'M. Nekrassov states that he is well acquainted with Robert Duval and Charles Maistre.' I've never said any such thing.

VERONIQUE: I thought not. As a matter of fact, that's why I came to see you.

GEORGES: Robert Duval? Charles Maistre? Never heard the names.

VERONIQUE: They're journalists on our paper. They have written against German rearmament.

GEORGES: Well?

VERONIQUE: You are expected to say that the Soviet Union paid them.

GEORGES: And if I do?

VERONIQUE: They will be committed to a military court on a charge of treason.

GEORGES: Don't worry. They won't get a word out of me. Do you believe me?

VERONIQUE: I believe you, but take care. They are no longer satisfied with your lies. They're beginning to make them up for you.

GEORGES: You mean that paragraph? That's some over-zealous

subordinate. I'll have him put in his place. I'm seeing Jules very shortly, and I'll order him to publish a denial.

VERONIQUE [*without conviction*]: Do what you can.

GEORGES: Is that all you have to tell me?

VERONIQUE: That's all.

GEORGES: Good night.

VERONIQUE: Good night. [*With her hand on the door-knob*] I hope you won't become too vicious. [*She goes out.*]

GEORGES [*to himself*]: That girl doesn't understand politics. A school-kid, that's what she is! [*Addressing the door*] Did you think I'd fall into your trap? I always do the opposite of what I'm expected to do. [*He crosses the room and goes to find his dinner jacket.*] We'll drive Billancourt to despair! I'll think up some terrible slogans. [*He goes to fetch a shirt and collar. He chants.*] Drive Billancourt to despair! Drive Billancourt to despair!

[*The telephone rings. He picks up the receiver.*]

Oh, it's you, Sibilot? Well? What? No, that's not possible. You've seen Jules himself? You told him that I insisted? Idiot! You didn't know how to speak to him. You're frightened of him. You ought to have brow-beaten him. He's going to old Mother Bounoumi's tonight? Good. I'll speak to him myself. [*He hangs up.*] They refuse me something! Me? [*He sinks into an armchair, temporarily over-whelmed.*] I've had a basinful of politics. A basinful! [*He gets up suddenly.*] They're after me. They're after me. Well, I have the feeling they are going to meet up with me. I accept the challenge. Indeed, I welcome it. It's time I exerted my authority. [*Laughing*] I'll send them scuttling underground.

[*Telephone. He picks up the receiver.*]

Hallo! You again! Excuse me, but who are you? Ah! Splendid! I was just thinking of you. A rat? Quite right, my dear sir. The low-est of rats. I go even further – a skunk. I get minor employees sacked. I hand journalists over to the cops. I drive the poor to despair, and that's only a beginning. My coming revelations will provoke a string of suicides. Now you, of course, you are an honest man. I can see that from here. Your clothes are worn, you take the

Metro four times a day, you smell of poverty. The deserving are not rewarded. I have money, glory, women. If you meet me when I am in my Jaguar, look out! I purposely graze the pavements to splash honest people. [*He hangs up.*] This time I was the one who hung up first. [*He laughs.*] She was right, that girl, and I'm going to become vicious. [*Kicking the rose-baskets over one by one.*] Vicious, vicious, vicious!

CURTAIN

*A small drawing-room being used as a buffet, and opening by means of
double doors on to a large room at the back. To the left is a window half open
to the night. Between the window and the doors there are tables covered with
white linen and laid with platters of petits fours and sandwiches. Through
the doors at the back, guests can be seen passing backwards and forwards.
There is a crowd in the large room. Some pass across the open doorway
without entering the small drawing-room, while others come and help
themselves at the buffet-bar. To the right is a closed door. There is very
little furniture apart from a few armchairs and tables, the room having been
cleared so that the guests can circulate freely. Baudouin and Chapuis enter
and introduce themselves to Mme Bounoumi.*

BAUDOUIN [*stopping* MME BOUNOUMI *and introducing* CHAPUIS *to
    her*]: Chapuis.
CHAPUIS [*introducing* BAUDOUIN]: Baudouin.
    [BAUDOUIN *and* CHAPUIS *take out their cards and present them to
    her simultaneously.*]
BAUDOUIN and CHAPUIS: Inspectors from the Department of
    Defence of the State.
BAUDOUIN: Specially entrusted by the Government . . .
CHAPUIS: To protect Nekrassov.
BAUDOUIN: Has he arrived?
MME BOUNOUMI: Not yet.
CHAPUIS: It would be unwise to bring him in through the front
    door.
BAUDOUIN: And, if you will allow us, we will give orders . . .
CHAPUIS: That he should come in through the servants' entrance . . .
BAUDOUIN [*pointing to the door on right*]: Which leads directly here.
MME BOUNOUMI: Why all these precautions?
CHAPUIS [*confidentially*]: The possibility of an attack cannot be ruled
    out.

MME BOUNOUMI [*taken aback*]: Ah!

BAUDOUIN: Don't be afraid, madam.

CHAPUIS: We are here!

BAUDOUIN: We are here!

[*They go out. Guests enter, among them* PERDRIÈRE, JULES *and* NERCIAT.]

NERCIAT [*putting his arm around* PERDRIÈRE]: Here is the prodigal son. I drink to Perdrière.

ALL: To Perdrière.

PERDRIÈRE: Ladies and gentlemen, I was an old fool. I drink to the man sent by Providence to strip the wool from my eyes.

JULES [*smiling*]: Thank you.

PERDRIÈRE [*not hearing him*]: To Nekrassov!

ALL: To Nekrassov!

JULES [*annoyed, to* NERCIAT]: Nekrassov! [*Shrugging his shoulders*] What would he be without me? [*He moves away.*]

NERCIAT [*to* PERDRIÈRE]: Say something about Palotin.

PERDRIÈRE: I drink to Palotin who ... who had the courage to publish Nekrassov's revelations.

SOME OF THE GUESTS: To Palotin.

JULES [*annoyed*]: People don't understand the power of the press.

PERDRIÈRE: I want to take this opportunity to ask you all to forgive my obstinacy, my stupid blindness, my ... [*He starts to cry. They surround him.*]

MME BOUNOUMI: My good Perdrière ...

PERDRIÈRE [*trying to gain control of himself*]: I ask you to forgive me! I ask you to forgive me ...

MME BOUNOUMI: Let's forget the past. [*She embraces him.*]

JULES [*to the* PHOTOGRAPHERS]: Photos!

[PERIGORD *is passing with a glass in his hand.* JULES *seizes him by the arm, spilling the contents of the glass.*]

Here!

PERIGORD: The idea, chief?

JULES: Yes, the idea. Take down everything I say. [*To* ALL] Friends

... [*They fall silent.*] You, I, Perdrière, all of us here, are future victims of the firing squad. I suggest that we transform this already memorable evening into a great moment in the tide of human affairs. Let us form the FFSV Club.

ALL: Bravo! Long live the FFSV.

JULES: During the evening we shall elect a provisional committee to draw up the constitution. I propose myself as president. [*Applause. To* PERIGORD] Front page tomorrow, with my picture.

[*Enter* MOUTON *and* DEMIDOFF.]

What's this? Mouton? [*He goes over to* NERCIAT *and* MME BOUN-OUMI.] Did you see?

MME BOUNOUMI: Oh!

NERCIAT: Who invited him?

MME BOUNOUMI: I didn't. Who's that with him?

JULES: Demidoff.

NERCIAT: That Russian? They have a nerve.

MME BOUNOUMI: My God! The attack!

NERCIAT: What?

MME BOUNOUMI: The possibility of an attack cannot be ruled out.

NERCIAT: They've come to ...

MME BOUNOUMI: I don't know, but I have two inspectors here, and I am going to warn them.

[*During this conversation,* MOUTON *has come forward among the guests. He smiles or holds out his hand to each in turn, but they all turn their backs on him. He bows to* MME BOUNOUMI.]

MOUTON: Madam ...

MME BOUNOUMI: No, sir. No! *We* are all going to die. We wish you a long life, but we do not acknowledge you.

THE GUESTS [*going out*]: Long live the FFSV! [*Turning to* MOUTON] Down with the future executioners! [*They go out.*]

[MOUTON *and* DEMIDOFF *are left alone.* DEMIDOFF *goes to the buffet and helps himself liberally.*]

MOUTON: Rather a chilly reception.

DEMIDOFF [*eating*]: I didn't notice.

MOUTON: You never notice anything.

DEMIDOFF: Never! I am here to expose the Soviet régime, and not to observe the customs of the West. [*He eats and drinks.*]

MOUTON: They take me for a Communist.

DEMIDOFF: That's strange.

MOUTON: No, it isn't strange. It's tragic, but it's not strange. You have to put yourself in their place. [*Suddenly*] Feodor Petrovitch!

DEMIDOFF: What?

MOUTON: That list is false, isn't it?

DEMIDOFF: What list?

MOUTON: The list of Future Firing Squad Victims . . .

DEMIDOFF: I know nothing about it.

MOUTON [*startled*]: What?

DEMIDOFF: I shall know when I've seen Nekrassov.

MOUTON: Then it could be true?

DEMIDOFF: Yes, if Nekrassov is really Nekrassov.

MOUTON: I should be lost.

    [DEMIDOFF *shrugs his shoulders.*]

What a position! If the Russians spare me, it must be because I
- am useful to them.

DEMIDOFF: Obviously.

MOUTON: But that's absurd! Feodor Petrovitch, you can't possibly believe . . .

DEMIDOFF: I believe nothing.

MOUTON: My life speaks for me. I have done nothing but fight them.

DEMIDOFF: How do you know?

MOUTON [*shaken*]: Ah! How do I know? To be quite frank, sometimes I feel I am being manoeuvred. I can recall some disturbing things. [*Pause.*] My secretary was a Communist. As soon as I found out, I dismissed him.

DEMIDOFF: Was there a scandal?

MOUTON: Yes.

DEMIDOFF: You played their game.

MOUTON: Do you think so, too? I didn't dare admit it to myself. [*Pause.*] During the last strikes, I was the only one in my industry who granted nothing to the strikers. Result: three months later, in the trade union elections . . .

DEMIDOFF: All your workers voted for the CGT.

MOUTON: How do you know?

DEMIDOFF: It's the usual thing.

MOUTON: In fact, I gave them recruits.

[DEMIDOFF *nods in agreement.*]

Alas! [*Pause.*] Feodor Petrovitch, look at me! Have I the face of an honest man?

DEMIDOFF: Of an honest Westerner.

MOUTON: But a fine-looking old man?

DEMIDOFF: An old Westerner.

MOUTON: Could I be a Communist with a face like this?

DEMIDOFF: Why not?

MOUTON: I built myself up with my own hands, by my own work.

DEMIDOFF: By luck, also.

MOUTON [*smiling slightly at his memories*]: Yes, I have had some luck.

DEMIDOFF: They were behind your luck.

MOUTON [*with a start*]: They?

DEMIDOFF: It is possible that they made your fortune because you were their tool without knowing it. Perhaps they arranged everything in such a way that, unknown to you, your every action produced the effect desired by Moscow.

MOUTON: Does that mean that my whole life has been nothing but a sham?

[DEMIDOFF *nods agreement. Suddenly*]

Tell me frankly; if everyone takes me for a revolutionary, and if all my actions are those required by the Party, what distinguishes me from an active Party member?

DEMIDOFF: You? Nothing. You are an *objective* Communist.

MOUTON: Objective! Objective! [*He takes out his handkerchief and wipes his forehead.*] Ah! I am possessed! [*Suddenly looking at the handkerchief.*] What this? The two of us are talking and I find myself waving a handkerchief. How did it get into my hand?

DEMIDOFF: You took it out of your pocket.

MOUTON [*distraught*]: I did . . . Oh, it is worse than I thought. They have arranged for me to give the signal. What signal? To whom? To you, perhaps? How do I know that you aren't one of their agents? [DEMIDOFF *shrugs his shoulders.*] You see, I am going mad. Feodor Petrovitch, I beseech you, decommunize me!

DEMIDOFF: How?

MOUTON: Expose that blackguard!

DEMIDOFF: I will expose him if he is an impostor.

MOUTON [*seized with anxiety again*]: And suppose he really is Nekrassov?

DEMIDOFF: I shall brand him before everyone.

MOUTON [*with a start.*]: Brand him . . .

DEMIDOFF: I contend that all those who left the Soviet Union after I did are accomplices of the régime.

[GOBLET *appears in the background.*]

MOUTON: It would be best to treat him as an impostor, in any case.

DEMIDOFF: No. [*At a gesture from* MOUTON.] Say no more. I am incorruptible.

[MOUTON *sighs.*]

Well! What are you waiting for? Let's find him.

MOUTON: I have called in an inspector of the Sûreté. If the so-called Nekrassov is an impostor, he must be an international crook. I will have him imprisoned for life. [*Seeing* GOBLET.] Ah, Goblet! Come in.

[GOBLET *approaches.*]

Look very carefully at the man I shall point out to you. If he is an habitual criminal, arrest him on the spot.

GOBLET: In front of everyone?

MOUTON: Naturally.

GOBLET: Is he handsome?

MOUTON: Not bad.

GOBLET [*sadly*]: People will again see the contrast.

MOUTON: What contrast?

GOBLET: Between his face and mine.

MOUTON: You refuse . . .

GOBLET: I don't refuse at all. Only I prefer to arrest them when they are ugly, that's all.

[BAUDOUIN *and* CHAPUIS *enter*.]

BAUDOUIN [*showing his card to* MOUTON]: Defence of the State. Your papers?

MOUTON: I am Charles Mouton . . .

CHAPUIS: Exactly! A suspect.

[MOUTON *shrugs his shoulders and shows his identity card*.]

BAUDOUIN: Good. [*To* DEMIDOFF] We know you. Off with you, and don't forget that you are a guest of France.

CHAPUIS: Make yourselves scarce. We want to have a word with Inspector Goblet.

MOUTON [*to* GOBLET]: We're going to have a look around to see if our man has arrived. Wait for us here.

[DEMIDOFF *and* MOUTON *go out*.]

BAUDOUIN [*barring* GOBLET's *exit*]: And what are *you* up to here?

GOBLET: I'm a guest.

CHAPUIS: A guest? With a mug like yours?

GOBLET: If you're guests with your mugs, why shouldn't I be with mine?

CHAPUIS: We're not guests. We're here on duty.

GOBLET: Well, so am I!

BAUDOUIN: Would you be looking for someone?

GOBLET: That's none of your business.

CHAPUIS: But look here, friend . . .

BAUDOUIN: Leave him alone; he's a close one. [*To* GOBLET] Look for anyone you like, but don't get in our way.

GOBLET [*bewildered*]: In your way?

CHAPUIS: Lay off Nekrassov!

GOBLET [*bewildered*]: Eh?

BAUDOUIN: Lay off him, pal, if you value your job.

GOBLET [*still trying to understand*]: Nekrassov?

CHAPUIS: Yes, Nekrassov. Don't touch him!

GOBLET: I don't take orders from you. I'm from the crime section, and I take my orders from my superiors.

CHAPUIS: That may be so, but your superiors take their orders from ours. Good night, pal.

BAUDOUIN [*smiling*]: Good night. Good night.

[BAUDOUIN *and* CHAPUIS *go out.*]

GOBLET [*under his breath*]: Go to hell! [*Thinking*] Nekrassov! I've seen that name in the papers ...

[*Enter* GEORGES, SIBILOT *and the two* BODYGUARDS.]

GEORGES [*to the two* BODYGUARDS]: Go and play. [*He shuts the door on them. To* SIBILOT] Stand up straight! For God's sake look as if you're somebody! [*He ruffles his hair.*] Take it easy! There!

SIBILOT: Let's go in.

[GEORGES *holds him back.*]

What's the matter with you?

GEORGES: I feel dizzy. I shall go in. They will throw themselves at my feet. They will kiss my hands. It makes my head swim. How can one man be the object of so much love and so much hatred? Reassure me, Sibilot. It is not I whom they love, nor I whom they hate. I'm only a symbol, aren't I?

[MOUTON *and* DEMIDOFF *pass across at the back.*]

SIBILOT: I ... [*Seeing* MOUTON] Turn round!

GEORGES: What is it?

SIBILOT: Turn round, I tell you, or we shall be lost.

[GEORGES *turns round, facing out front.*]

Mouton has just passed by with Demidoff. They're looking for you.

GEORGES: To hell with Demidoff. It's Jules and Nerciat I'm concerned about. Those idiots think they can work me with strings.

SIBILOT: Listen, Nikita ...

GEORGES: Be quiet! I'll show them who's the master. Madam Castagnié will be back at her job tomorrow, or else ... [*He stamps his foot with irritation.*] To hell with it!

SIBILOT: What's wrong now?

GEORGES: This evening I have to play the decisive round, and I don't feel in the mood for winning it. What's this?

[*A* GUEST *staggers in. He leans against the buffet, picks up a glass, drinks and holds the glass as if drinking a toast.*]

GUEST: Present! Fire! Long live France! [*He collapses.*]

GOBLET [*springing forward*]: Poor chap! [*He kneels beside him.*]

GUEST [*opening one eye*]: What an ugly mug! Give me the *coup de grâce.*

[*He falls asleep.* GOBLET, *furious, pushes him under the buffet and pulls the tablecloth down over him.* GEORGES *sees him.*]

GEORGES [*to* SIBILOT]: Goblet! [*He turns his back quickly on* GOBLET.]

SIBILOT: Where?

GEORGES: Behind you. That's a bad start.

SIBILOT [*sure of himself*]: I'll take care of him.

GEORGES: You?

SIBILOT: He likes me. [*He goes towards the inspector, with open arms.*] Well, I *am* glad to see you.

GOBLET [*startled*]: I don't know you!

SIBILOT: Don't say that. Why, I'm Sibilot. Don't you remember me?

GOBLET [*still suspicious*]: Yes.

SIBILOT: Well then, let's shake hands.

GOBLET: No.

SIBILOT [*in a heartrending voice*]: Goblet!

GOBLET: You've changed.

SIBILOT: Go on with you!

GOBLET: You're dressed differently.

SIBILOT: Is that all? I was sent here by my editor and I borrowed these clothes so that I'd look smart.

GOBLET: You didn't borrow that face.

SIBILOT: What's wrong with my face?

GOBLET: It's a two hundred thousand franc face.

SIBILOT: Are you mad? The face goes with the outfit. [*He takes* GOBLET *by the arm.*] I won't let you go. Are you thirsty?

GOBLET: Yes, but I can't swallow.

SIBILOT: Your throat, eh? Choked up? I know how it is. Ah! We're out of place here. Do you know what we ought to do?

The pantry is light, airy, and spacious; plenty of nice-looking maids. Let's go down there and have a drink.

GOBLET: But I have to wait for . . .

SIBILOT: A drink, inspector, a drink. We'll feel at home. [*He pulls him out.*]

GEORGES [*alone*]: Ooh!

CHAPUIS [*appearing at a door*]: Psst!

BAUDOUIN [*at the other door*]: Psst!

GEORGES: Eh?

BAUDOUIN: We are Inspectors from the Defence of the State.

CHAPUIS: And we have come to welcome you . . .

BAUDOUIN: To the State which we defend.

GEORGES: Thank you.

CHAPUIS: Don't you worry about anything . . .

BAUDOUIN: Rely completely on us.

CHAPUIS: At the moment of danger, we shall be there.

GEORGES: The moment of danger? Is there any danger?

BAUDOUIN: The possibility of an attack cannot be ruled out . . .

GEORGES: An attack on whom?

BAUDOUIN [*smiling*]: On you!

CHAPUIS [*laughing openly*]: On you!

GEORGES: Well, well! But tell me . . .

BAUDOUIN: Sh! Sh! We are on the look out!

CHAPUIS: We are on the look out!

[*They vanish as* MME BOUNOUMI *and her guests enter.*]

MME BOUNOUMI: Here is our saviour!

ALL: Long live Nekrassov!

A MAN: Sir, you are a man!

GEORGES: Sir, you are another!

A WOMAN: How handsome you are!

GEORGES: For your pleasure, madam.

ANOTHER WOMAN: Sir, I would be proud to have a child by you.

GEORGES: Madam, we will consider the matter.

MME BOUNOUMI: Dear friend, will you say a few words?

GEORGES: Certainly. [*Raising his voice.*] Ladies and Gentlemen, civilizations are mortal, Europe can no longer think in terms of liberty, but only in terms of destiny. The wonder of Greece is in danger. We must save it.

ALL: We shall die for the wonder of Greece! We shall die for the wonder of Greece!

[*Applause.* MME BOUNOUMI *pushes* PERDRIÈRE *towards* GEORGES.]

MME BOUNOUMI [*to* GEORGES]: Here is someone who admires you.

GEORGES: You admire me, sir? That is enough to make me love you. Who are you?

PERDRIÈRE: I am everlastingly obliged to you, sir.

GEORGES [*astonished*]: To me? I have obliged someone?

PERDRIÈRE: You have obliged me to stand down.

GEORGES: Perdrière! [PERDRIÈRE *tries to kiss his hand. He prevents it.*] Well, I am delighted to meet you. [*They embrace.*]

MME BOUNOUMI: Photos! [*Flashes. She takes* GEORGES *by one arm,* PERDRIÈRE *takes his other arm.*] Now, the three of us. Take the group.

JULES [*quickly*]: Do you mind? [*He takes* PERDRIÈRE'*s arm.*]

GEORGES: No, my dear Jules, no. Later.

JULES: Why do you systematically refuse to be photographed with me?

GEORGES: Because you fidget. You'd spoil the film.

JULES: If you don't mind . . .

GEORGES: No, my dear chap, I have my public. People buy your rag in order to cut out my picture and they have the right . . .

JULES: You may have your public, but these are *my* photographers, and I consider it inadmissible that you should prevent them from photographing me.

GEORGES: Quickly, then. [*Flash.*] There, there. That's enough. Now I want a word with you.

[GEORGES *takes* JULES *by the arm and leads him downstage.*]

JULES: What do you want with me?

GEORGES: I want you to reinstate the seven employees whom you have dismissed.

JULES: What, again! But that's none of your business, old man. It's strictly an internal affair.

GEORGES: Everything to do with the paper is my business.

JULES: Who is the editor? You or I?

GEORGES: You are. But you won't be for long if you play at that game. I'll ask the Board to get rid of you.

JULES: Very well, here is Nerciat, whom they elected as chairman on Thursday in place of Mouton. You have only to ask him.

GEORGES [taking NERCIAT by the arm and leading him down to JULES]: My dear Nerciat . . .

NERCIAT: My dear Nekrassov . . .

GEORGES: May I ask you a favour?

NERCIAT: It's granted before you ask it.

GEORGES: Do you remember that poor Madame Castagnié?

NERCIAT: Good gracious, no.

GEORGES: The secretary whom you dismissed.

NERCIAT: Ah, yes. She was a Communist.

GEORGES: She is a widow, my dear Nerciat.

NERCIAT: Yes. A Communist widow.

GEORGES: She has a sick daughter.

NERCIAT: Sick? A bad egg. A Communist brat.

GEORGES: She only had her wages to live on. Do you want her to put her head in the gas-oven?

NERCIAT: That would be two Communists less. [Pause.] What do you want?

GEORGES: I want you to give her back her job.

NERCIAT: But, my dear Nekrassov, I cannot do anything by myself. [Pause.] Believe me, I will transmit your request to the Board. [GEORGES is furious, but he contains himself.] Is that all?

GEORGES: No. [Taking Soir à Paris from his pocket.] What's this?

NERCIAT [reading]: 'Nekrassov states: I know the journalists Duval and Maistre personally.' Well? That is a statement you made.

GEORGES: I did not.

NERCIAT: You didn't make it?

GEORGES: Certainly not.

NERCIAT: Ho, ho. [*To* JULES, *severely*] My dear Jules, you astonish me. You know the slogan of our paper – 'The Naked Truth'!

JULES [*taking hold of* PERIGORD *as he is passing*]: Perigord, I am very surprised. Here is a statement attributed to Nekrassov, which he has never made.

PERIGORD [*taking the paper and reading it*]: Ah! It must have been little Tapinois!

JULES: Little Tapinois!

PERIGORD: She must have thought she was doing the right thing.

JULES: We can't have that on our paper, Perigord. 'The Naked Truth.' Sack Tapinois.

GEORGES: I'm not asking for that!

JULES: Sack her, sack her.

GEORGES: No, Jules, please. We've had enough dismissals.

JULES: Well, give her a good telling off, and tell her that she has kept her job only through the personal intervention of Nekrassov.

GEORGES: That's right. [*Pause.*] As far as I'm concerned I shall be satisfied with a denial.

JULES [*taken aback*]: With a what?

GEORGES: A denial which you will publish tomorrow.

JULES: A denial?

NERCIAT: A denial?

PERIGORD: A denial?

[*They look at each other.*]

JULES: But, Nikita, that would be the worst blunder.

PERIGORD: They'd wonder what had come over us.

NERCIAT: Have you ever seen a paper deny its own statements, unless forced to do so by the courts?

JULES: We should immediately draw public attention to this unfortunate little paragraph.

PERIGORD: Which I am sure no one has read.

JULES [*to* NERCIAT]: Did you notice it, my dear chairman?

NERCIAT: I? Not at all. Though I read the paper from beginning to end.

JULES: If we start that little game, what will it lead to? Do we want to devote each issue to contradicting the previous one?

GEORGES: Very well. What do you propose doing?

NERCIAT: About what?

GEORGES: About this statement.

JULES: Just say no more about it. Bury it in the next day's news. That's always the best way. Do you think that our readers remember what they have read from one day to the next? My dear chap, if they had any memory we couldn't even publish the weather forecast!

NERCIAT [rubbing his hands]: Well, everything is settled.

GEORGES: No.

NERCIAT: No?

GEORGES: No! I insist that you publish a denial.

NERCIAT: You insist?

GEORGES: Yes, by virtue of the services which I have rendered you . . .

NERCIAT: We've paid you for them!

GEORGES: By virtue of the fame which I have acquired . . .

JULES: My poor Nikita, I didn't want to tell you, but your fame is on the down grade. On Thursday we reached a top circulation of two million. But since then we've dropped to 1,700,000.

GEORGES: That is still well above your normal circulation.

JULES: Wait till next week.

GEORGES: Next week?

JULES: We'll drop back to 900,000, and then what will you be? A steep rise on our sales graph, a steep fall, and then nothing more – death.

GEORGES: Not so fast. I still have some sensational revelations!

JULES: Too late! It's shock tactics that count. The readers are saturated. If you were to tell them tomorrow that the Russians eat their children, it would no longer have any effect on them.

[Enter MOUTON and DEMIDOFF.]

MOUTON [in a loud voice]: Gentlemen!

[Everyone becomes silent and turns towards him.]

You have been betrayed.

[*Murmurs of surprise from the guests.*]

NERCIAT: Why have you come here, Mouton?

MOUTON: To expose a traitor. [*Pointing to* DEMIDOFF] Here is Demidoff, the Soviet economist, who worked in the Kremlin for ten years. Listen to what he has to tell us. [*To* DEMIDOFF, *pointing to* GEORGES] Have a good look at that man who is passing himself off as Nekrassov. Do you recognize him?

DEMIDOFF: I must change my glasses. [*He takes off his glasses, puts on another pair, and looks around him.*] Where is he?

GEORGES [*throwing himself upon him and embracing him*]: At last! I have been looking for you for such a long time.

[MOUTON *pulls him back.*]

MOUTON [*to* DEMIDOFF]: Do you recognize him?

GEORGES: Everyone leave the room; I have a secret message for him.

MOUTON: We won't leave until this business is settled.

[*The Inspectors of the Defence of the State enter.*]

BAUDOUIN [*looming in front of* MOUTON]: Oh, yes, sir, you'll go.

MOUTON: But I . . .

BAUDOUIN: Defence of the State. It's an order.

CHAPUIS [*to the others*]: You as well, gentlemen, if you please.

[*They usher all the guests out.* DEMIDOFF *and* GEORGES *remain alone.*]

DEMIDOFF [*who has been examining* GEORGES, *and has noticed nothing else*]: This man is not Nekrassov.

GEORGES: Save your energy – we are alone.

DEMIDOFF: You are not Nekrassov. Nekrassov is short, and stocky, and has a slight limp.

GEORGES: He limps? I am sorry I didn't know that before. [*Pause.*] Demidoff, I've been wanting to speak to you for a long time.

DEMIDOFF: I don't know you.

GEORGES: But I know you very well: I have found out a great deal about you. You arrived in France in 1950. At that time you were a Leninist-Bolshevik and you felt very lonely. For a time you turned to the Trotskyists and became a Trotskyist-Bolshevik. After the failure of their group, you went over to Tito, and called yourself a Titoist-Bolshevik. When the Soviet Union became reconciled with Yugoslavia, you set your hopes on Mao Tse-tung, and called yourself a Tungist-Bolshevik. But China did not break with the Soviets, so then you called yourself a Bolshevik-Bolshevik. Is that right?

DEMIDOFF: It is correct.

GEORGES: All these great changes merely took place in your head and you have always been alone. At one time your articles were published in *Soir à Paris*, but now nobody wants them. You live in an attic with a goldfinch. Soon the goldfinch will die and the landlord will evict you, and you will have to sleep in a Salvation Army home.

DEMIDOFF: I'm not afraid of poverty. I have only one aim: to annihilate the Soviet bureaucracy.

GEORGES: Well, the game's up, old chap. The West has devoured you. You don't count any more.

DEMIDOFF [*catching him by the throat*]: You dirty snake!

GEORGES: Let go, Demidoff, let me go! I'm going to show you a way out.

DEMIDOFF [*letting him go*]: It's no use.

GEORGES: Why?

DEMIDOFF: You are not Nekrassov, and I have come here to say so.

GEORGES: Don't say it. You would be helping your enemies. Your hatred of the Soviets cannot be very strong if it has not silenced your love for the truth. Think! Mouton has brought you out of oblivion in order to bring about my downfall. When that's done, he'll drop you again. One day you will be found dead in a ditch, the victim of frustration and repressed hatred, and who will have the last laugh? All the bureaucrats in Russia!

DEMIDOFF: You are not Nekrassov. Nekrassov limps.

GEORGES: Yes, yes, I know. [*Pause.*] Demidoff, I want to join the Bolshevik-Bolshevik Party.

DEMIDOFF: You?

GEORGES: Yes. Do you realize the giant stride you have just taken? When a party has but one member, there is little chance that it will ever have two. But once it has two members, what is to prevent it from having a million? Do you accept?

DEMIDOFF [*stunned by the news*]: My party will have two members?

GEORGES: Yes, two.

DEMIDOFF [*suspicious*]: You know that we are based on the principle of centralization?

GEORGES: I know.

DEMIDOFF: And our rule is authoritarian democracy?

GEORGES: I know.

DEMIDOFF: I am the leader.

GEORGES: I will be the rank and file.

DEMIDOFF: The first sign of fraction work, and I'll expel you.

GEORGES: Don't worry, I'm devoted to you. But there's no time to lose. Today I am famous. Tomorrow, perhaps, I shall be forgotten. Seize the opportunity. My articles are being read all over the world. I shall write them at your dictation.

DEMIDOFF: Will you denounce the generation of technicians which has supplanted the old revolutionaries?

GEORGES: In every column.

DEMIDOFF: Will you say what I think of Orloff?

GEORGES: Who is Orloff?

DEMIDOFF: He was head of my department. A jackal!

GEORGES: Tomorrow he will be the laughing stock of Europe.

DEMIDOFF: Splendid! [*He holds out his hand.*] Put it there, Nekrassov.
    [GEORGES *shakes his hand. The guests appear hesitantly at the door.*
    MOUTON *and some guests come in.*]

MOUTON: Well, Demidoff, who is this man?

DEMIDOFF: Him? He is Nekrassov!
    [*Applause.*]

MOUTON: You lie! What have you two concocted while you were alone?

GEORGES: I have been giving him news of the underground resistance which is being organized in the Soviet Union.

MOUTON: Impostor!

GEORGES [*to the guests*]: I call your attention to the fact that this individual is playing the game of the Communists!

GUESTS [*to* MOUTON]: Go back to Moscow! Go back to Moscow!

MOUTON: You are driving me to suicide, you scoundrel, but I'll take you to the grave with me. [*He pulls out a revolver and points it at* GEORGES.] You may thank me, gentlemen. I am ridding the earth of a blackguard and of an objective Communist!

MME BOUNOUMI: The attack! The attack!

[BAUDOUIN *and* CHAPUIS *throw themselves upon* MOUTON, *and disarm him. The two* GUNMEN *enter at a run from the door on the right.*]

CHAPUIS [*to the two* BODYGUARDS, *pointing to* MOUTON]: Take the gentleman away.

MOUTON [*struggling*]: Leave me alone! Leave me alone!

GUESTS: Go back to Moscow! Go back to Moscow!

[*The* BODYGUARDS *pick him up and carry him out by the door on the right.*]

BAUDOUIN [*to the* GUESTS]: We have foiled the attack. Ladies and gentlemen, the danger is over. Please return to the other rooms. We wish to be alone with M. Nekrassov for a few moments in order to discuss with him measures for ensuring his safety, but have no fear; we shall return him to you soon.

[*The* GUESTS *leave.*]

BAUDOUIN: You must admit, sir, that we are your guardian angels.

CHAPUIS: And that, without us, that scoundrel would have shot you dead.

GEORGES: I thank you, gentlemen.

BAUDOUIN: Don't mention it. We were only doing our duty.

CHAPUIS: And we are very happy to have rescued you.

[GEORGES *bows slightly, and starts to go out.* BAUDOUIN *takes him by the arm.*]

GEORGES: But . . .

CHAPUIS: We have our difficulties, you know.

BAUDOUIN: And we would like you to give us a helping hand.

GEORGES [*sitting down*]: How can I be of service to you?

[*The* INSPECTORS *sit down.*]

CHAPUIS: Well, we are working on a serious case affecting national morale.

GEORGES: Is the morale of France in danger?

CHAPUIS: Not yet, sir. We are keeping watch.

BAUDOUIN: But the fact is that attempts are being made to undermine morale.

GEORGES: Poor France! And who dares . . .

CHAPUIS: Two journalists.

GEORGES: Two out of forty million? This country must be easily demoralized.

BAUDOUIN: These two men are only symbols. And the government wants, through them, to strike at an obnoxious press which misleads its readers.

CHAPUIS: We must strike swiftly and hard.

BAUDOUIN: We plan to arrest them tomorrow. The day after at the latest.

CHAPUIS: But we've been told to obtain proof that the two accused have deliberately taken part in a plot against national morale . . .

BAUDOUIN: Which we think is quite unnecessary . . .

CHAPUIS: But which the legal authorities consider it necessary to demand . . .

BAUDOUIN: But, for once, luck is on our side . . .

CHAPUIS: We've got you.

GEORGES: You've got me?

BAUDOUIN: Don't you get it?

GEORGES: Indeed I do; or at least I think I do.

CHAPUIS: Well, you will be our witness.

BAUDOUIN: In your capacity as a Soviet Minister, you must have employed these journalists.

CHAPUIS: And you would do us a great favour by confirming it.

GEORGES: What are their names?

CHAPUIS: Robert Duval and Charles Maistre.

GEORGES: Maistre and Duval ... Duval and Maistre. ... No, I don't know them.

BAUDOUIN: Impossible!

GEORGES: Why?

CHAPUIS: You stated yesterday, in *Soir à Paris*, that you knew them very well.

GEORGES: They attributed words to me that I never used.

BAUDOUIN: That may be. But the article is there. And in any case, they are Communists. Duval is a leading member of the CP.

CHAPUIS: Come, come, Duval. You must know him.

GEORGES: In the Soviet Union each Minister has his own personal agents who are not known to the others. You need the Ministry of Propaganda, or Information, or perhaps Foreign Affairs. I, as you know, was Minister of the Interior.

BAUDOUIN: We appreciate your scruples ...

CHAPUIS: ... and in your place we should have the same scruples.

BAUDOUIN: But since Duval is a Communist ...

CHAPUIS: It isn't necessary for you actually to have seen his name.

BAUDOUIN: And you can be morally certain that he is a Soviet agent.

CHAPUIS: You could therefore testify without any qualms that he was paid for his work.

GEORGES: I am sorry, but I shall not testify.

[*Pause.*]

BAUDOUIN: Very well.

CHAPUIS: Good.

BAUDOUIN: France is the land of liberty. Here everyone is free to speak or to be silent.

CHAPUIS: We bow to your wishes.

BAUDOUIN: And we hope that our chiefs will do so as well.

[*Pause.*]

BAUDOUIN [*to* CHAPUIS]: Will they?

CHAPUIS [*to* BAUDOUIN]: Who knows? The difficulty is that M. Nekrassov has many enemies.

BAUDOUIN [*to* GEORGES]: People who are annoyed by your fame ...

CHAPUIS [*to* GEORGES]: And who claim that you were sent here by Moscow . . .

GEORGES: That's nonsense!

CHAPUIS: Of course.

[*They get up and stand on either side of him.*]

BAUDOUIN: But these slanders must be silenced.

CHAPUIS: By an act which definitely commits you.

BAUDOUIN: After all, only last month, you were the sworn enemy of our country . . .

CHAPUIS: . . . and there is nothing to prove that you aren't still . . .

BAUDOUIN: We have been told many times that we are failing in our duty . . .

CHAPUIS: And that we should take you straight back to the frontier.

BAUDOUIN: Imagine what would happen if we were to hand you over to the Soviet police!

CHAPUIS: You'd have a bad time, after the statements you've made.

GEORGES: You'd be heartless enough to throw me out? After I have put my trust in French hospitality?

CHAPUIS [*laughing*]: Ha, ha!

CHAPUIS [*to* BAUDOUIN]: Hospitality!

BAUDOUIN [*to* CHAPUIS]: Why not the right of asylum?

CHAPUIS: He thinks he's living in the Middle Ages!

BAUDOUIN: We are hospitable to English lords . . .

CHAPUIS: . . . German tourists . . .

BAUDOUIN: . . . American soldiers . . .

CHAPUIS: . . . and to those expelled from Belgium . . .

BAUDOUIN: But frankly, you wouldn't want us to be hospitable to Soviet citizens!

GEORGES: It's blackmail, then?

CHAPUIS: No, sir, it's a dilemma.

BAUDOUIN: I would even say: an alternative. [*Pause.*]

GEORGES: Take me to the frontier. [*Pause.*]

BAUDOUIN [*changing his tone*]: My dear Georges, so you're going to be difficult?

CHAPUIS: You're going to play tough?

GEORGES [*jumping up*]: What?

BAUDOUIN: Sit down.

[*They make him sit down.*]

CHAPUIS: You can't scare us, you know!

BAUDOUIN: We've seen real tough characters – men.

CHAPUIS: Everyone knows that swindlers are only cissies.

BAUDOUIN: Women.

CHAPUIS: Once you've had a little going over . . .

BAUDOUIN: You'll start talking . . .

GEORGES: I don't understand what you mean.

CHAPUIS: Oh yes, you do.

BAUDOUIN: We mean that you are Georges de Valéra, the small-time crook, and that we could turn you over right away to Inspector Goblet, who is after you.

GEORGES (*trying to laugh*): Georges de Valéra? It is a misunder-standing! I . . .

CHAPUIS: Take it easy. For the past week your bodyguards have been photographing you on the sly from every angle. They have even taken your fingerprints. We only had to compare the results with your police dossier. You've had it.

GEORGES: Hell! [*Pause.*]

BAUDOUIN: You know, we're not bad chaps.

CHAPUIS: And swindlers are not in our line.

BAUDOUIN: That's the business of the criminal branch, and our department doesn't think much of that lot.

CHAPUIS: We'll tell Inspector Goblet where to get off.

BAUDOUIN: We want those two journalists, that's all.

CHAPUIS: And if you give them over to us, you can be Nekrassov as much as you like.

BAUDOUIN: You will do us a few little favours.

CHAPUIS: We shall point people out to you from time to time.

BAUDOUIN: You will say that you know them. Just to please us.

CHAPUIS: And in exchange, we'll keep our mouths shut.

BAUDOUIN: We are the only ones who know, you see.

CHAPUIS: Of course, the Prime Minister has been told.

BAUDOUIN: But that doesn't matter. He doesn't know.

CHAPUIS: He said, 'I don't want to know it.'

BAUDOUIN: And he knows what he wants to know!

CHAPUIS: Get the idea, son?

BAUDOUIN: On Thursday we'll come for you and take you to the examining magistrate.

CHAPUIS: He will ask you if you know Duval . . .

BAUDOUIN: And you will say, 'Yes' because you can't do otherwise.

CHAPUIS: Good night, pal. At your service.

BAUDOUIN: See you Thursday, and don't forget. [*They go out.*]

    [GEORGES *is left alone.*]

GEORGES: Well! Well, well, well! . . . Well, well, well, well, well! [*He goes to the mirror.*] Farewell great Russian steppe of my childhood, farewell, fame! Farewell, Nekrassov! Farewell, you dear great man! Farewell traitor, skunk, farewell, rat! Long live Georges de Valéra! [*He looks through his pockets.*] Seven thousand francs. I have shaken the world, and it has brought me seven thousand francs. What a dog's game! [*To the mirror*] Georges, my good old Georges, you've no idea how glad I am to find you again. [*Recovering.*] Ladies and gentlemen, Nekrassov is dead, and Georges de Valéra is about to take French leave. [*He thinks.*] The main door – impossible, the cops are watching it. The servants' entrance . . . [*He opens a door at the right.*] Hell! My two gunmen are guarding the corridor. [*He crosses the room.*] The window? [*He leans over.*] It's a forty-foot drop. I'd crack my skull. No gutters? [*He climbs on the window-sill.*] Too far away. My God, if I could find a way of keeping my two gunmen busy . . .

    [DEMIDOFF *has come in, and seizes him round the waist, pulling him off the window-sill.*]

DEMIDOFF: Don't do that, member. I forbid it.

GEORGES: I . . .

DEMIDOFF: Suicide, yes, you think of it for the first three months. Then you get over it, you'll see. I've been through it. [*Confidentially*] I left the main room because I have had a little to drink. I mustn't get drunk, member. See that I don't. I'm terrible when I get drunk.

GEORGES [*very interested*]: Oh!

DEMIDOFF: Yes.

GEORGES: Really terrible?

DEMIDOFF: I smash everything. Sometimes I kill.

GEORGES: That's very interesting.

[MME BOUNOUMI *and* GUESTS *burst in.*]

MME BOUNOUMI [*to* GEORGES]: At last we can get together with you. You are not leaving, I hope? We're going to begin the party games.

GEORGES: Games?

MME BOUNOUMI: Yes.

GEORGES: I know one that used to make everyone in the Kremlin laugh till tears came to their eyes.

MME BOUNOUMI: You intrigue me. What is it?

GEORGES: At times when we were feeling good, we used to make Demidoff drunk. You can't imagine the wonderful ideas he has when he is drunk. He's a real poet.

MME BOUNOUMI: How delightful! Shall we try?

GEORGES: Pass the word round, and I'll do the rest.

MME BOUNOUMI [*to a* GUEST]: We must make Demidoff drunk. It seems that he is very amusing when he has had a few drinks.

[*The word gets round.*]

GEORGES [*to* DEMIDOFF]: Our friends want to drink a toast with you.

DEMIDOFF: Good. [*Looking at the glasses which a servant is bringing round*]: What's this?

GEORGES: Dry Martini.

DEMIDOFF: No American drinks. Vodka!

MME BOUNOUMI [*to the* SERVANTS]: Vodka!

[SERVANT *brings glasses of vodka on a tray.*]

DEMIDOFF [*raising his glass*]: I drink to the destruction of the Soviet bureaucrats!

MME BOUNOUMI *and* GUESTS: To the annihilation of the bureaucrats!

GEORGES [*taking a glass from the tray and giving it to* DEMIDOFF]: You are forgetting the technocrats.

DEMIDOFF: To the destruction of the technocrats! [*He drinks.*]

GEORGES [*handing him another glass*]: What about Orloff? [*To the* GUESTS] He was his boss.

DEMIDOFF [*drinking*]: To the hanging of Orloff!

GEORGES [*handing him a glass*]: This is the moment for a toast to the Bolshevik-Bolshevik Party.

DEMIDOFF: Do you think so?

GEORGES: Of course. It's your chance to make it known. Think of the publicity.

DEMIDOFF [*drinking*]: To the Bolshevik-Bolshevik Party!

GUESTS: To the Bolshevik-Bolshevik Party!

[*The majority are drunk by now. Paper hats, streamers and toy trumpets appear. During the ensuing scene* DEMIDOFF'*s tirades are punctuated by the sounds of the toy trumpets.*]

DEMIDOFF [*to* GEORGES]: What shall I drink to now?

GEORGES [*holding out a glass*]: To your goldfinch!

DEMIDOFF: To my goldfinch!

GUESTS: To his goldfinch!

[GEORGES *hands him another glass.*]

DEMIDOFF: And now?

GEORGES: I don't know. . . . What about France? That would be polite.

DEMIDOFF: No. [*Raising his glass.*] I drink to the good little Russian people, who are kept in chains by bad shepherds.

GUESTS: To the Russian people!

DEMIDOFF: You will free them, won't you? My poor little people; you're going to free them?

ALL: We will free them! We will free them! [*Trumpets.*]

DEMDIDOFF: Thank you. I drink to the deluge of fire and steel which will sweep down on my people.

ALL: To the deluge! To the deluge!

DEMIDOFF [*to* GEORGES]: What am I drinking?

GEORGES: Vodka.

DEMIDOFF: No.

GEORGES: Look!

[*He picks up the bottle and shows it to him.*]

DEMIDOFF: Stand clear, everyone! This is French vodka! I am a traitor!

GEORGES: Now, now, Demidoff.

DEMIDOFF: Silence, member! Any Russian who drinks French vodka is a traitor to his people. You must execute me. [*To* EVERYONE] Come on! What are you waiting for?

MME BOUNOUMI [*trying to calm him*]: My dear Demidoff, we wouldn't dream of such a thing.

DEMIDOFF [*pushing her away*]: Then liberate them, all of them, all of them, all the Russians! If a single survivor remains, he will point his finger at my breast and say to me: 'Feodor Petrovitch, you drink French vodka.' [*Replying to an imaginary questioner*] It's Orloff's fault, little father. I couldn't stand him any longer. [*He drinks.*] I drink to the liberating bomb!

[*A terrified silence. He turns threateningly to* PERDRIÈRE.]

Drink, you!

PERDRIÈRE: To the bomb!

DEMIDOFF [*threatening*]: To *which* bomb?

PERDRIÈRE: I ... don't know. ... To the H bomb.

DEMIDOFF: You skunk! You jackal! Do you think you can put a stop to history with a firecracker?

PERDRIÈRE: But I don't want to put a stop to it.

DEMIDOFF: And I want to put a stop to it at once. Because I know who is writing it. It is my little people with their bad shepherds. Do you understand? Orloff himself is writing history, but I have fallen out of it, as a little bird falls out of the nest. [*His eyes follow an invisible flying object flying across the room at great speed.*] How quickly it goes! Stop it! Stop it! [*Taking a glass.*] I drink to the Z bomb which will blow up the earth! [*To* PERDRIÈRE] Drink!

PERDRIÈRE [*in a choked voice*]: No.

DEMIDOFF: Don't you want the earth to blow up?

PERDRIÈRE: No.

DEMIDOFF: But how will you stop man's history unless you destroy the human race? [*At the window.*] Look! Look at the moon! Once upon a time it was a world. But the lunar capitalists had more sense than you. When they began to smell heresy there, they blew up the moon's atmosphere with cobalt bombs. That explains the silence of the heavens. Millions of moons are circling in space. Millions of clocks stopped at the same moment of history. There is only one left ticking around the sun, but if you have courage we can put an end to this disgraceful noise. I drink to the moon of the future! To the earth! [GEORGES *tries to slip away.*] Where are you going, member? Drink to the moon!

GEORGES: To the moon!

DEMIDOFF [*drinks and spits in disgust*]: Pah! [*To* GEORGES] Understand, member, I am on the future moon, and I am drinking French vodka. Ladies and gentlemen, I am a traitor. History will win. I am going to die, and my children will write my name in books: Demidoff, the traitor, drank French vodka at Madame Bounoumi's. I have done wrong, ladies and gentlemen. Wrong in the eyes of centuries to come. Raise your glasses; I feel lonely. [*To* PERDRIÈRE] You, you jackal, shout with me: Long live the historical process!

PERDRIÈRE [*terrified*]: Long live the historical process!

DEMIDOFF: Long live the historical process, which will crush me like a flea, and which will smash the old society as I am going to smash this table.

GEORGES [*opening the door at the right and letting in the two* BODY-GUARDS]: He's gone mad! Get hold of him!

[*The* BODYGUARDS *throw themselves on* DEMIDOFF *and try to control him.* GEORGES *gets ready to flee, but he finds himself face to face with* GOBLET, *who comes in by the door at right carrying* SIBILOT, *who is blind drunk, over his shoulders.*]

GOBLET [*putting* SIBILOT *down in an armchair*]: Lie down, old man. Wait while I get a cold compress for you.

SIBILOT: Good old Goblet; you're a mother to me. [*Bursts into tears.*]

I have betrayed my mother. I dragged you into the kitchen to prevent you arresting a crook.

GOBLET [*drawing himself up*]: What crook?

SIBILOT: Georges de Valéra.

[*During this time* GEORGES *makes a detour in order to reach the door at the right without passing in front of* SIBILOT *and* GOBLET.]

GOBLET: Georges de Valéra? Where is he?

[GEORGES *has reached the door on the right.*]

SIBILOT [*pointing with his finger*]: There! There! There!

GOBLET: Good God!

[*He pulls out his revolver and dashes off in pursuit of* GEORGES, *firing as he goes.*]

GUESTS [*terrified*]: The shooting's begun! The shooting's begun!

DEMIDOFF [*in ecstasy*]: At last! At last! This is history!

[BAUDOUIN *and* CHAPUIS *dash off in pursuit of* GOBLET. DEMIDOFF *frees himself from the* BODYGUARDS *and dashes off in pursuit of the* INSPECTORS. *The* BODYGUARDS *recover themselves and also dash off in pursuit.*]

CURTAIN

Sibilot's 1925 drawing-room.

> [*It is night.* GEORGES *comes in by the window.* VERONIQUE *then comes in and puts the light on. She is wearing the same clothes as in Scene Three and is getting ready to go out.* GEORGES *comes behind her, hands raised and smiling.*]

GEORGES: Good evening.

VERONIQUE [*turning round*]: Hello! Nekrassov!

GEORGES: He is dead. Call me Georges, and draw the curtains. [*He lowers his hands.*] You have never told me your name, girl.

VERONIQUE: Veronique.

GEORGES: Dear France! [*He drops into an armchair.*] I was sitting in this same armchair, you were getting ready to go out, and the cops were prowling around the house. We're back to where we started. How young I was! [*Listening.*] Did you hear a whistle?

VERONIQUE: No. Are they after you?

GEORGES: They have been ever since I was twenty. [*Pause.*] I have just shaken them off. But not for long.

VERONIQUE: What if they come here?

GEORGES: They'll come. Goblet through habit, and the DS by following the scent. But not for another ten minutes.

VERONIQUE: You've got the DS after you?

GEORGES: Inspector Baudouin and Inspector Chapuis. Do you know them?

VERONIQUE: No. But I know the DS. You are in danger.

GEORGES [*ironically*]: A little!

VERONIQUE: Don't stay here.

GEORGES: I must talk to you.

VERONIQUE: About yourself?

GEORGES: About your friends.

VERONIQUE: I'll see you tomorrow, wherever you like, and at whatever time you suggest. But, run!

GEORGES [*shaking his head*]: If I leave you now, you will never see me again. They'll get me. [*At a gesture from* VERONIQUE] Don't argue. You get to feel these things when you're in the profession. Besides, where do you expect me to go? I haven't a friend to hide me. At midnight, a man in a dinner jacket is not noticed, but wait till tomorrow in broad daylight. [*Seized with an idea.*] Where are your father's old suits?

VERONIQUE: He gave them to the concierge.

GEORGES: And his new ones?

VERONIQUE: They aren't ready, except for what he's wearing.

GEORGES: You see. Luck has deserted me. Veronique, my star has fallen and my genuis is fading. I'm finished. [*He walks about.*] They are going to arrest someone tonight, that's certain. But whom? Who is going to be arrested, can you tell me? Goblet is chasing Valéra and the D S is after Nekrassov. Whoever catches me first, I shall become what he wants me to be. What's your bet. The CD or the DS, Georges or Nikita?

VERONIQUE: I bet on the DS.

GEORGES: Me too. [*Pause.*] Warn Maistre and Duval.

VERONIQUE: What do you want to warn them of?

GEORGES: Listen, my girl, and try to understand. [*Patiently*] What will the Defence of the State branch do with me? Put me in gaol? They aren't so stupid. Nekrassov is the guest of France. They've probably rented a suburban villa for me, fairly isolated, with beautiful sunny rooms. They will instal me in the most beautiful of these rooms, and there I'll keep to my bed night and day. Because Nekrassov is very weak, poor chap. He has suffered so much. That won't prevent your father from continuing my sensational revelations. He has captured the style and can manufacture them without me. [*Imitating the cry of newsboys*] 'Maistre and Duval went to Moscow secretly. Nekrassov paid them in dollars!' That's what I believe they call creating the psychological climate. When they have been thoroughly dragged through the mud, the public will think it quite natural that they should be charged with treason.

VERONIQUE: The court won't take any notice of my father's articles. They'll need witnesses.

GEORGES: How do you know I won't give evidence?

VERONIQUE: You?

GEORGES: Yes. On a stretcher. I don't like being beaten up, and if they beat me every day I shall give way in the end.

VERONIQUE: You think they'll beat you up.

GEORGES: They won't stand on ceremony. [*Pause.*] Oh! you can despise me. I am too much of an artist to have physical courage.

VERONIQUE: I don't despise you. And who said anything about physical courage? It's enough to know what you want.

GEORGES: If only I knew!

VERONIQUE: Do you want to become an informer?

GEORGES: No, but I don't want to have my face smashed in. So there's the choice.

VERONIQUE: You have far too much pride to talk.

GEORGES: Have I any pride left?

VERONIQUE: You are bursting with it.

GEORGES: Listen to that! Never mind. I'd be very relieved if Duval and Maistre were out of harm's way.

VERONIQUE: What difference would that make?

GEORGES: When I've had as much as I can stand, I could name them. At least I'd know they wouldn't go to gaol.

VERONIQUE: But if you name them, they'll be convicted.

GEORGES: The conviction wouldn't matter, so long as they couldn't arrest them.

VERONIQUE [*disarmed*]: My poor Georges!

GEORGES [*not listening to her*]: You understand, kid. I shall disappear. You go and tell them to get away somewhere.

VERONIQUE: They won't run away.

GEORGES: With the cops after them and five years' gaol hanging in front of them? You're crazy.

VERONIQUE: They won't run away because they are innocent.

GEORGES: And you were trying to get me to run away because I'm guilty? Fine logic! Follow your advice, and all the guilty in France would be quietly fishing for trout while the innocent were rotting in prison.

VERONIQUE: That's just about what does happen.

GEORGES: No smart talk, kid. The fact is you're letting them in for it.

VERONIQUE: Wait till they're arrested, then you'll see.

GEORGES: I see it all. You'll go and yell in the streets. Posters, meetings, processions. A regular circus. And where will your two friends be? In the cells. Of course, it's in your interest for them to be locked up as long as possible! [He laughs.] And I, poor fool, put my head in the lion's mouth to warn them. Warn them? You people don't care a rap about it. What a fool I am! I don't blame you – every man for himself. But I'm a bit digusted with you, all the same, because I shall be going to gaol myself, and I have a feeling of solidarity with these two poor chaps you're sacrificing.

[VERONIQUE dials a telephone number.]

What are you doing?

VERONIQUE [into the telephone]: Is that you, Robert? I'm putting you on to someone who wants to talk to you. [To GEORGES] It's Duval.

GEORGES: The line may be tapped.

VERONIQUE: That doesn't matter. [She gives him the receiver.]

GEORGES [into the telephone]: Hullo, Duval? Listen carefully, old chap, you are going to be arrested tomorrow, or the day after at the latest, and most likely convicted. You haven't even got time to pack a bag. Make your getaway as soon as you put the receiver down. Eh? Oh! Oh! [Putting the receiver down.] Did he let me have it!

VERONIQUE [into the receiver]: No, Robert, no, take it easy; he's not a provocateur. Nothing of the sort. I'll explain everything. [To GEORGES] Do you want me to call Maistre?

GEORGES: It's not worth it. I understand. [He bursts out laughing.] For the first time in my life I wanted to do someone a good turn. It will certainly be the last. [Pause.] There's nothing left for me but to go. Good night. I'm sorry to have troubled you.

VERONIQUE: Good night.

GEORGES [*suddenly exploding*]: They are idiots, that's what they are! Poor types with no imagination. They have no idea what gaol is like. But I have.

VERONIQUE: You haven't been in gaol.

GEORGES: No, but I am a poet. Prison has been hanging over me all evening and I feel it in my bones. Do they know there's a five to two chance they'll come out with tuberculosis?

VERONIQUE: Duval went to prison on October 17th, 1939, and came out on August 30th, 1944. He's tubercular.

GEORGES: Then, there's no excuse.

VERONIQUE: But, my dear Georges, he's doing exactly what you're doing – acting in his own interests.

GEORGES: His interests, or yours?

VERONIQUE: His, mine, ours. They are all one. You have nothing much except your own skin, and you want to save it. That's quite natural. Duval wants to save his skin, but he doesn't keep thinking about it. He has his Party, his work and his readers. If he wants to save *all* that he is, then he must stay where he is. [*Pause.*]

GEORGES [*violently*]: Dirty egoists!

VERONIQUE: I beg your pardon.

GEORGES: Everyone will be happy. He will have his crown of thorns and you will have your circuses. But what about me, you rotten lot? What do I become? A traitor, a stool-pigeon, an informer!

VERONIQUE: You've only to . . .

GEORGES: Oh, no! I'll be tied to a prison bed and the cops will beat me up three times a day. They'll stop for breath from time to time. Then they'll ask me, 'Will you give evidence?' I'll be cornered. Bells will be ringing in my ears. My head will feel like a pumpkin, I'll think of those two martyrs, those two innocents who are playing a dirty trick on me by not running away, and I'll say to myself, 'If you rat, they'll be in for five years.' If I rat, of course, you'll all be very pleased. There's no Christ without

Judas, eh? Well, poor Judas. Here's a Judas with a heavy heart. I understand him, and I honour him. If I don't rat . . . Well! I'll still be getting the beatings because of you. And what will my reward be? To be spat upon. Your father will have filled *Soir à Paris* with my false statements, while your rags will celebrate the acquittal of Duval and the ignominious defeat of that slanderer Nekrassov. You will carry your friends in triumph and as they march, your joyful crowds will be treading on my face. Manipulated, just like a child! And by everybody.

There, I was the instrument of hatred; here, I am the instrument of history. [*Pause.*] Veronique! If you were to explain my position to your pals do you think they would be good enough to run away?

VERONIQUE: I'm afraid not.

GEORGES: The swine! I ought to kill myself, right here in front of you, and dirty your floor with my blood. You're lucky that I no longer have the courage to do it. [*He sits down again.*] I no longer understand anything about anything. I used to have my own little philosophy. It helped me to live. I've lost everything, even my principles. Ah! I ought never to have gone into politics!

VERONIQUE: Go, Georges. We ask nothing of you, and you don't owe anything to anyone. Please go.

GEORGES [*at the window, draws the curtains back a little*]: Night. The streets are deserted. I'll have to slink along by the walls until morning. After that . . . [*Pause.*] Shall I tell you the truth? I wanted them to catch me here. When you retire from the world, what counts is the last face you see. You remember it a long time. I wanted it to be yours. [VERONIQUE *smiles.*] You ought to smile more often. It makes you beautiful.

VERONIQUE: I smile at people whom I like.

GEORGES: There's nothing about me for you to like, and I don't like you. [*Pause.*] If I could prevent those fellows going to gaol, what a good trick I'd be playing on all of you! [*He walks up and down.*] To the rescue, my genius! Show me you are still alive!

VERONIQUE: Genius, you know . . .

GEORGES: Quiet! [*He turns his back on* VERONIQUE *and bows.*] Thank you, thank you! [*Turning back to* VERONIQUE] I regret to inform you that your pals won't be arrested. Good-bye to your circuses and your martyrs' crowns. Madame Castagnié will get her job back, and who knows if Perdrière's hundred thousand votes won't go to the Communist candidate on Sunday. I'll show you that no one can pull my strings as they like.

VERONIQUE [*shrugging her shoulders*]: You can't do anything.

GEORGES: Find someone to hide me. Come and see me tomorrow, and I'll give you an interview with exclusive world rights.

VERONIQUE: What, again!

GEORGES: Don't you want it?

VERONIQUE: No . . .

GEORGES: I had such a lovely title too: 'How I became Nekrassov', by Georges de Valéra.

VERONIQUE: Georges!

GEORGES: I'll stay with your friend for a fortnight. Photograph me from every angle, with and without the eye-patch. I know them all: the Palotins, Nerciats and Moutons. I'll give you revelations with chapter and verse.

VERONIQUE: As soon as the first article appears, they'll send the police to us. If we refuse to give you up, they'll publish everywhere that your statements are all lies.

GEORGES: Do you think they'll dare to arrest me once the first article is published? I know too much. And what if they do? If they want my address, you can give it to them. You make me sick, you and your martyrs. If you must have one, why not me?

VERONIQUE: You see, you're bursting with vanity.

GEORGES: Yes. [*Pause.*] Do you agree about the interview?

VERONIQUE: Yes. [*She kisses him.*]

GEORGES: Keep your distance. [*He laughs.*] So I've won in the end. Your progressive paper will publish an article by a crook. That won't make much of a change for me. I dictated to the father, and I'll dictate to the daughter.

VERONIQUE: I'll go with you. It'll be safer.

[BAUDOUIN *and* CHAPUIS *come in through the window.*]

CHAPUIS: Good morning, Nikita.

BAUDOUIN: Inspector Goblet is looking for you.

CHAPUIS: But don't be afraid. We are going to protect you.

VERONIQUE: It's all up!

GEORGES: Who knows? I have found my genius again. Perhaps my star is not dead.

BAUDOUIN: Come with us, Nikita. You are in danger.

CHAPUIS: This girl is in with the Communists.

BAUDOUIN: Perhaps they've given her the job of murdering you.

GEORGES: I am Georges de Valéra, the swindler, and I demand to be handed over to Inspector Goblet.

CHAPUIS [*to* VERONIQUE]: Poor Nikita!

BAUDOUIN [*to* VERONIQUE]: Your Russian friends have just arrested his wife and his sons.

CHAPUIS [*to* VERONIQUE]: His mind has been unhinged by sorrow, and he doesn't know what he's saying.

[BAUDOUIN *goes to the front door and opens it. Two* MALE NURSES *come in.*]

BAUDOUIN [*to the* NURSES]: There he is. Be very gentle.

CHAPUIS: You need a rest, Nikita.

BAUDOUIN: These gentlemen are going to take you to a nice clinic.

CHAPUIS: With a lovely sunny garden.

GEORGES [*to* VERONIQUE]: You see what they've thought up. It's even worse than the suburban villa.

BAUDOUIN [*to the* NURSES]: Take it away!

[*The* NURSES *come forward, leaving the door open. They seize* GEORGES. GOBLET *comes in.*]

GOBLET: Naturally, ladies and gentlemen, you haven't seen a man five feet ten in height . . .

GEORGES [*shouts*]: Here I am, Goblet! I am Georges de Valéra!

GOBLET: Valéra!

GEORGES: I confess to two hundred swindles! You will be Chief Inspector before the end of the year.

GOBLET [*coming forward, fascinated*]: Valéra!

BAUDOUIN [*blocking his way*]: A mistake, colleague. It's Nekrassov.

GOBLET [*avoiding him and throwing himself on* GEORGES, *whom he pulls by one arm*]: I've been looking for him for years!

CHAPUIS [*taking* GEORGES *by the other arm*]: We tell you that this man is a lunatic who thinks he is Valéra!

GOBLET [*pulling on* GEORGES' *arm*]: Let go of him! He's my property. He's my living, my man, my game.

CHAPUIS [*pulling*]: Let go of him yourself!

GOBLET: Never!

BAUDOUIN: We'll have you suspended.

GOBLET: You try! There'll be a row!

GEORGES: Courage, Goblet, I'm with you.

BAUDOUIN [*to the* NURSES]: Take them both away!

[*The* NURSES *fall on* GEORGES *and* GOBLET.]

VERONIQUE: Help!

[CHAPUIS *gags her with his hand, and she struggles violently. At this moment,* DEMIDOFF *appears, fighting mad.*]

DEMIDOFF: Where is my member?

GEORGES: Help, Demidoff!

DEMIDOFF: My God! My member! Give me my member! I want my member!

BAUDOUIN [*to* DEMIDOFF]: Who asked you to interfere?

DEMIDOFF: Interfere? [*He knocks him down. The others throw themselves on him.*] Long live the Bolshevik-Bolshevik Party! Keep it up, member! Down with the cops! [*He knocks down a* NURSE.] Ah, you want to split the Bolshevik-Bolshevik Party! [*He knocks* CHAPUIS *over.*] You'd try to stop the onward march of the revolution!

[*He knocks* GOBLET *over.* GEORGES *and* VERONIQUE *look at each other and get away through the window.* DEMIDOFF *knocks out the other* NURSE, *looks around him and goes out through the door shouting.*]

Hold on, member, I'm coming.

GOBLET [*coming to, sadly*]: Didn't I say I wouldn't catch him! [*He falls back unconscious.*]

CURTAIN

SCENE EIGHT

Palotin's office. Dawn. Grey light. The electric lights are on. Nerciat, Charivet, Bergerat, Lerminier and Jules are present. Nerciat is wearing a paper hat. Bergerat blows into a toy trumpet. Charivet and Lerminier are seated, helpless, with streamers twined around their dinner jackets. Jules is walking about, a little apart. They all look tired and lost. They are wearing badges of the Future Firing Squad Victims – large rosettes on which the audience can see, in letters of gold, FFSV. During the scene it becomes gradually lighter, becoming fully light only after Jules has left.

CHARIVET: I've got a headache!

LERMINIER: So have I!

BERGERAT: And I!

NERCIAT [*dryly*]: And so have I, my friends. What now?

CHARIVET: I want to go to bed.

NERCIAT: No, Charivet, no! We are waiting for Nekrassov, and you will wait with us.

CHARIVET: Nekrassov! He's still running!

NERCIAT: They promised to bring him back before dawn.

CHARIVET [*pointing to the window*]: Before dawn? It's dawn now.

NERCIAT: Exactly. Everything will soon be settled.

CHARIVET [*goes towards the window and recoils in disgust*]: How horrible!

NERCIAT: What is?

CHARIVET: The dawn! I haven't seen it for twenty-five years. Hasn't it aged! [*Pause.*]

NERCIAT: Friends . . .

    [BERGERAT *blows into his toy trumpet.*]

For the love of God, Bergerat, don't blow that thing any more.

BERGERAT: It's a trumpet.

NERCIAT [*patiently*]: I can see that, old man, but would you do me a favour and throw it away?

BERGERAT [*indignantly*]: Throw away my trumpet? [*After a moment's reflection*] I'll throw it away if you'll take off your paper hat.

NERCIAT [*thunderstruck*]: My what? You're drunk, old man. [*He puts his hand to his head and feels the hat.*] Oh! [*He throws the hat away with disgust and pulls himself together.*] A little dignity, gentlemen. We're holding a meeting. Get rid of those streamers.

[BERGERAT *puts his trumpet on the desk. The others brush themselves.*]

Good!

[JULES, *who has all this time been walking up and down, deep in thought, goes over to the desk, opens it and takes out a bottle of spirits and a glass. He is about to pour himself a drink.*]

No, my friend, not you! I thought you never drank.

JULES: I'm drinking to forget.

NERCIAT: To forget what?

JULES: To forget that I am in possession of the best piece of news in my whole career, and that I am forbidden to publish it. 'Nekrassov was Valéra.' Ha! There's a mouthful for you! Two celebrated men in one. Two headlines in one. The biggest plum in journalism!

NERCIAT: You don't know what you're saying, my dear chap.

JULES: I was dreaming. [*He goes on walking.*] Oh, to be a left-wing paper for one day! For a single day! What a headline! [*He stops, in ecstasy.*] I can see it. It covers the whole of the front page, continues on page two, invades page three . . .

NERCIAT: That's enough!

JULES: All right. All right. [*Sadly*] After the Battle of Tsushima the editor of a leading Japanese paper was confronted with a similar dilemma. He committed hara-kiri.

NERCIAT: Have no regrets, my friend. Nekrassov is Nekrassov. He ran away just now because he thought he was the object of a Communist attack. [*Looking* JULES *straight in the eye*] That's the truth.

JULES [*sighing*]: It's less beautiful than the dream. [*There is a knock at the door.*] Come in.

[BAUDOUIN *and* CHAPUIS *enter. Their heads are covered in*

bandages. CHAPUIS *has his arm in a sling.* BAUDOUIN *is on crutches.*]

ALL: At last!

NERCIAT: Where is he?

BAUDOUIN: We surprised him at Sibilot's . . .

CHAPUIS: Carrying on a gallant conversation with a Communist girl . . .

JULES: With a . . . Sensational!

　　[*He reaches for the telephone, but* NERCIAT *stops him.*]

NERCIAT [*to the* INSPECTORS]: Continue!

BAUDOUIN: He was about to sell his story to *Libérateur.*

CHAPUIS: 'How I became Nekrassov,' by Georges de Valéra.

LERMINIER: To *Libérateur*?

BERGERAT: By Georges de Valéra?

CHARIVET: What a narrow escape we've had!

NERCIAT: Of course you arrested him?

CHAPUIS: Of course.

ALL [*except* JULES, *who is still dreaming*]: Excellent, gentlemen, excellent!

CHARIVET: Shut him up in a fortress!

LERMINIER: Send him to Devil's Island!

BERGERAT: Put him in an iron mask.

BAUDOUIN: The fact is . . . [*He hesitates.*]

NERCIAT: Speak up! Speak!

CHAPUIS: We had just captured him, when a score of Communists . . .

BAUDOUIN: . . . threw themselves on us and knocked us senseless.

CHAPUIS [*pointing to their bandages*]: Look at our wounds.

NERCIAT: Yes, yes. . . . What about Nekrassov?

CHAPUIS: He . . . he escaped . . . with them.

LERMINIER: Imbeciles!

CHARIVET: Fools!

BERGERAT: Idiots!

BAUDOUIN [*pointing to his crutches*]: Gentlemen, we have fallen victims to our duty.

NERCIAT: Not enough! I am sorry you didn't get your necks broken. We'll complain to the Prime Minister.

BERGERAT: And to Jean-Paul David.

NERCIAT: Get out!

[BAUDOUIN *and* CHAPUIS *go out.*]

BERGERAT [*sadly takes off his rosette and looks at it*]: Finished!
[*He throws it away.*]

LERMINIER [*same action*]: Finished!

CHARIVET [*same action*]: We'll die in our beds. [*Pause.*]

JULES [*to himself, sadly*]: He's lucky!

NERCIAT: Who?

JULES: The editor of *Libérateur*.

NERCIAT [*violently*]: That's enough. [*He takes the bottle and glass from* JULES *and throws them on the floor. To the other three*] Buck up, my friends. Let's consider the future with clear heads.

BERGERAT: There is no future. Tomorrow is the day of execution. *Libérateur* will publish Valéra's confession, and our evening rivals will take great pleasure in reproducing it in full. We shall be drowned in ridicule.

CHARIVET: In shame, my friend, in shame!

LERMINIER: We'll be accused of having played the game of the Communists!

BERGERAT: We are ruined and dishonoured.

CHARIVET: I want to go to bed! I want to go to bed!
[*He tries to go out, but* NERCIAT *holds him back.*]

NERCIAT: What a mania for getting to bed. There's no hurry, since you're sure to die there.
[BERGERAT *blows his trumpet.*]
As for you, my friend, for the last time, stop blowing that thing . . . that trumpet!

BERGERAT: At least I have the right to drown my sorrows in music.
[*At a look from* NERCIAT] All right, all right . . . [*He throws the toy away.*]

NERCIAT [*to all*]: Nothing is lost, but we must think. How are we going to save the paper? [*Long pause.*]

JULES: If you would allow me . . .

NERCIAT: Speak!

JULES: We could steal a march on *Libérateur* and publish the news in our afternoon edition.

NERCIAT: What?

JULES [*reciting his headline*]: 'Bigger than Arsène Lupin! Valéra hoaxed all France.'

NERCIAT: I ask you to be quiet.

JULES: We should sell three million copies.

ALL: Stop it! Stop it!

JULES: All right, all right. [*He sighs.*] This is the torture of Tantalus! [*Pause.*]

NERCIAT: On second thoughts, I support Palotin's idea, but I would take it a step further. Our revelations will arouse public anger . . .

BERGERAT: That's true.

NERCIAT: We'll appease it with a human sacrifice. We'll say that our good faith was abused. One of us will take all the blame. We'll denounce his criminal carelessness in the paper and dismiss him ignominiously.

[*Pause.*]

CHARIVET: Who were you thinking of?

NERCIAT: The Board of Directors does not handle news as such. None of its members is guilty.

ALL: Bravo! [*They applaud.*]

JULES [*stops clapping*]: In that case I don't see . . .

[*He stops. Everyone looks at him. He walks up and down. Their eyes follow him.*]

Why are you looking at me?

NERCIAT [*coming up to him*]: My dear Palotin, courage!

BERGERAT: We regard this paper, in a way, as our child.

CHARIVET: It won't be the first time that a father has given his life for his child.

JULES: Ah! Ah! You want me to . . . [*Pause.*] I accept.

ALL: Bravo!

JULES: I accept, but that won't help much. What am I? A humble employee. The public doesn't even know my name. But if you want to create a real sensation, my advice is sacrifice your Chairman.

BERGERAT [*taken aback*]: Well!

LERMINIER: Well! Well!

CHARIVET: Palotin is not altogether wrong.

NERCIAT: My dear friend . . .

CHARIVET: Ah! You would be making a real gesture!

NERCIAT: And you'd take my place as Chairman? I am sorry, but it was Palotin who introduced Valéra to us.

CHARIVET: Yes, but you accepted his statements without verifying them.

NERCIAT: So did you.

CHARIVET: I was not Chairman of the Board.

NERCIAT: Nor was I. Mouton was Chairman.

CHARIVET [*walking towards* NERCIAT]: Mouton was suspicious, poor chap!

LERMINIER [*walking towards* NERCIAT]: It is not his fault that we fell into the trap.

BERGERAT: It was you, Nerciat, who drove him out with your intrigues.

[NERCIAT, *stepping back, knocks against the attaché case.*]

CHARIVET [*with a cry*]: Look out!

NERCIAT [*turning round*]: Eh?

ALL: The case! [*They look at it with terror, at first. Then suddenly, they become angry.*]

NERCIAT [*to the attaché case*]: Trash! [*He gives the case a kick.*]

BERGERAT [*to the case*]: I'll give you radioactive powder! [*Kicks the case.*]

CHARIVET [*pointing to the case*]: That's the cause of all the trouble!

LERMINIER: Death to Valéra! [*A kick.*]

ALL: Death! Death!

[*They go on kicking the case.* MOUTON *enters, followed by* SIBILOT.]

MOUTON: Bravo, gentlemen! Take some exercise. You're just the age for it.

NERCIAT: Mouton!

ALL: Mouton! Mouton!

MOUTON: Yes, my friends, Mouton, your former chairman, to whom honest Sibilot just confessed everything. Come in, Sibilot, don't be afraid!

SIBILOT [*coming in*]: I ask you all to forgive me.

JULES: Blundering idiot!

MOUTON: Silence! My good Sibilot, don't apologize. You have done us a great service. If we save the paper, it will be thanks to you.

CHARIVET: Can it be saved?

MOUTON: If I doubted it, would I be here?

BERGERAT: And you know the way?

MOUTON: Yes.

CHARIVET [*grasping his hand*]: It was criminal of us ...

BERGERAT: How can you forgive us ...

MOUTON: I never forgive. I forget, if you know how to make me forget. *Soir à Paris* is a cultural asset. If it disappears, France will be the poorer. That is why I am prepared to let bygones be bygones.

CHARIVET: What do you suggest?

MOUTON: I don't suggest anything. I demand.

BERGERAT: Demand, then!

MOUTON [*first demand*]: It goes without saying that I remain your Chairman.

NERCIAT: Allow me, my friend, a proper vote was taken ...

MOUTON [*to the others*]: Think only of the paper. If Nerciat can save it, I'll withdraw.

CHARIVET: Nerciat? He's incompetent.

NERCIAT: I insist that ...

ALL [*except* JULES *and* MOUTON]: Resign! Resign!

[NERCIAT *shrugs his shoulders and leaves the group.*]

MOUTON [*second demand*]: You dismissed seven innocent employees. I expect them to be reinstated and compensated.

LERMINIER: Certainly!

MOUTON: Gentlemen, now I come to the main point. For the past year the paper has been on the down grade. We have thought only of increasing sales. The staff has been engaged in a frantic search for sensational news. We have forgotten our stern and splendid slogan: the Naked Truth. [*He points to the poster on the wall.*]

LERMINIER: Alas!

MOUTON: What is the root of the evil? Gentlemen, it is because we entrusted the editorship of our paper to an adventurer, a man without principles and without morals. I mean Palotin!

JULES: There we go! Of course, you've always wanted to get rid of me.

MOUTON: Gentlemen, you have to choose: him or me?

ALL: You, you!

JULES: I was the heart of the paper and my pulse was felt in every line. What will you do without the Napoleon of the objective press?

MOUTON: What did France do after Waterloo? She lived, sir, and we shall live.

JULES: Badly! Beware! [*Pointing to* MOUTON] There's Louis XVIII. There's the Restoration. I'm off to St Helena. But beware the July Revolutions!

MOUTON: Get out!

JULES: With pleasure! Stagnate, gentlemen! Stagnate! From this morning the news is on the left. The daily sensation is on the left! The new thrill is on the left. And since they are on the left, I'll go after them. I'll found a progressive daily that will ruin you!

SIBILOT: Chief, chief, forgive me, the lie was choking me, and . . .

JULES: Stand back, Judas! Go and hang yourself!

   [*He goes out.*]

MOUTON: No regrets! It was a public cleansing operation. [*Pointing to the window*] Look! Palotin leaves us, and the sun comes out. We shall tell the truth, gentlemen, we shall shout it from the house-tops. What a fine profession is ours. Our paper and the sun have the same mission: to enlighten mankind. [*He approaches them.*] Swear to tell the truth, the whole truth, and nothing but the truth.

ALL: I swear it!

MOUTON: Come here, Sibilot. I ask you to entrust this great and honest man, our saviour, with the editorship of the paper.

SIBILOT: Me? [*He faints.*]

MOUTON: Here is my plan. I telephoned the Minister just now. Naturally, he is dropping the charge against Duval and Maistre. There are no clear grounds.

CHARIVET: He must be furious.

MOUTON: He was, but I calmed him down. We agreed on the steps to be taken. At dawn tomorrow, three thousand people will mass in front of the Soviet Embassy. By ten o'clock there will be thirty thousand. The police cordon will be broken three times, and seventeen window-panes will be broken. At three o'clock in the afternoon a question will raised in the Chamber of Deputies by a government supporter. He will ask that the Embassy be searched.

CHARIVET: You're not afraid of a diplomatic incident . . .

MOUTON: I hope for one.

CHARIVET: We'll risk a war!

MOUTON: That's what you think. The Soviet Union and France have no common frontier.

NERCIAT: Where's the sense in all this and why all this fuss?

MOUTON: To smother in advance the fuss that *Libérateur* will make. For it is we, friends, who will start the dance. Today's issue of our paper is going to stir up public anger and the anti-Soviet demonstrations. [*He shakes* SIBILOT.] Sibilot!

SIBILOT [*coming to himself*]: What?

MOUTON: To work, my friend. The front page must be reset. Put first, as a lead-in: 'Georges de Valéra sells out to the Communists.' The main headlines must take up half the page: 'Nekrassov kidnapped by the Soviets during a reception at Mme Bounoumi's.' Then you'll have another sub-heading: 'After spending twelve hours in the embassy cellars, the hapless victim was sent off to Moscow in a trunk.' Understand?

SIBILOT: Yes, Mr Chairman.

MOUTON: Take six columns and pad it out as you fancy.

CHARIVET: Will they believe us?

MOUTON: No, but neither will they believe *Libérateur*. That's the main thing. [*To* SIBILOT] By the way, my friend, the police found a further list among Nekrassov's papers . . .

CHARIVET: A list of . . .

MOUTON: Of Future Firing Squad Victims, of course. [*To* SIBILOT] You will publish the principal names on the front page: Gilbert Becaud, Georges Duhamel and Mouton, your Chairman.

[*He bends down, picks up an FFSV rosette, and pins it to his button-hole.*]

CHARIVET: Can I go to bed now?

MOUTON: Certainly, my friend. I'll look after things.

[*He pushes his colleagues towards the door.* NERCIAT *shows signs of resisting.*]

You too, Nerciat, you too. When you have your head firmly on the pillow, I know that you are not doing anything stupid. [*On the threshold,* MOUTON *turns towards* SIBILOT.] If you need me, Sibilot, I'll be in my office.

[*They go out.* SIBILOT *gets up and walks up and down, at first slowly, and then more and more quickly. Finally he takes off his jacket, sends it flying on to an armchair, opens the door and calls*]

SIBILOT: Tavernier, Perigord – front page conference!

[TAVERNIER *and* PERIGORD *come running in, see* SIBILOT, *and stop, amazed.* SIBILOT *looks into their eyes*]

Well, boys, do you love me?

CURTAIN

THE TROJAN WOMEN

EURIPIDES

Adapted by Jean-Paul Sartre

English Version by Ronald Duncan

INTRODUCTION

Why The Trojan Women? *Greek Tragedy is a beautiful monument which we inspect with interest and respect with a scrupulous interpreter by our side. But it is a ruin where nobody would want to live. Devotees of classic drama periodically attempt to resuscitate Aeschylus, Sophocles and Euripides, and present them in their original style. But we are left feeling remote from such pious parodies. The reason why we find it difficult to connect with such productions is that these plays were inspired by an essentially religious conception of the world which is now completely strange to us. Though their language can seduce us, it no longer convinces us. Our aversion to such revivals is not helped by the many bad versions of the plays which abound. And when Jean-Paul Sartre chose to adapt a classic tragedy for the Théâtre National Populaire, and of all the tragedies the one which is the most static and the least theatrical, indeed, one which even the Athenians themselves did not take to immediately, I wanted to know what made him choose this play. This is how he justified it.*

It is generally assumed that Greek tragedy is both elemental and unsophisticated, but this is not true. We think of the actors today leaping about the stage and falling into prophetic trances, but Greek actors were highly stylized and even wore special masks and boots. Classic drama is essentially as artificial as it is rigorous. It is first and foremost a liturgy which sets out to impress the audience rather than to move them. Its horror is majestic, its cruelty is solemn. This is true of Aeschylus, who wrote for a public who still believed in the great myths and in the mysterious power of the gods. But it is even more true of Euripides who marks the end of one tradition and the transition to another, the comedies typified by Menander. When Euripides wrote *The Trojan Women*, these myths were already becoming suspect. Although it was too early to overthrow the old idols, the critical minds of the Athenians were already questioning them. The play has its liturgical element. One can see that the Athenians have already become more interested in what the dramatist is saying than how it is said. Though the audience was offered many of the traditional gestures for which it had a connoisseur's taste, yet it reacted to these with a new detachment. From being a mere ritual, tragedy now became a vehicle for thought. Though Euripides used the traditional form which superficially resembled that of his predecessors, he knew that his audience was critical of his content, and consequently his play carries overtones even when he is writing within the convention. Beckett and Ionesco are doing the same thing today, that is, using a convention to destroy a convention. And this method is sound strategy and it also makes for good drama. The Athenians probably reacted to *The Trojan Women* in a similar way to that in which contemporary audiences received *Waiting for Godot* or *The Bald-headed Prima Donna*. That is, they were aware that they were listening to characters who had beliefs which they no longer held themselves.

All of which makes a translator's job very difficult. If he keeps to the text he finds himself writing lines like: '*The dawn breaks on white wings*' and producing a romantic pastiche. Though I kept to the classic form, I was not unaware that I was writing for an audience which no longer subscribes to the religious beliefs which the play carries, and therefore would only receive them in inverted commas. Whereas the translation published by Bude, which is excellent in many respects, attempts to reassert those beliefs rather than accept the fact that they are no longer valid. The same problem will arise in four or five centuries from now when Beckett's and Ionesco's comedies are revived – that is, how to bridge the gap which will separate the audience then from the climate of opinion which obtained when the plays were written.

There was an implicit rapport between Euripides and the audience for which he was writing. It is something which we can see but not share. Since this relationship was implicit, a translation cannot reproduce it. It was therefore necessary to adapt the play.

It would have done no good to try to imitate the style of its language. It would have been equally unprofitable to try to render it into the contemporary French idiom. What I tried to do was to find a style that would be both acceptable to the modern ear and yet sufficiently removed from it to give the play its proper perspective.

I decided to write in verse in order to maintain the liturgical and rhetorical character of the original. I kept the language supple, modified the accent so that my verse could carry the contemporary idiom. As I have said, Euripides wrote for a sophisticated audience which no longer wholly subscribed to the legends he referred to and he was thus able to obtain some ironic effects by reference to them. But my problem was to make the audience take these myths sufficiently seriously to be surprised when they discover that they are no longer effective. We can, of course, still respond to a good deal of Euripides' humour, especially in the character of Talthybios, the prototype of the middleman who is the instrument in events which do not concern him. Our reaction to Helen is, of course, now tainted by Offenbach. Euripides himself could afford to be reckless. He was writing against a solid cultural and religious background, a stability which no longer obtains. I therefore had to construct some of this conformity of belief before I could, as it were, destroy it.

The question of style is one thing, but the problems which arise because of the differences between Greek culture and our own are altogether another. Euripides' text contains innumerable allusions which the Athenian public immediately understood. These mean nothing to us; we have forgotten the legends to which they refer. Consequently I deleted many of them and developed others. Cassandra did not have to explain herself to a Greek audience, nor tell them at length what would be Hecuba's final fate. Everybody knew only too well that, transformed into a dog, she would climb the mast of the ship which was to carry her from Troy and then would fall into the water. But when we see her go off at the end of the play, we do not know this: we believe that she goes to Greece. What I had to stress was that all Cassandra's predictions came to pass. Ulysses would take ten years to find his way home, the Greek navy would be destroyed, Hecuba would never leave Trojan soil. And to emphasize the tragic dénouement, I found it necessary to add Poseidon's final monologue.

Similarly the Athenian audience knew only too well that Menelaus, after having rejected Helen, would end up by taking her on his own boat. In Euripides the chorus makes a discreet allusion to this. But there is nothing in the original text to enable a French audience to anticipate this sudden change after Menelaus' previous protestation. It was therefore necessary to make the chorus express the indignation which the audience feel at this point, when the ship carried Menelaus and Helen away.

In some respects I have modified the general style of the play itself. *The Trojan Women* is not a tragedy in the sense that *Antigone* is: it is more of an oratorio. I have therefore tried to increase the dramatic tensions implicit in the original text by emphasizing some of the conflicts, such as that between Andromeda and Hecuba, the ambivalent attitude of Hecuba herself who, at times, is content to abandon Troy to its misfortune, while at others she rails against the injustice which has caused it. And the sudden switch of that little *bourgeoise*, Andromeda, who first produces all the attitudes of a wife, and then switches to those of a mother. And finally I emphasized the erotic perversity of Cassandra, who throws herself into Agamemnon's bed, knowing that she will perish there.

These difficulties, you may say, do not justify the choice of the play. But I think its subject does. *The Trojan Women* was produced during the Algerian War, in a very faithful translation by Jacqueline Moatti. I was impressed by the way this version was received. I admit it was the subject of this play which first interested me. This is not surprising. The play had a precise political significance when it was first produced. It was an explicit condemnation of war in general, and of imperial expeditions in particular. We know today that war would trigger off an atomic war in which there would be neither victor nor vanquished. This play demonstrates this fact precisely: that war is a defeat to humanity. The Greeks destroy Troy but they receive no benefit from their victory. The gods punish their belligerence by making them perish themselves. The message is that men should avoid war. This is Cassandra's affirmation, which is taken so much for granted that it is unnecessary to state it. The effects are obvious enough. It is sufficient to leave the final statement to Poseidon: *Can't you see war will kill you: all of you?*

The only place where I have actually interpolated anything new into the text was in reference to the Colonial War where I allowed myself to use the word Europe which is, of course, a wholly modern term. I did so because it is the equivalent of the ancient antagonism which existed between the Greeks and the barbarians, that is, between Greece and the civilization around the Mediterranean, and the gradual infiltration into Asia Minor where Colonial Imperialism arose. It was this colonialism of Greece into Asia Minor that Euripides denounced, and where I use the expression 'dirty war' in reference to these expeditions I was, in fact, taking no liberties with the original text.

I did not tamper with any references to the deities. Their position in the drama is extremely interesting. I have kept close to Euripides here. The only thing I have done is to try and re-state the gods' position, so as to make the criticism of them intelligible to a contemporary audience. In *The Trojan Women* these deities are powerful and ridiculous at the same time. On the one hand they dominate the world. The Trojan War is entirely their work but we see that they do not conduct themselves as gods but rather as men suffering from human vanities, grudges and jealousies. '*The gods have broad backs,*' Hecuba says when Helen blames them for the consequences of her own bad conduct. In the prologue we see that the goddess betrays her own heavenly colleagues for so little that we are shocked by it. It is as if she had sold heaven for the price of a lipstick. One sees that Euripides' purpose is to use the convention only to destroy it; he accepts a traditional belief only to make it appear ridiculous. The moving prayer which Hecuba makes to Zeus, which so astonishes Menelaus, and seems to anticipate a sort of fervent religiousness à la Renan, suggests that the chaos of human events finally has to submit to divine reason, and appears credible, at least for a moment, for we then see that Zeus has no more respect for human values than either his wife or his daughter. He himself does nothing to save Troy from its fate, and it is one of the paradoxes of the play that the only thing that brings the gods together is their determination to destroy Troy.

T – T.P. – K

The play ends in total nihilism. But whereas the Greeks had to live with gods who were capricious, we, seeing their predicament from outside, realize that they were, in fact, rejected by the deities. I have tried to emphasize this, and Hecuba's final despair is the human reply to Poseidon's terrible ultimatum, in which the gods break finally with men and leave them to commune with their own death. This is the final note of tragedy.

JEAN-PAUL SARTRE

(From an article by Bernard Pingaud in *Bref*, the monthly journal of the Théâtre National Populaire, February 1965.)

ADAPTOR'S NOTE

I must stress that this version is a free adaptation and not a translation. A casual comparison between the English and French texts would show that I have taken as many liberties with M. Sartre as he has with Euripides. I have paraphrased some passages and deleted others: cutting many references to the gods and paring Andromeda's dirge. With Racine in the background, the French have still an appetite for rhetoric which a contemporary English audience will not swallow. I have merely sought to give this version impact and I am sure that M. Sartre, being a man of the theatre, does not object to the liberties I have taken.

RONALD DUNCAN

The Trojan Women *was first produced in this version on 29 August 1966 at the Assembly Hall as part of the Edinburgh International Festival. The cast at this production was:*

POSEIDON	Edward Jewesbury
PALLAS ATHENE	Cherry Morris
HECUBA	Flora Robson
CHORUS LEADER	Diana Churchill
CHORUS	Patricia Kneale
	Charmian Eyre
	Joanna Wake
	Suzanne Mockler
	Janet Moffatt
	Cherry Morris
	Joy Ring
TALTHYBIOS	Michael Murray
CASSANDRA	Jane Asher
ANDROMEDA	Cleo Laine
ASTYANAX	Gavin Orr
HELEN	Moira Redmond
MENELAUS	Esmond Knight
SOLDIERS	Alan Foss
	Tom Baker
	Michael Irving
	Charles Noble

Directed by Frank Dunlop
Scenery and costumes designed by Carl Toms
Lighting by Francis Reid

CHARACTERS

POSEIDON
PALLAS ATHENE
HECUBA
CHORUS LEADER
CHORUS

TALTHYBIOS
CASSANDRA
ANDROMEDA
ASTYANAX
HELEN
MENELAUS
SOLDIERS

The action takes place by the walls of Troy.
The play is performed without an interval.

SCENE ONE

[*Enter* POSEIDON]

POSEIDON: I, Poseidon, God of the Sea,
        Have abandoned my shoal of lively Neireides
           And risen from the deep
        To gaze upon this bonfire that was Troy.
          Many years ago with our own hands Phoebus and I
        Piled stone upon stone
           And built the walls of that proud city;
             Since then,
        I have loved every stone of it.

[*Pause. He looks down at the ruins.*]
          Nothing but ash will be left.
        Now there are no priests in the sacred groves:
          Only corpses.
        Our temples bleed. The Greeks laid waste to every one.
        On the very steps of the Altar to Zeus,
        King of all the Gods, and my own brother,
          They slit Priam's throat.

[*Pause.*]
        These Grecian vandals, who sacked my city,
          Will carry their plunder off with them
            To deck out their wives and children
           With the gold and jewels of Phrygia.
        Ten times the season for sowing the corn came round.
          Still the Greeks stayed there, watching,
            growing old,
        Obstinately besieging the city.
          But now it's all over.
        Their ships are ready and only wait for the wind.
          It is not courage, but cunning which triumphs.
        Now the Trojans are dead: all of them

But these are their women:
Some to become officers' concubines; others mere
　　slaves.
That one over there with a fat belly,
Is the poor Queen. She is weeping,
　Grieving for her husband and her sons.
It is I who have been defeated;
　For now who will serve or worship me
In all these streets of ash? Nobody.
　Hera, my own sister-in-law, Goddess of Argos;
My niece, Pallas Athene, Goddess of Attica,
　　Combined their powers to destroy my
　　　precious Phrygians:
　To break my heart.
　　I am defeated: I give in.
What can I do with these ruins?
　Farewell, noble city,
I shall never look upon your ramparts
　Or gaze upon your glistening towers again.
My masterpiece is destroyed. Farewell!
　But for Pallas Athene's spite
　　Proud Troy would stand here still.

SCENE TWO

[PALLAS *enters and goes up to him.*]
PALLAS:　　　Poseidon!
[*He turns, sees her and angrily goes to leave.*]
　　　No, stay
　　　Most powerful God, whom we lesser deities worship,

Whom my own Father looks up to.

POSEIDON: When you're polite, Athene, you put me on my
guard.

PALLAS: If I can put our undying hatred to one side
Will you listen to me?

POSEIDON: Why not?

It's always pleasant to have a family chat
Amongst mortal enemies.

PALLAS: Quite. Let's be civilized.

I've a proposition to make.

It's to our mutual interest: it concerns Troy.

POSEIDON: You can see yourself what's left of it.

It's a little late to have any regrets.

PALLAS: Don't worry. I'm not going to feign sorrow
over your city.

I decided to wipe it from the face of the earth.
And that's what I did.

[Pause.]

What I want to do is to punish those Greeks.

POSEIDON: The Greeks?

PALLAS: None other. Will you help me?

POSEIDON: But they're your allies. You've only just given them
this victory.

For the Goddess of Reason, aren't you being a
trifle unreasonable?

I've never known any other God switch so capriciously
as you do
from love to hate.

PALLAS: They have insulted me. Cassandra took refuge in
my temple.

Ajax dragged her out of it by her hair.

And do you know not a single Greek
Laid a hand on him or tried to prevent him from
perpetrating

This piece of sacrilegous profanity. Not one.

              And to top that, the temple dedicated to me now
                  burns.

POSEIDON: Mine too.

PALLAS: Both of us desecrated.
              Will you help me?

   [POSEIDON *hesitates.*]

              And comfort your Trojan dead?

POSEIDON: You are my neice. But you have done me a terrible
                  injury:
              Don't imagine I shall forget it,
          Or omit to take me revenge.
              But I will help you.

PALLAS: We must bring about a catastrophic return journey.
              Zeus has promised me rain, hail and a hurricane
              And will hurl his shafts of lightning against their
                  fragile fleet.
              You must gather up all your waves
          Into one great wall of water.
                  And when it is as high as a mountain
                  Fling it down upon them.
                  As for those who reach the Straits of Euboea,
          Let the sea open up beneath them
                  To suck them all down to oblivion.
              Let every single one drown;
                  So long as Greece learns respect for me.

POSEIDON: It shall be done.
              On the beaches of Mykonos, from Scyros to Lemnos,
                  Against the reefs of Delos,
              At the base of the promontory of Caphareus,
                  My innumerable mouths shall vomit their corpses.
              Return to Olympus, niece. Watch.
                  When they start to cast off their ropes
              Ask your father to send down his thunderbolts.

   [*They part, each to their side of the stage.*]

SCENE THREE

[HECUBA *is now seen for the first time. She is lying on the ground.*]
HECUBA [*trying to get up*]:
              Up you get, you poor old crone,
         Never mind your broken neck. You're on your knees
                   today: but tomorrow you may fall on your feet.
         Be patient, philosophical.
         Being sorry for yourself won't get you anywhere;
              It never does, it never did.
         Don't try to swim against the current,
              When destiny wants to destroy you: let it.
         But it's no use:

                             Not even my courage
         Can stand up to the flood of my grief
              In its full spate of sorrow.
         Now there is no sorrow in all the world
              Which is not my sorrow.
         I was a Queen: my husband, a King.
              I bore him fine sons.
         The Greeks cut them down, one by one.

         As for my husband, Priam,
         These same eyes that weep,
              Watched when they bled him on the steps of the
                   altar
         And saw his throat open like a mouth
              And his blood flower, then flow, over his golden
                   skin;
         While my daughters,

Who were to be betrothed
To the greatest kings of Asia,
They have all been dragged off to Europe
     As chattels to bad masters.

O Troy,
Your full sails were bellowed with your own glory.
     They cracked in the sun and sagged.
It was only hot air that had filled them.

[*Pause.*]

I talk too much, but I cannot remain silent.
     And silence cannot feel any more than words can.
Shall I then weep? I cannot: I have no tears left
          within me.
     I can only throw my body upon the indifferent
          ground
And let it mourn noiselessly
          rolling from side to side
          like an old hulk in a tempest.

[*She goes to throw herself down again, but stops.*]

          No.
Misery is like loneliness in this:
     that both are left a voice with which to sing
That's where all song comes from,
          So I shall sing:

          O ships of Troy,
Did you know where you were going
     ten years ago
When your rowers sweated,
And your proud beams parted
     The passive seas of the World?
When every port was your harbour
Did you know then where you were heading?
     All your voyages had one destination;

You were going to seek that Grecian traitor,
Helen, wife to Menelaus,
   and bring her back to be
   Death to every Trojan.

   O ships of Troy,
From those white decks iron men once sprang,
For ten long years now you have lain
   Anchored in our own harbours.
But today you are to sail away again
Taking me, the Queen of your city, with you
   With shaven head and ravaged face

To be a servant at a servant's table.
Did you have to do all this for this:
   To bring a blood bath on my people,
Plunge me and all these women into mourning,
All because you wanted the glory once again
   Of sailing across to Greece
   To anchor where shame is fathomless?

[*She claps her hands.*]
   Get up there
Your Trojan widows, Trojan virgins, all mated to the
   dead.
Have the guts to look down upon these smouldering
   ruins
   For the last time
   And articulate your grief.

LEADER OF THE CHORUS:
   Your anguish, Hecuba, has ripped open our tent.
   Fear feeds at our breasts,
   Claws at our hearts.
   What do you want us to do?

HECUBA: Look down at those ships in the bay

A WOMAN: The Greeks are hoisting their sails.

ANOTHER WOMAN: I can see men carrying oars.

ALL: They are leaving.

LEADER [*to others off-stage*]:

Come out and see what's in store for you.

The Greeks are getting ready to go home,

You poor wretches, come out here and see for yourselves.

All of you!

HECUBA: No, no, not all of you.

Not Cassandra. Keep her inside. She's mad.

At least spare me the last humiliation

Of letting the Greeks see me blush with shame.

A WOMAN: What will they do?

Put us to the sword?

ANOTHER WOMAN: Abduct us, ravage us?

HECUBA: Think of the worst.

It will be that.

[*To herself*]

A slave.

Whose? Where?

In Argos? in Phthia?

On some island off the coast?

A pitiful old woman

More dead than alive,

A useless hornet in a foreign hive,

Dragging out her last few days.

Or I will have to squat night and day

Outside somebody's door

at their beck and call;

As nurse to some Greek matron's brats;

Or worse, stuck in their kitchen baking bitter bread;

With nothing but rags to cover the ruins of my body

And only an earth floor to lie down upon?

[*Pause.*]

And I was Queen of Troy.

A WOMAN: If I throw my shuttle from side to side for ever
          It will never be on the looms of Ida again.
ANOTHER WOMAN: Every member of my family is dead. My home
                burned to the ground.
            Looking on these walls which smell so acrid
            I know that I am seeing them for the last time.
LEADER: Be quiet.
            Preserve your strength,
            Worse misfortunes yet await you.
A WOMAN: Are there worse than these?
ANOTHER WOMAN: Yes. One night some drunken Greek
            Will drag you to his filthy bed.
FIRST WOMAN: The thought of what my body may do
            Makes me loathe each limb of it.
OTHER WOMAN: Uprooted.
            To live away from here will be to live in hell.
ANOTHER WOMAN: I shall probably have to carry their slops.
ANOTHER WOMAN: Maybe I'll be a servant in Attica?
                On the fertile plain of Penee,
            At the foot of Mount Olympus.
            They say life is good there,
            Even for slaves.
FIRST WOMAN: Anything's better than to be taken to the banks of
            the Eurotas.
            There I'd see Helen triumphant
            And have to obey Menelaus,
            The butcher of Troy.
LEADER: Someone's coming.
OTHERS: Who is it?
LEADER: A Greek. Look how he runs.
            He's coming to tell us what they're going to do with
            us.
            This is the end. Though we haven't yet left our native
            land,
            We are foreign to it;

As we are now things that belong to Greece,
Their slaves. Even here, their slaves.

SCENE FOUR

[*Enter* TALTHYBIOS. *He speaks to* HECUBA.]

TALTHYBIOS: You know who I am, noble lady,
      Talthybios, herald to the Greek Army.
    I often entered the gates of your city,
      To deliver messages from our generals.
    And I am now instructed to convey an edict to you.

HECUBA: The moment we feared has come.

TALTH: I suppose it has: your future has been decided.

HECUBA: Where are we to go?

TALTH: You are all to be separated.
    Each to different masters.

HECUBA: What masters?
    Are we all to be treated exactly alike?
      No exception made for anyone?
        Surely not?

TALTH: No. Give me time: I will tell you.

HECUBA: I am waiting.
    [*Pause.*]
    Cassandra?

TALTH: You've guessed right.
    She is to be one of the lucky ones:
    Agamemnon himself wants your daughter.

HECUBA: As a servant to Clytemnestra?
      It is as I feared.

TALTH: Not at all.

The King of Kings wants her as his concubine.

HECUBA: His harlot?

TALTH: He might even marry her. . . . in secret.

HECUBA: So.

You know that she is already betrothed to the Sun,
To him alone,
And that the golden-headed god
insists she remains a virgin.

TALTH: Of course. It's because her virginity can be guaranteed,
she being a prophetess,
That she's so attractive to His Majesty.

HECUBA: Throw away the Temple keys, poor child;
Tear off your holy fillet
And cover your hair with ash.

TALTH: Come now, worse things could happen to her
Than sharing a bed with a King.

HECUBA: And what have you done with my daughter Polyxena?

TALTH: She serves Achilles.

HECUBA: But Achilles is dead.

TALTH: She still serves him.

HECUBA: What strange customs you Greeks have.
To think that I gave her life
For her to spend it in a tomb.

TALTH: She's one of the lucky ones, I can tell you.
Even Cassandra will often wish she was with her.

HECUBA: Why?

TALTH: She has found peace there.

HECUBA: Is she alive? Can she still see the sky
Or the stars at night?
Tell me.
Your look of shame's your answer.

TALTH: We have given her shelter.

HECUBA: Shelter from what?

TALTH: The World.

HECUBA: True.

[*Pause.*]

And Andromeda?

TALTH: Well, of course, being Hector's wife,
          She was considered something special
          And goes to Achilles' son.

HECUBA: And what of me? Broken with age,
              Unable to walk without this stick.
          What work can I do?
          Who could possibly want me?

TALTH: Ulysses. A slave in his household.

HECUBA: No. No. Anybody but him.
          I spit on that dog.
          On that double tongued monster
              Who breathes hatred and discord
          Wherever he finds friendship.
          Ulysses! O Women of Troy,
          Now weep for me, your Queen
              in misery alone.

CHORUS: And what about us?
          What is to become of us?

TALTH: How should I know?
          It's not my business.
          The small fry will be sorted out in lots.

[*To the* GUARDS]

          Go and fetch Cassandra.
              Agamemnon wants her within the hour.
          What's that? The tent's all red.
              Quick, stop any Trojan women
          From burning themselves alive.
              I can understand that a free people
          Don't easily knuckle under to a catastrophe like this,
          But I don't want any embarrassing suicides on my
              hands.
              Do you understand?
          And certainly no human torches.

That might be a way out for them
But it would be a bore to me.
HECUBA: It isn't a fire there at all.
It's Cassandra.
She's mad.

SCENE FIVE

[*Enter* CASSANDRA.]
CASSANDRA: May this flame,
This gentle flame,
Rise slowly, dance fiercely,
Round this torch of me,
And lift its impetuous pride
Against the thighs of night
And stand up straight within the supple air.
May Hymen bless the union that it makes
And grant that I, who was a virgin of the sun,
Shall its full quietus make, as I lie beside the King.
[*To* HECUBA]
Hold this torch, Mother,
Lead the cortège.
What's wrong? Why are you crying?
Because of my father, because of my brothers?
It is too late to grieve for them
For I am to be married,
Your tears should be of joy, of joy!
Take it.
[*She holds out the torch to* HECUBA.]
You refuse? Very well,

My own hands shall coax and carry this flame
    To Hymen's couch
Where a Greek is to take me.
For even if the Queen of the Night
Set a light to all her stars,
    And the entrails of the hemisphere debowelled burned
        in their orbits
I would not have light enough:
Darkness would mark my way
    As I walked towards that bed
        Where I am to be joined to the enemy.

So may this flame rise higher and higher
        till it licks the sky,
For this is the day my life has grown to.
    Now Phoebus, God that is my God,
        Conduct this choir that is my choir,
        And you, my Mother, dance;
        Join in this dance for her who was your daughter.
Oh please, Mother, to please me. . . .
    And why are these Women of Troy
Not dressed for a carnival and singing hilariously?
Come, now all together, after me:
        Oh woe, woe, woe.

LEADER OF THE CHORUS [*to* HECUBA]:
    Hold her back, Your Majesty,
    Hold on to her,
        She doesn't know what she's doing
        And might even jump straight into his bed.

HECUBA: Give me that torch, child,
    You're not holding it upright.

CHORUS: Her ecstasy is all despair,
    Misery has not made her sane.

CASSANDRA: They think that I'm mad.
        Listen, Mother, I tell you

You should rejoice at this betrothal.
    And if you see me
    suddenly timid,
      I want you to thrust me into Agamemnon's arms
        and let him carry me off to Argos.
For once there, I will turn our marriage bed into his
    tomb.
Helen had a thousand thousand Greeks killed beneath
    our walls.
But I shall do even worse to them.
    Cassandra will be their doom.
Through me, and because of me,
    Their King, their great King, shall perish.
By my sacrifice their Royal house shall fall.
And I shall destroy his people
    As he has destroyed our own.
So now is not the time to weep
Unless tears of joy,
    So laugh as the wind laughs;
    Let there be a gale of laughter;
For I swear my father and my brothers
      will be revenged.

HECUBA: How? By you?

CASSANDRA: By me.

HECUBA: My child, you will be a slave, helpless . . .
      How can you . . .?

CASSANDRA: With an axe.
      There, right in the skull.
   I'm not saying it will be I who strikes the blow,
      But I guarantee this King of Kings will bleed all the
        same.
      Oh, how he'll bleed!

[*Joyfully*]
      As for me, they'll cut my throat.

[*Pause.*]

A long time later, the son will kill his own Mother
And flee – dogs at his heels.
That will be the end of the House of Atreus.
Nobody will ever fear them again.

CHORUS: Don't, Cassandra.
You are embarrassing us,
And you are making your Mother feel ashamed.
Not in front of the Greeks, we beg you . . .
Don't let our conquerors
Hear your prophecies
And smile at your distraction.

CASSANDRA: Why should I be silent?
I speak of what the Sun has told me.
I could tell you more
But it is too horrible.
You are right. I will say no more.

[*To* HECUBA]
Don't cry.
The Greeks are victorious. But what now?
What happens to them?
I will tell you:
they will be beaten, they will be humiliated:
Some will fall outside Troy, others on the plains.
They will perish in their thousands,
Not in defence of a city on their native land
As our men did:
They will die for nothing.
Few of them will ever see their homes again,
They will not even be buried;
Nobody will say a prayer over them;
Trojan earth will digest their flesh
And their wives will never find their bones.
These wretches are all recruits,
a slaughtered but unburied army.
The vultures wait,

And oblivion awaits them.
> Not a trace of these conquerors will remain;
>> Not even their shadow.
> Except for a handful
>> who will crawl back to Greece
> Only to find themselves unwanted and unwelcome.

Apollo himself has told me
> How Clytemnestra has behaved in Agamemnon's
>> absence.
>> But I won't repeat it.
> And all this, for what?
>> Ten years to seek out one adulteress;
> And their victory will be to find
>> Their own wives have been faithless to them –
> And every man's a cuckold!

[*To* TALTHYBIOS]
> This is what you call winning the war.
>> True, we have lost it;
>> But not our honour.
> We have fallen on our own soil
> Defending our own city.

Gentle hands waited to nurse our wounds,
And watching eyes waited to weep
> When we could bleed no more.
> When our King fell
>> Troy itself was his widow.

[*To* HECUBA]
> You should be grateful to these Greeks.
> They even turned Hector
Who was a modest gentle man
> Into an immortal legend of courage.
> We who defended our native land are glorified,
But those who conquered us shall be cursed.
> They started this filthy war:
They will die as stupidly as they lived.

[*To the* TROJAN WOMEN]

    Lift up your heads: be proud,
      Leave your revenge to me;
    He who embraces me will be destroyed by me.

A WOMAN: I wish I could believe you;
    I wish I could laugh
      And be as crazily defiant as you are.
        But look at us,
      Take a look at yourself.
    All your singing and spitting won't get you anywhere.
      It's all words,
        impotent words.

TALTHYBIOS: And they'd prove rather expensive
    If we didn't know she was insane.

[*Aside*]

    The more I see of the intimate lives of the great
      The more I realize they're as petty and perverse as
        the next man.
      As for the most mighty King of Argos
    Who has taken it into his head
      to desire this creature who's not right in hers,
    All I can say is: a poor devil like me
      Wouldn't want her for all the gold in all the World.
        But there it is:
    So come on, my pretty, follow us.
      Let's get going.
      You heard them: words won't help you now.

[*To* HECUBA]

    I'll come back for you
    Immediately Ulysses sends for you.
      You won't find it so bad with him,
    As servant to Penelope.
      People speak rather well of her.

CASSANDRA: Servant? There's only one servant here
      And that: you,

You insolent and obsequious lout
With the manners of a farm hand.
You don't know what you're talking about.
My mother won't be going to Ithaca.
Apollo has assured me
She will die here, in Troy.

TALTH: Not if I have anything to do with it, she won't.
Her suicide would finish me.

CASSANDRA: Who said anything about suicide?

TALTH: How else?

CASSANDRA: You'd like to know, wouldn't you?
But I shan't tell you.
As for Ulysses and all his double talk,
That man doesn't know what he's in for.
He's got another ten years,
Another ten years of mud and blood,
before he sees Ithaca again.
Oh yes, I know everything's ready and he's about to
set sail,
But the end is often only another beginning.
The giant flesh-eating Cyclops
squats on his rock,
his mouth watering, waiting for him.
So does Circe who turns men into pigs;
Not to mention Scylla and Charybdis
who lick their lips at a smell of a shipwreck.
I tell you the only place Ulysses is going to is Hell.
We know a few who are waiting for him there.

[To the WOMEN]
I can assure you Ulysses will suffer.
Whatever your misfortunes are,
He will envy them.

[She looks into the distance.]
That's it. When he eventually climbs out of Hades
And lands on his own island

He finds that it too has been conquered.

[*She emerges from her trance.*]

But what's Ulysses to me?

[*To* TALTHYBIOS]

Well, what are we waiting for?

I'm impatient to be joined to my betrothed:

for better or worse.

No, just the worst.

So toll the wedding bells!

Our marriage shall be a cortège down the road to Hell

And this generalissimo,

this King of Kings,

Who wants to embrace the daughter of the Sun

Will never see the light again.

Endless night will devour you,

And your body will be chucked over a cliff.

Toll the wedding bells!

For our broken bodies will be naked together

And vultures alone will be satisfied;

Their beaks will be intimate with my breast;

Their claws shall caress your manhood.

Here I'll tear the veil of my virginity,

Of prophecy,

While my body is still unravished.

May the gentle breeze

waft it to the true God of Love:

The Sun, the Sun.

Now which is my boat? Where do I embark?

Since I am death,

See that a black flag

Flies at the mast of the ship which carries me.

Good-bye, Mother,

Be calm; you're going to die soon.

Father, I am coming,

I am coming to join you in your grave;

> I won't keep you waiting,
>> I am coming to you at the head of a hideous cortège
>> Made up of the entire house of Atrides
>> Who slaughtered you.
>> Toll the wedding bells!

[*She goes off with the* SOLDIERS.]

> Dong! Dong!
> Toll the wedding bells!

[HECUBA *faints.*]

LEADER OF THE CHORUS:
> Quick, Hecuba's collapsed.
> Don't stand there. Lift her gently:
> She's still our Queen.

[*They do so.*]

HECUBA: I did not seek your concern
> And I do not thank you for it.
> What I wanted was to embrace the earth,
>> to yield myself into its blind unconsciousness.
> For you see, we are all blind too;
>> We can do nothing but submit.
> But unhappily, though we are blind,
>> we alone are conscious.

CHORUS: Oh Royal Lady,
> Pray to the Gods.

HECUBA [*savagely*]:
> No. They are allies
> Not to be relied upon.
> Let us be silent.

CHORUS: Silence is something we fear.

HECUBA: Then stop complaining.
> Better, think when you were last happy.

CHORUS [*alternating verses*]:
> That was yesterday.
> It was only yesterday
>> that we were happy.

That was the same day Troy fell.
   In the morning, we saw from the ramparts
That the beach was deserted
   And their fleet had left our bay;
There in the middle of the plain
   Stood a great wooden horse on wheels,
A wooden horse with a golden harness.
   The People of Troy, seeing this idol
From the rock of the citadel,
   cried out: 'It is over. The siege is finished.
The Greeks are gone. Our suffering is at an end,
   So hoist their wooden idol into our Acropolis
As an offering to Pallas Athene,
   Zeus' noble daughter, who has forgiven us.'
      Everyone was shouting and singing;
Strangers kissed in the streets;
Old men asked what all the excitement was about.
   'It's peace, it's peace,' we cried,
and lifted them off their feet.
      We tethered ropes round this idol to haul it to
         Athene's Temple.
Everyone lent a hand, some pulling, others pushing.
   It took all day, not till dusk was it there;
Then our victory songs and the sound of Lydian lutes
         enlivened the night.
That was yesterday.
   All the houses in the city were dark and empty;
Everybody was out in the streets: dancing with torches,
Singing; nobody slept, it was a night of carnival,
A carnival of peace.
   That was how Troy went down:
In riotous joy!
   And that was only yesterday.

LEADER OF THE CHORUS:
   Nothing is more deceptive than happiness.

> Joy is a cheat which covers up for the misery
>> stalking behind the grin.
> At midnight we were still singing,
>> then suddenly the whole city
> rang with one refrain:
>> it was the cry
>>> of death.
>> War was back again:
>> Pallas had forgiven nothing.
> The Greeks had leapt out of the idol
> And were slaughtering our men and boys.
>> That was how our night of celebration ended
>> with the dawn of death.

HECUBA: Troy wasn't conquered:
The Trojans weren't defeated.
> They were betrayed by a Goddess:
It's always a mistake to worship a woman.

LEADER OF THE CHORUS:
> Look, Your Majesty,
> A chariot is coming.

[HECUBA *doesn't move.*]

A WOMAN: It's Andromeda, Hector's wife,
> carrying Astyanax in her arms.

[*To* ANDROMEDA]
> Where are you taking him?

ANDROMEDA: To my master.

[HECUBA *now turns, looks coldly at* ANDROMEDA, *and sees*
ASTYANAX *who carries a small basket.*]

HECUBA: Misery. Everywhere I look: misery.

ANDROMEDA: What are you crying about?
> It's my loss.

HECUBA: It's ours.

ANDROMEDA: No, mine.

HECUBA: You are all my children.

ANDROMEDA: Were.

HECUBA: I mourn for all my sons.

ANDROMEDA: But I only for one, Hector.

HECUBA: I weep for our burning city.

ANDROMEDA: I weep for Hector's city.

HECUBA: For our royal home.

ANDROMEDA: Only for the house where I became a woman:
                          Where I gave birth to Astyanax.

HECUBA: It's burning: it's burnt.
                  Everything's flattened; a shambles of ash.

ANDROMEDA: You are to blame.
                  It was you who gave birth to Paris:
                      that damned adventurer.
                  Didn't the Gods themselves, foreseeing his future,
                      order you to smother him?
                  You refused: it is we who are punished for that:
                        for your pride
                      Which you hawked around as a Mother's love.
                  It was this precious infant of yours
                      Which smashed Troy like a toy;
                      And now Pallas alone can laugh
                  At the heap of corpses piled up at the foot of her statι
                      While these vultures encircle us;
                      and we stand here as slaves.

HECUBA [*broken, her face in her hands*]:
                  If Priam
                      could cry out from Hell
                  He would shout: 'You lie, you lie.'

ANDROMEDA: If Hector could come back
                  He would save me. He would revenge me.

          [*Then quietly but without gentleness*]
                  I have never liked you.
                  You have never liked me.
                      But you're an old woman:
                      I feel sorry for you.

      [*Pause.*]

Polyxena is dead.

HECUBA: Dead? What a coward I am.

That's what Talthybios was trying to tell me.

And I hadn't the courage to understand.

Dead. How?

ANDROMEDA: They cut her throat on Achilles' tomb.

[*Pause.*]

I saw her body.

I covered her face with a black veil.

HECUBA: Slaughtered on a tomb:

Like a goat, or an ox.

What a terrible death.

ANDROMEDA: Why terrible?

She is dead. That's all.

Better off than I who live.

HECUBA: What do you know of death or life?

I tell you death is a nothingness;

however painful life is

it is better than death: it has hope.

I prefer life at its worst to death at its best.

ANDROMEDA: Your will to live's insane.

You know very well you've nothing to live for,

Your sons are all dead,

And your belly is too old to breed any more.

Your future is completely hopeless.

So much the better for you.

You can give in and sink in your circumstances

Rather than cling on to a life that's finished

As far as you're concerned.

If you do that you won't suffer so much.

For death is a void,

A void that is eternal and peaceful.

Listen to me: It is the same for Polyxena now

As it was before she was born.

For now she is dead, she can't suffer any more,

and is unaware of the suffering she once
experienced:
 her sheet is wiped clean again.
But I still suffer, and I still know I suffer:
 Life has more to scribble over me.
I was a good wife and devoted Mother;
 Some of us are. But as many of us know:
It doesn't matter how a woman behaves.
 The world thinks the worst of us,
And slanders us if we give it half a chance.
 I didn't give it that chance. I stayed at home,
 Where the gossips couldn't get at me.
It was no sacrifice: I was happy
 Devoting myself wholly to Hector.
But you see, old woman, my virtuous life
 has been my undoing,
And my reputation for being chaste recoils on me;
  for it is that
Which now makes Neoplotemus,
 the son of the man who murdered my husband,
Demand me for his bed.
 I am frightened. I am frightened
 And it is myself I fear.
For I do not want my memory of Hector to be erased.
 But I am a woman,
And a woman is only a woman.
 They say it takes just one night of pleasure to
  master her:
A woman is only an animal.
 That is why I am frightened.
Hector was the only man I ever knew;
 I loved his courage, his wisdom, and his gentle-
  ness,
The touch of his hands on my body.
And now the thought that this same body

May groan for joy when some other man lies upon it,
Makes me want to tear it limb from limb.
Polyxena was lucky:
She was murdered still a virgin.

[*To* HECUBA]

Liar. You say life is hope.
Look at me. I'm alive. What hope have I?
None.
I know what life's going to write on me.

LEADER OF THE CHORUS: You are a Princess,
But misfortune levels us.
By telling us of your fears
You make me aware of my own.

HECUBA: When the sea is rough
Sailors sail into it bravely;
But when there's a tempest,
They haul their canvasses down,
And let the waves drive them where they will.
I do that: I yield and I advise you to do the
same:
My child, Hector, is dead. Your tears won't bring
him back.
Forget him: devote the virtues which he loved to
your new husband.

ANDROMEDA: You disgusting old slut,
To think that Hector's own Mother
Should turn pimp.
You're nothing but a whoremonger.

HECUBA: Do what I say,
For Astyanax's sake.
He is the son of my son,
And the last of his race.
Do it for his sake,
So that he,
Or his son's son,

> May one day refound this city,
> And revenge us.

[*Enter* TALTHYBIOS.]

> What now?

TALTHYBIOS [*going to* ANDROMEDA]:
> Don't hate me.

ANDROMEDA: Why not?

TALTHYBIOS: I am only a messenger.
> It is my distasteful duty
> To tell you what my masters have decided.

ANDROMEDA: Come to the point.
> Don't be afraid to speak.

TALTH: Your son.

ANDROMEDA: Are they going to separate us?

TALTH: In a way. Yes.

ANDROMEDA: We shan't have the same masters?

TALTH: He won't have one at all.

ANDROMEDA: You're leaving him here?

TALTH: I don't know how to tell you.

ANDROMEDA: Spare me your scruples,
> Get on with your job, lackey.

TALTH: They're going to kill him.

[*Pause. She clasps her child to her, staring at him. He continues quickly*]

> It was Ulysses who persuaded them.
> He urged the Greek Assembly
> Not to spare the life of the heir to the Trojan throne,
>> because he might sometime become the focal point of rebellion.
>> The Assembly accepted his resolution.

[*Pause.*]

> So it's no use holding on to him like that.
> Give him to me.

[*She resists.*]

> Come on now. Hand him over.

There's nothing else you can do.
Neither your city, nor your husband,
    can protect you now:
    neither exist any more.
Don't you understand, we give the orders now?
    Do I have to tear him from you?
Don't be silly. Bow to the inevitable,
    Accept it with dignity.

[*Pause.*]

For God's sake, isn't there anything
    that can make you hand that child over?
Can't you see you won't gain anything
    By trying my patience
    Or making the soldiers angry?
If you do that, they'll just leave him to the vultures.
But if you hand over quietly,
    we might even let you bury him,
and our generals will treat you with more considera-
tion.

ANDROMEDA [*to the* SOLDIERS]:
    Don't you dare lay hands on him!
    I'll hand him over. Later.

[*They back away, watching her. She looks down at her child in silence.
Then slowly lifts up its hands one at a time, examining the small
fingers. She then holds one of its feet in her hands; then runs her
forefinger over the line of the child's mouth and eyes as though she
had never seen the child, or any child, before. The* SOLDIERS *approach
her. She looks up. They stop. She walks towards them holding out
the child.*]

ANDROMEDA: Here you are, take it: kill it.
    Hit it with an axe. Throw it on a fire:
        It's yours.
    I can't protect it: I could only give life to it.
        What are you waiting for?
        Take it.

[*The* SOLDIER *goes to lead the child off when* ASTYANAX *spills his basket of sea shells. The* SOLDIER *bends down to pick them up and places them in the basket, then leads the child off.*]

TALTH [*to the* SOLDIERS]:

Carry it to the ramparts.

Wait for me there.

[*To himself*]

All very distasteful. I feel quite sick.

That's the worst of war:

Those who give the orders

Seldom see the mess it makes

When you hold a child by the feet

And bash its head in against a wall.

HECUBA: That child was my son's son.

There goes our future, mine and yours.

[*She puts her hands over her eyes.*]

What a blessing blindness would be.

[*Exit* OMNES *except* HECUBA *and the* CHORUS. *It is now dawn.*]

CHORUS: Once again

The gentle dawn illumines a burned-out city.

This is the second time in our history

The brazen dawn has revealed

a tangle of limbs in our gutters,

Rubble spewing over our streets.

This is the second time

The Greeks have liberated us.

The first time, it was many years ago.

They invaded us from Salamis.

They told us then that they were bringing

Greek culture and European enlightenment

to the backward people of Asia:

Our city burned with progress,

Our young men had their limbs

amputated by philosophy.

The Greeks always envied our harvests,

     their soil was eroded, ours still fertile;
That was all there was to it, many years ago.
But that time, though they sacked our city,
     they did not lay waste to the countryside;
They went away
       leaving us with the strength to rebuild.
     Our Gods were merciful then.
       But now they have abandoned us.
Though we lift our hands to heaven and cry:
     Save us! Save us!

[A pause.]

     Nobody answers. Only Echo.
     This dawn is indifferent: our Gods are deaf.

[They sink to the ground. Enter MENELAUS with SOLDIERS.]

MENELAUS: What a glorious morning!
     This is the day of all days.
     The day I've lived for;
       There that slut sits now
     Squatting in a hovel, a prisoner
       at my mercy; I have no mercy.
     Now is the moment I have lived for:
       when I caught up with her again,
     And could make her suffer
       as she made me suffer . . .
     You will have guessed that I'm King Menelaus,
       well known for his misfortunes.
     Some people at home criticize me:
       They say I started this terrible war
     Merely because of a woman.
       But that's not fair.
     It was because of a man.
       And that man was Paris,
     The shit whom I took into my palace
       and who ran off with my wife.
     That's why this war's been fought.

And I'm grateful that the Gods
have punished Paris for his perfidy:
   Neither her, nor his city, exist any more.
And now it's this woman's turn:
   this woman whose name sticks in my throat;
Whose name I've never spoken for years, ten years.
   I have two alternatives:
Either to have her executed here
   Amongst the ruins of the city she chose for her
      home,
Or to take her back to Sparta
   and settle her account there.
I've decided to do precisely that:
   for by postpoing her punishment, I increase it.
When she reaches Sparta
   The mothers and widows of the Greeks
Whose men fell here
   will lynch her, stone her to death;
That'll be her end.

[*To the* SOLDIERS]
    Get her.
Drag her out by her hair.
   Make her grovel at my feet.
Then I promise you we'll hoist sails
   and only wait for a wind.

HECUBA: At last.
[*Pause.*]

At last I can believe in you, Zeus.
     You,
       the unknown
      and the unknowable,
     You,
Who seated at the centre of the earth
   can, at the same time,
hold the world in your hands

        like a ball in space,
            at last you have my grudging belief.
      At any rate, I believe in your justice
      For by this, I see that you do punish the wicked.

MENELAUS: That's a strange sort of prayer.
      Who are you?

HECUBA: Hecuba, Queen of Troy.

MENELAUS: I didn't recognize you.

HECUBA: Are you really going to punish Helen?

MENELAUS: I gather from your prayer
      that you'd like to see her put to death?

HECUBA: Of course.

MENELAUS: So would I. So would I.

HECUBA: That's what I meant by saying Zeus was just.
        Do it. But when you do it,
           Don't look at her.

MENELAUS: Why not? It's ten years since I saw her.
      I want to see what those years
        have done to her too.

HECUBA: Nothing. You should know that.
      Women like her keep their beauty
        because life doesn't touch them.
      They're indifferent to the misery they cause.
        They age late and then suddenly.
      Her eyes are still beautiful,
        though death looks out of them;
      Her skin is still smooth,
        For her lips, men will still slaughter each other,
          and cities burn.

[HELEN *comes out from the tent.*]
        Go now. Don't look at her.
      You think your desire for her is dead.
        She will rekindle it,
      And you'll be in her clutches again.

MENELAUS: Nonsense.

[*He turns and looks at* HELEN.]

[*Pause.*]

Release her.

HELEN: You need not have used force
     to have me brought to you.
  The instant I saw you, I wanted to run to you.
     For though you hate me, I still love you.
     I have wanted you. I have waited for you.

[*Pause.*]

  Let me ask you one question:
     I will never ask another:
  What do you want to do to me?

MENELAUS: I?

HELEN: You.

MENELAUS: To kill you.

HELEN: If you, my love, want my death,
     then I, my love,
        desire my own death too.
  But just let me explain.

MENELAUS: No. I don't want to hear your explanations.
     You're going to die. That's all.

HELEN: Are you afraid to listen?

MENELAUS: Aren't you afraid to die?

HECUBA: It's too late now. I begged you not to look.
     But you may just as well let her talk.
       There's no risk there
       Whatever she has to say. I have an answer to it.
  And will stuff her lies down her throat,
     So let her talk of your past;
  It will give you the courage
     to see that she has no future.

MENELAUS: You needn't worry. There's nothing she can say
     that will have any effect on me.
  But I'll let her talk, since you want me to.
     She knows only too well

There's nothing she can say, or do,
    that will have any effect on me.
She's already dead as far as I'm concerned.

HELEN [*placing herself in front of him*]:
    No, do not turn away.
       Look at me.
    Have the courage to look at me for the last time.
    Look on every part, then know what it is you're
        killing.
    You hate me? I do not hate you.
       If only you knew. . . . Yes,
      There are some things you should know. . . .
    Oh, I know the sort of things I've been accused of. . . .
      But I've an explanation for each.
    I don't know whether you'll believe me or not,
      But let me speak and have the courage to listen.

[*Pause.*]

    Do you want to know who is really to blame
      for all this misery?
    She is. That old woman. She was the start of it all.
      It was she who gave birth to Paris.
    The Gods themselves were alarmed.
    They foresaw that that scoundrel would ferment a
        war – and what a war.
      They ordered her to smother him.
       Did she do it?
    No. And King Priam was too weak to make her.
      All of this stems from that;
     That was the beginning of it all.
    Paris was only twenty when three Goddesses
      competed for his favours.
    Pallas herself offered him the whole of Greece
      if he'd choose her.
    And with her behind him
      he'd have overrun it in no time.

And what was Hera's bribe?
    She offered him Asia Minor.
And the whole of Europe.
    But Cypris offered nothing.
Nothing except me. She merely described me.
    She won. Paris chose her for his Goddess,
Then worshipped me.
        You were lucky then.
For if he'd chosen either of the other two,
    he would have conquered Greece.
If it were not for this body,
    which your soldiers have so misused,
You yourself would be a subject of that barbarian.
    But your luck was my misfortune.
        That you might escape
    I became the victim: Cypris sacrificed me.
And my beauty, my beauty became my shame.

MENELAUS: You slut. Why did you go?

HELEN: Darling, it was you, not I, who left.
        You were a careless husband
When you went off to Crete
    and left me alone with your lecherous guest.

MENELAUS: You could have resisted.

HELEN: I, a mere mortal,
Resist the goddess, Aphrodite?
    Could you do that?
A pity you cannot punish her
    for what she did to me.
If you could, you'd be stronger than Zeus himself,
    For even the King of the Gods
Is as much her slave as everybody else is.
        Why did I go?
    That's a question I've often asked myself.
And the answer is always the same:
        It was not I who left;

But somebody who was not me.
Aphrodite was an unseen guest in your palace,
  like an invisible shadow to Paris;
And as you know, Cypris had made a bargain with
      Paris
  to give me to him as long as he lived.
There was nothing I could do
  to break that odious but sacred tie.
But the moment Paris was dead, I was free.
  Immediately I did everything, everything I could
To get back to you.
  At night, I climbed up on the city walls,
Tied ropes together to carry me to the ground
  where I might run to you.
Your own guards can prove it:
  because they always caught me.
That's all I have to say: that's my story.
  I am the victim of circumstance;
Destiny's plaything: abducted;
  married against my will to a man I loathed;
  forced to live in a foreign city I despised.
All this I endured to save my country.
  My own chastity was my contribution;
And there is nothing more precious to a woman than
      that.
  Yet, in spite of this sacrifice,
  they are wanting to stone me to death.
I am hated by the Greeks, detested by the Trojans,
Alone in the world, understood by none.
  Now tell me this:
Do you think it is right to put me to death
When it was the Gods, not I, who sinned?
  If you don't, then take me where I belong:
In our bed, on your throne;
  To do less would be to insult the Gods

Who, for all their mistakes,
    do not err in justice.

HECUBA: I'm beginning to doubt it.

CHORUS: Don't let her get away with it, Your Majesty.
    This woman is dangerous.

Puncture her eloquence with a few facts.

HECUBA: Very ingenuous.

You'd like us to believe that the three Goddesses
    were as vain as you are?

That they would trade their holy cities
    to corrupt a jury at a beauty contest?

Is it likely that Hera would give
    Argos sanctuary?

Or Athene would ever deliver Athens to the Trojans?
    They were merely teasing Paris.

By trying to suggest that the Goddesses are vain too
    You do not diminish your own viciousness.

    As for all this about Aphrodite:

You make me laugh, if I could laugh.
    Though I must say I liked your bit about
        Aphrodite

Entering the Palace as a shadow to my son.
    Tell me why would she bother to do that

When she can control us like marionettes
    from the comfort and security of heaven?

If King Menelaus wants to know the truth,
    all he has to do is to remember
    how handsome my son Paris was.

Immediately this woman saw him, she wanted him.
    That's all there was to it.

I'm tired of hearing people
    blaming Aphrodite for lusts which are all their own.

Paris was very good looking. He stayed with you.
    He was a Prince of Asia:

She was also impressed by the golden ornaments he wore.

Greed added to her lust,
She didn't rest till she'd satisfied both desires.

[*To* HELEN]

You always had to make do with the second best
didn't you?

Sparta is a poor country. There, even the Queen has
to be economical.

And you wanted luxury:
You wanted to be able to copulate all night
and chuck bucketfuls of gold out of your windows
during the day.

So you ditched your husband for a man you lusted
after and traded your shabby little kingdom in
for the richest city in the whole of Asia.
It was good business, wasn't it?

Yet you try to make out you were carried off
against your will.

Will. Odd that nobody saw this abduction.
Strange you didn't cry out.

Or if you did nobody heard you.

And when your own people declared war,
Came here to fetch you, and besieged this city,

How many tears of remorse did you shed
when you saw piles of Greek bodies

In heaps against these walls? Not one.

When things were going well for them,
you conveniently remembered
Menelaus was your husband:

His name used to spring to your lips then
to keep Paris up to scratch.

But when the Greeks suffered any reverse,
you forgot your first husband's name again.

Always an opportunist:
Always keeping your eye on the main chance,
Never on virtue, never on loyalty to either.

And of course now the Greeks have won,
You come here with some cock and bull story
about trying to tie ropes together to make your
escape
and that the guards witnessed these attempts of
yours.
You bitch, you know damn well
all these men have been butchered
and this because of you.
Unfortunately for you, and for me, too:
I'm still alive.
You have one witness and this my evidence:
How many times did I come to you
And beg you to leave my son
and go home to Greece?
I pleaded with you to do that,
knowing Paris would, in time, forget you
and marry again.
If you had gone through those walls
the war would have stopped instantly.
And didn't I offer, again and again,
To have you conducted secretly
back to your own people?
But you never listened, did you, my beauty?
You didn't like the idea
Of quitting that palace where you strutted like a
strumpet,
Where every man ogled you, including King Priam.
Just look at yourself now
Decked out with Trojan jewels,
Your vapid face thick with make-up.
The lot. And the man you're trying to seduce now
Is your own husband.
You should be throwing yourself at his feet,
wearing rags, you wig cropped,

cringing for forgiveness.

Menelaus, be firm. Don't listen to her.

There'll be no peace for Greece

Till she's done away with

Give the order, make an example of her.

CHORUS: Your ancestors will curse you

If you hesitate.

Your country will reproach you

if you are weak.

Be strong, noble. Punish her.

MENELAUS: That is my intention.

I am convinced she left Sparta

Of her own free will.

All this talk about Aphrodite

Is entirely irrelevant.

[*To* HELEN]

You dishonoured me:

You shall die.

The army will stone you.

You are lucky: you won't suffer for very long.

We endured ten years.

HELEN: You are my husband.

You are my King.

I implore you to forgive me.

I have done nothing. No, that's not true, my darling.

I know that I have hurt you

But blame the Gods for that, not me.

Forgive me, take me back!

HECUBA: Let me speak now, not for my sake,

Or Troy's sake.

But for my enemies: the Greeks who died.

Do not betray them.

Do not betray their children.

MENELAUS: Be quiet, old woman!

[*Indicating* HELEN]

That creature doesn't mean anything to me.

[*To the* SOLDIERS.]

Take her aboard my ship.

HECUBA: But only a minute ago
You were going to have her killed immediately.

MENELAUS: I was angry then.
I now realize my original decision was correct.
It is better she should die in Greece.

HECUBA: Perhaps it is.
But don't let her go on your boat.

MENELAUS: Why not?

HECUBA: Because once a man has loved,
As you have loved,
His love does not die,
even when it seems to be dead.

MENELAUS: That's true.
But she whom I loved is no more.
I never loved that
Or if I did, it was not me.
But I'll take your advice, old woman;
maybe it is wise.
She can go on some other ship,
And when she reaches Greece
the wretch will die as wretchedly as she deserves.
I'll make an example of her:
It's not easy to make women chaste
But where inclination fails
I'll make terror teach them.

[*He exits.*]

CHORUS: Do you believe he will kill her?

HECUBA: It's an even chance.

CHORUS: Look! Look at the coward.
What a liar he is.
There she goes now right onto his own ship,
And he trailing behind her.

              Now the game's up.
           She'll bring him to heel
           And reign unpunished over Sparta.
           Nothing pays off like crime.

HECUBA: And I thought you were just, Zeus.
           I must be going mad.
           Nothing will now ever assuage
             the bitterness our dead must feel
           As they, in their invisible battalions,
               crowd the beach
                 to watch that brazen hussy
                 step onto that ship,
           Knowing they died for nothing.

CHORUS: Absolutely nothing.
           Helen will see Sparta again.
             There she will reign:
               Nothing pays off like crime.
           Zeus has deprived us of everything:
             Our temples, our incensed altars;
           Our city, our fertile fields, our harbours,
           and you leave us with nothing, though we were
                 innocent;
             while you allow Helen
             To show her heels with Menelaus,
             and reign over Sparta again
             as if nothing had happened.
               Nothing pays off like crime.
           The men whom we loved,
             Who fathered our children,
           will haunt these blackened stones
             With all the anguish of the unburied dead,
           While we, their widows, wander
             in far-off lands with loneliness as our companion,
             growing old, growing ugly,
           and some of us becoming whores;

While that most honourable lady
  calls for her golden mirror again
  and sits contemplating her own smug beauty.
    That's what it will be.
  Nothing pays off like crime!

HECUBA: A pleasant journey, Helen.
  May you drop dead on it.
  If there's a God anywhere amongst all these Gods,
    May he grasp all his lightning like a dagger
  and strike that ship with it.
    May it catch fire, sink.
  And you, Menelaus, you impotent old cuckold,
    May you drown too.
  I'd like the sea to swallow you both up
    then spew your swollen bodies on some beach
  where your compatriots could contemplate your
        beauty:
      skin mottled and putrid,
      flesh slipping from the bone;
  Then they could see:
      If crime pays off so well.

[*Enter* TALTHYBIOS *carrying the body of* ASTYANAX.]

CHORUS: Look, look, look;
  Here's the little corpse of Astyanax.
  They dropped him like a stone from a high tower.

TALTHYBIOS: Hecuba, all our ships have now put to sea,
        except one,
  It waits for you and the rest of the booty.
  Achilles' son has had to leave in a hurry;
    War has started again in his country.
  A usurper has seized his father's kingdom.

HECUBA: Ten years of it here.
  Now it starts up somewhere else again.
    Always war somewhere.
  Has his father lost his throne?

Don't expect me to be sympathetic.
And Andromeda?

TALTH: He took her with him.
Before she left, she went and knelt by Hector's tomb.
I found it moving, very moving.
Neoptolemus was compassionate enough
to allow a sepulchre to be built.
And look at this.

HECUBA: His shield. Hector's shield.

TALTH: By custom, of course, it belongs
to the son of his conqueror.
But in this instance, he's waived that right;
So we won't be taking it with us
To hang in the palace at Phthia.
We thought that it might distress Andromeda
To see this relic of Hector's
Hanging on the walls of her new bridal chamber.
And we didn't want to upset her.
That would have been cruel,
And we Europeans are both civilized
and sensitive.
So you needn't bother to try to find planks
to make a coffin for Astyanax,
Here it is! He can rest on his father's shield.
My instructions are
To hand over the body to you
since his mother has already left.
Here, take it.
Perhaps you'll let me help you
Bury it?
As you see, I've already cleaned it up
Or tried to; there was a lot of blood.
Here will do, won't it?
I'll help you dig; it needn't be very deep.
As I say, our ship's waiting.

After ten years, I can hardly believe it.

HECUBA: Lay this shield
Upon the earth
    it protected.
        I loved him.
This ring is still polished
    where it was rubbed by his arm.
And now this eye of brass,
    which once turned back the sun,
Will lie where no light can look on it
    As a coffin for his son.

[*She takes* ASTYANAX *in her arms.*]
    Bloody Greeks!
Drunk with power
    yet frightened of a child.
With Hector dead, our army slaughtered
        and our city a cinder
    you were still frightened of a child.
If you feared him, you will soon fear one another:
    Civil war will do to you
    what you have done to us.
And when both Troy and Greece
    have been levelled as war levels,
All that will remain
    will be this little tomb
    standing among these shattered columns.
On it, it shall bear this inscription:
    'Here lies a child
        murdered
    because he frightened Greece.'

[*Over the body*]
    Little one,
You will never grow to strength,
    Or know that love
Which makes a man equal to a God.

        Nor will you fall or fail
      As men do, from weakness or from age;
         But if men can be happy,
      You could have been happy,
         All life's possibilities
      Were held in this tiny hand. . . .
      I always said he had his father's hands.
      Now that which moved is still,
          forever still,
      and the blood congeals on his battered skull.
         What waste, waste, waste.

[*To the* WOMEN]

      Go and find something
      With which we can wrap his body.

[*Some* WOMEN *go into the tent.* HECUBA *lays the corpse on the shield.*]

      And to think I used to believe
         in happiness.
      I tell you destiny is drunk
         and the Gods are blind, clumsy, deaf and in-
            different.
      A man's a fool if he thinks he's achieved happiness
         Unless he's on his death bed.
      Now I'll bind these wounds which will never heal.

[*They return.*]

      Did you find anything?

A WOMAN: Only these rags.

HECUBA: Rags will do.
      The dead are not particular.

[*The* SOLDIERS *place the body on the shield again and take it off.* HECUBA *watches this silently. Then she suddenly explodes with anger.*]

      You filthy Gods,
      You always hated me.
         And of all cities

Troy was the one city
You detested.
Why? Didn't we mumble prayers enough?
Make ritual and habitual sacrifice?
And all for what?
Today we suffer in hell.
And you smirk at us from heaven.
Keep your heaven!
Go on licking your lips
Over human misery.
But I tell you, this time
You omniscient immortals
have made one small mistake:
You should have destroyed us with an earthquake
if you wanted to sweep us out of the way.
If you'd done that
Nobody would have ever mentioned Troy again.
But as it is, we held out for ten years
against the whole of Greece,
And then were only beaten by a cheap trick.
We die, but we do not die.
Two thousand years from now,
our courage will still be talked about;
It was something real
like your injustice.
You have condemned me. Now I'll condemn you:
Soon all of you immortals
Will be as dead as we are!
Come on then, what are you waiting for?
Have you run out of thunderbolts?

[*Pause.*]

Filthy cowards!

LEADER OF THE CHORUS:
Don't. We beg you.
You'll bring down other misfortunes on us.

There's always something worse.
  Here it comes.
Look, they're setting light to the Acropolis.

[*Enter* TALTHYBIOS.]

TALTH: My orders were to destroy anything left standing.

[*To an* OFFICER *of his suite*]
  Burn Troy.
  See that nothing remains.

[*To the* WOMEN]
  When you hear a trumpet,
  File down in an orderly fashion to the beach,
  It will be the signal for you to leave.

[SOLDIERS *enter.*]

[*To* HECUBA]
  Ulysses has sent these men to fetch you.
  Poor old woman, you'd better follow them.

HECUBA: Now is the mountain of my misfortune capped:
  To be carried off
Leaving my Troy in flames.
  I salute those flames.
The greatest city the world has ever seen:
  To be populated by rodents,
  Decorated by brambles.
I said the Gods were deaf.
  That was not true:
They are evil.
  It's a waste of time to ask them for help.
Better to rely on my legs.
  Come on, old bones, don't let me down.

[*She tries to walk away.*]

TALTHYBIOS: Where's she off to? Stop her.
  She must have gone out of her mind.

HECUBA: Oh the pity of it. Poor Troy.

CHORUS: Troy is no more. But a memory. Our memory.

HECUBA: Oh the waste of it.

So many hands,
So many hours and hours of work.
Its glory was that it was home.
Now ash settles on what we were
And smoke describes what we've become.

CHORUS: The pity of it.
The waste of it.

HECUBA [*kneeling and beating the ground*]:
Oh earth, dear earth,
Be merciful.
Open up, take us into yourself.
Don't let them part us from you.

CHORUS: What was that? That noise?

HECUBA: That groan was the sound
A city makes when dying.
The walls of Troy collapse. Stand firm.
Now make them drag us off.
No Trojan feet will ever walk
willingly from Troy.

[*They are all dragged off. Black out.*]

[POSEIDON *appears and looks down at the prisoners waiting on the beach.*]

POSEIDON: Poor Hecuba,
You shall not die among your enemies.
I shall let you go on board
Then later take you down
Into my kingdom of the sea.
And I will raise up a rock to you
near your native land
So that my waves will break over you ceaselessly,
Repeating your innumerable sorrows.

[*He turns and calls*]
Pallas! Pallas Athene!
Let's get to work.

[*There is a flash of lightning. Then a pause.*]

Idiots!
We'll make you pay for this.
You stupid, bestial mortals
    Making war, burning cities,
    violating tombs and temples,
    torturing your enemies,
    bringing suffering on yourselves.
        Can't you see
        War
        Will kill you:
        All of you?

CURTAIN

MORE ABOUT PENGUINS
AND PELICANS

For further information about books available from Penguins please write to Dept EP, Penguin Books Ltd, Harmondsworth, Middlesex UB7 0DA.

In the U.S.A.: For a complete list of books available from Penguins in the United States write to Dept CS, Penguin Books, 625 Madison Avenue, New York, New York 10022.

In Canada: For a complete list of books available from Penguins in Canada write to Penguin Books Canada Ltd, 2801 John Street, Markham, Ontario L3R 1B4.

In Australia: For a complete list of books available from Penguins in Australia write to the Marketing Department, Penguin Books Australia Ltd, P.O. Box 257, Ringwood, Victoria 3134.

In New Zealand: For a complete list of books available from Penguins in New Zealand write to the Marketing Department, Penguin Books (NZ) Ltd, P.O. Box 4019, Auckland 10.

JEAN-PAUL SARTRE IN PENGUIN PLAYS

For the classic exponent of existentialism, literary invention is a natural medium and Sartre has established himself as a great dramatist of our age. His plays put the issues of the real world on trial.

ALTONA AND OTHER PLAYS

Three plays dealing with problems of human freedom. *The Flies* (1942) presents Sartre's interpretation of the Greek legend of Orestes. *Men Without Shadows* (1946) is a brutal study of the effects of torture on captured members of the Maquis. *Altona* (1959) comments on the acquisitive aspects of capitalism as seen in a family of rich German industrialists.

THE RESPECTABLE PROSTITUTE
LUCIFER AND THE LORD

In these two plays the classic exponent of existentialism puts the issues of the real world on trial. *The Respectable Prostitute* indicts the corrupt moral code of the American South when a prostitute is forced to perjure herself in a Negro rape case. *Lucifer and the Lord* is one of Sartre's best works – rich in ideas, dialectic, drama and feeling. Set in Germany at the time of the Lutheran Reformation, it describes the struggles of a notoriously cruel young general who accepts a challenge to do nothing but good. Its exploration of good and evil through the suffering of one man puts this drama on the level of Sophocles' *Antigone*.

ROADS TO FREEDOM
Jean-Paul Sartre's trilogy in Penguins

THE AGE OF REASON

This novel covers two days in the life of Mathieu Delarue, a teacher of philosophy, and in the lives of his acquaintances and friends. Individual tragedies and happiness are etched against the Paris summer of 1938, with its night clubs, galleries, students, and café society.

But behind it all there is a threat, only half realized at the time, of the coming catastrophe of the Second World War.

'Constantly delights with its brilliance' – *Spectator*
'A dynamic, deeply disturbing novel' – Elizabeth Bowen

THE REPRIEVE

The Reprieve includes many of the characters of *The Age of Reason*. It surveys that heat-wave week in September 1938, when Europe waited tensely for the result of the Munich conference. Sartre's technique of almost simultaneous description of several scenes enables him to suggest the mood of all Europe as it tried hard to blinker itself against the threat of war.

'His method is consummately able. It is only a writer with an exquisite sense of rhythm who can mix episode with episode as M. Sartre does here' – *Observer*

IRON IN THE SOUL

In *Iron in the Soul* the same characters at last face reality, in the shape of defeat and occupation. Around a graphic narrative of the fall of France, Sartre weaves a tapestry of thoughts, feelings, and incidents which portrays – as few books about war have done – the meaning of defeat. As in the earlier books, the school master Mathieu is the most articulate character: able to reflect on the nature of freedom even as he fires his last rounds against the oncoming enemy.